SELECTIONS

FROM

EARLY CHRISTIAN WRITERS

SELECTIONS FROM
EARLY WRITERS

ILLUSTRATIVE OF

CHURCH HISTORY
TO THE TIME OF CONSTANTINE

BY

HENRY MELVILL GWATKIN, M.A.

SOMETIME DIXIE PROFESSOR OF ECCLESIASTICAL HISTORY IN THE UNIVERSITY OF
CAMBRIDGE HON. D.D. EDINBURGH

Wipf & Stock
PUBLISHERS
Eugene, Oregon

Wipf and Stock Publishers
199 W 8th Ave, Suite 3
Eugene, OR 97401

Selections from Early Writers
Illustrative of Church History to the Time of Constantine
By Gwatkin, Henry Melvill
ISBN: 1-59752-178-7
Publication date 5/6/2005
Previously published by Macmillan Company, 1902

PREFACE

IT is hoped that the present volume will be found within its limits a fairly representative selection of original documents for the use of students. Attention has been directed, not only to the general course of events, but to the history of the New Testament Canon, and to the personal opinions of conspicuous writers. It has been thought best to give a translation for the benefit of such as are but mean scholars, and in the second edition a few introductory notes were given.

My best thanks are due to the Trustees of the Lightfoot Fund, to Mr. Parker, of Oxford, and to Messrs. T. and T. Clark, of Edinburgh, for the use of translations mentioned below[1]; also to Dr. Zahn, of Erlangen, for the Latin text of the *Canon Muratorianus*, and to Professor (now Dean) Robinson for the Greek text of certain passages[2], for certain translations, and for much help in many directions.

[1] Translations marked L. are due to Lightfoot's *Apostolic Fathers*; R. to Dean Robinson; N.L. to the *Library of Nicene and Post-Nicene Fathers*; A.N.L. to the *Ante-Nicene Christian Library*.

[2] These are numbered XXI *a*, XLVIII, XLIX, LI *a*, LI *b*, LII.

CONTENTS

			PAGE
1.	The Neronian Persecution	*Tacitus*	2
2.	Opening of Clement's Letter to the Corinthians	*Clement of Rome*	2
3.	The Neronian Persecution	do.	4
4.	Arrangements settled by the Apostles	do.	6
4a.	The Persecution of Domitian	*Dio Cassius*	10
5.	Ignatius on Episcopacy	*Ignatius*	12
6.	Ignatius on Docetism	do.	12
7.	The Christians in the World	*Ep. ad Diognetum*	12
8.	Church Order of the Didaché	*Didache*	18
9.	Pliny's Correspondence with Trajan	*Pliny*	26
10.	The Neronian Persecution	*Eusebius*	30
11.	Of the Canonical Epistles	do.	32
12.	Of the Canon of the New Testament	do.	34
13.	Papias	do.	38
14.	Quadratus on our Lord's Miracles	do.	44
14a.	The Apology of Aristides	*Vita Barlaam*	44
15.	Heathenism the work of demons	*Justin*	46
16.	Christianity before Christ	do.	48
17.	Christian Worship	do.	50
18.	The Jewish interpretation of Isa. vii. 14	do.	56
19.	The Christian interpretation of various passages	do.	56
19a.	Hegesippus	*Eusebius*	58
19b.	The Encratites	do.	62
20.	Letter of Dionysius of Corinth to the Romans	do.	62
20a.	Tatian's Conversion	*Tatian*	64
21.	The Persecution at Lyons and Vienne	*Eusebius*	66
21a.	The Scillitan Martyrs		78

Contents.

			PAGE
22.	Fragment of Muratori on the Canon		82
23.	Origin of the Gospels	Eusebius	88
24.	Montanism	Hippolytus	90
25.	Letter of Irenaeus to Florinus	Eusebius	92
26.	Letter of Polycrates to Victor	do.	94
27.	Marcion	Irenaeus	96
28.	The Argument of Irenaeus from Tradition	do.	98
29.	A Tradition of the Elders	do.	104
30.	Philosophy a preparation for the Gospel	Clement of Al.	106
31.	The true Gnostic	do.	106
32.	Faith and Knowledge	do.	108
33.	Misuse of Scripture by Heretics	do.	108
34.	Bad Emperors the only Persecutors	Tertullian	110
35.	Testimony of the Soul	do.	112
36.	Christians not disloyal	do.	114
37.	Numbers of the Christians	do.	114
38.	Christian Worship	do.	116
38a.	Non-Scriptural Customs	do.	118
39.	Philosophy the Mother of Heresy	do.	118
40.	The Argument of Tertullian from Tradition	do.	120
41.	Disorderly Worship of Heretics	do.	122
42.	The Roman Bishop's Edict	do.	124
43.	Inconveniences of a mixed Marriage	do.	124
44.	The Misdeeds of Praxeas	do.	126
45.	Infant Baptism	do.	128
46.	Misdeeds of Callistus	Hippolytus	128
47.	Origen's conception of Education	Eusebius	130
48.	The Letter and the Spirit	Origen	132
49.	The Argument from our Lord's Miracles	do.	132
50.	Celsus on the Lord's Resurrection	do.	134
51.	The Gospel not specially addressed to Fools	do.	134
51a.	The true ground of Old Testament Inspiration	do.	136
51b.	The parabolic element in Scripture Narratives	do.	138
52.	The Method of God's dealing with Sinners	do.	140

Contents.

			PAGE
53.	Porphyry's Objections to Allegorical Interpretations	*Eusebius*	142
54.	Origen on the Authorship of the Epistle to the Hebrews	*do.*	142
54a	A Libellus of the Decian Persecution		144
55.	Dionysius of Alexandria on Novatian	*do.*	146
56.	The Unity of the Church	*Cyprian*	146
57.	On Church Discipline	*do.*	148
58.	Appointment of Bishops	*do.*	150
59.	Schismatical Baptism worthless	*do.*	152
60.	Heretical Baptism invalid	*do.*	152
61.	Firmilian's Letter to Cyprian	*do.*	154
62.	The Edict of Valerian	*do.*	154
63.	Dionysius of Alexandria on the authorship of the Apocalypse	*Eusebius*	156
64.	The Rescript of Gallienus	*do.*	160
65.	Aurelian's Decision of the Bishopric of Antioch	*do.*	160
66.	The Edicts of Diocletian	*do.*	162
67.	Our Lord's Miracles	*Arnobius*	162
68.	Lactantius criticizing earlier Apologists	*Lactantius*	164
69.	Misgovernment of Diocletian	*do.*	164
70.	The Toleration Edict of Galerius	*do.*	168
71.	The Edict of Milan	*do.*	170
72.	Constantine's Cross	*Eusebius*	174
73.	The Letter of Eusebius	*Theodoret*	176
74.	Select Canons of Councils		186
75.	Roman Religion		190

INTRODUCTORY NOTES.

CORNELIUS TACITUS (b. *cir.* 54) reached the consulship 97, wrote his *Annales cir.* 115, and died a few years later.

Extract I gives a heathen view of the Neronian persecution. The standpoint is that of a Roman aristocrat, to whom the Christians are detestable enough, but who is too intent on blackening Nero to go far out of his way for them.

Clement of Rome may have been a freedman of the T. Flavius Clemens consul 95, and put to death by his cousin Domitian. He wrote the letter of the Church of Rome to the Church of Corinth (95 or 96). His so-called Second Epistle is a sermon preached perhaps at Corinth about half a century later.

Extract II is the opening of the letter, with its picture of the Corinthian Church in its past prosperity. In Extract III is a Christian view of the Neronian persecution, and it records the execution of the two great apostles. Extract IV recites that the apostles made arrangements for the orderly government of the Churches, so that the Corinthians have done wrong in turning blameless presbyters out of office.

Cassius Dio Cocceianus (b. 155: governed several provinces: second consulship 229) wrote a history of Rome to his own time in eighty books, of which the last twenty or so are preserved chiefly in the Epitome of Joannes Xiphilinus, a Byzantine writer of the eleventh century.

Extract IVa is our fullest account of Domitian's persecution. It is certain from the evidence of the catacombs that Domitilla was a Christian: and there cannot be very much doubt of the consuls Glabrio and Clement (91 and 95).

Introductory Notes.

Ignatius of Antioch was given to the beasts by Trajan (98-117), but we cannot fix the date more nearly. The seven letters which seem proved genuine were written from Smyrna and Troas on his way to the amphitheatre at Rome.

Extracts V and VI represent two of his most prominent topics. In Extract V we see the stress he lays on the bishop's office, in Extract VI his earnest assertion of the reality of our Lord's humanity. It also glances at a third—his overwrought desire for martyrdom.

The Letter to Diognetus is by an unknown writer, perhaps 130-150. It is the most striking of Christian pamphlets before the *de Incarnatione* of Athanasius; and its powerful language is a strong contrast to the plainer style of Aristides and Justin.

Extract VII begins with his famous picture of Christian life, then points to its contrast with heathenism, and ends with a difficult passage where that contrast is appealed to in proof of Christianity.

The *Didaché* or *Teaching of the Apostles* (published in 1883 by Bishop Bryennius) is also the work of an unknown writer. Its date is uncertain; possibly even in the first century: its place also; possibly the mountains of Peraea. It represents a very early stage of Church government, before the rise of (monarchical) episcopacy.

Extract VIII gives an account of Baptism (earliest mention of affusion: peculiar form of the Lord's Prayer) and of the Lord's Supper (still in the evening). Then come stringent regulations for apostles and prophets (not to stay too long, or to ask for money, or to eat of a special *agapé*: yet not to be tried presumptuously) and for travelling Christians. A prophet desiring to settle down is worthy of his meat. Then directions for Sunday worship (confession before Lord's Supper), and finally instructions to appoint worthy men as bishops and deacons.

C. Plinius Caecilius Secundus (62-113) reached the consulship 100, and in the year 111 was sent by Trajan on a special mission to set in order the cities of Bithynia.

Extract IX shows his hesitation in dealing with the Christians. Obstinate offenders, of course, he puts to death: but what was to be done with those who renounced their offence, or had long ago given

Introductory Notes.

it up? Was it good policy to use indiscriminate severity? Trajan answers that convicted offenders must be punished, though they are not to be searched for, and that all suspected persons who renounce Christianity are to be set free.

Papias, bishop of Hierapolis in Phrygia (*cir.* 130), is chiefly known to us from the chapter of Eusebius here given. It will be noted that Eusebius dislikes him for his Millenarianism, and probably does him less than justice.

Extract XIII begins with a statement of Irenaeus, that Papias was a disciple of St. John. Against this Eusebius quotes Papias' preface, in which he seems to distinguish his own informant, the elder John, from the Evangelist. After mentioning sundry marvellous stories, he gives the words of Papias about our two first Gospels. It will be noted (*interpreted*, not *interprets*) that the Hebrew Matthew was out of use in his time. Last of all comes the story of the woman taken in adultery, which may (Ewald) have been the tradition told by Papias in illustration of John viii. 15.

Quadratus was one of the earliest Apologists, if he addressed his work to the Emperor Hadrian (117-138), as Eusebius states.

Extract XIV is the only fragment of it which remains. He seems to be contrasting the lasting results of our Lord's miracles with the passing effects produced by the magicians.

Aristides, the philosopher of Athens, is also said by Eusebius to have presented his *Apology* to Hadrian. The work was lost: but when a Syriac translation was discovered (disc. and ed. by Mr. Rendel Harris, 1891), its inscription pointed to Antoninus Pius (138-161). The Greek in an adapted form was recognized by Professor Robinson in the *Life of Barlaam and Joasaph*, which (as originally pointed out by Prof. Max Müller) is itself a Christian adaptation of a Buddhist romance. Found in the works of John of Damascus (*cir.* 730).

Extract XIVa is a simple account of Christian life, which should be compared with that of the writer to Diognetus.

Justin, the philosopher and martyr (b. *cir.* 100 at Flavia Neapolis, the ancient Shechem), owed his conversion to an old man he met on the seashore, perhaps at Ephesus. He continued to wear the philosopher's cloak, and taught as a philosopher at Rome, where

Introductory Notes.

he was put to death (163-167). The date of his *First Apology* is a difficult question; but the doubt seems to lie between 138 and *cir.* 150. Of his *Dialogue with Trypho*, all that can be said is that it was written later.

Extracts XV-XVII are from the *First Apology*. In Extracts XV and XVI we see his view of heathenism, that though its errors and persecutions are the work of demons, Christ the Reason is still the teacher even of heathens, as many as were willing to live with reason, like Socrates and others. They should be compared with Clement (Extract XXX) and contrasted with Tertullian (Extract XXXIX). The interest of Extract XVII is in the full account given of Baptism, of the Lord's Supper, and of the Sunday morning service as it was held at Rome in his time. The allusion to Gospels will be noted; also the parallel with the *Didaché* (Extract VIII).

Extracts XVIII and XIX, from the *Dialogue with Trypho*, are discussions of some of the chief Messianic prophecies which used to be quoted against the Jews.

Extract XIX a contains a fragment of Hegesippus, which has an important bearing on the early history of the Roman church (especially if διαδοχήν be read) and on the general agreement of churches in his time.

Dionysius was bishop of Corinth about 170. Eusebius gives us a general account of his numerous letters, and quotes the two passages here selected.

Extract XX is from his answer to Soter, bishop of Rome, and gives an interesting testimony to the early influence of the Church (not the bishop) of Rome, to the liturgical use of the Epistle of Clement, and to the corruption by some of Scriptures which Dionysius plainly counts canonical. Extract X may be from the same letter, and is the earliest direct assertion of Peter's visit to Rome. That of Caius, just before it, seems to be rather later.

Extract XX a, where Tatian explains his conversion, 'sums up in a nut-shell the whole case of the Apologists' (Harnack).

The *Letter* of the Churches of Lyons and Vienne gives an account

Introductory Notes.

of the persecution in Gaul in the days of Marcus Aurelius (177). Its simple words are best left to speak for themselves.

Attention may be called to a few points. (1) Intercourse between the Rhone district and the East: frequency of Greek names. (2) Persecution partly from the mob, partly official, and includes the searching forbidden (Extract IX) by Trajan. (3) Blandina, a slave-girl—one of Clement's παιδίσκαι (Extract III).

Extract XXI a is the official narrative of the trial of certain Christians from Scili in Africa before the proconsul Vigellius Saturninus. The date is 180 ('Coss. Praesente et Claudiano'). Note the proconsul's gentleness, and the defiant tone of Speratus. The question about the books may hint the possibility of a charge of magic; but the answer cannot be taken to mean (Harnack) that St. Paul's Epistles were not yet fully canonical.

The Fragment on the Canon published by Muratori in 1740 is commonly ascribed to a younger contemporary of Pius of Rome, so that its date will be *cir.* 170. It was written in Greek, and at Rome, and may be as late as 200 or even later.

It is given complete in Extract XXII, so that its fragmentary character will easily be seen, especially near the end.

Irenaeus (b. in Asia 120-130) was a disciple of Polycarp and of others who had seen St. John. He settled for some time in Rome, and finally succeeded Pothinus as bishop of Lyons in 177. His great work against the Gnostics was written in the next decade. The original is in great part lost; but we have it complete in an old Latin translation.

Extract XIX b (chiefly from Irenaeus) gives his account of the Encratites, and of Tatian in particular. Extract XXIII sums up his account of the origin of the Gospels, and gives his view of the Apocalypse (Domitianic date) and of some uncanonical books. Extract XXV is a fragment of a letter to his old friend Florinus, who had taken up Gnostic opinions, and in it he tells us of his teacher Polycarp. Extract XXVII is his account of Marcion: the Greek is partly preserved by Eusebius, *H.E.* iv. 11. Extract XXVIII

gives his argument from Tradition, which must be carefully distinguished from Tertullian's. It speaks also of the pre-eminence of the Roman Church, (c) and of its orthodoxy kept pure by constant streams of visitors (see Extract XX); and gives a further account of Polycarp. Extract XXIX is a tradition 'of the Elders,' which probably comes from the Commentary of Papias.

Polycrates of Ephesus is hardly known to us except from this Extract XXVI, which is his answer to Victor of Rome *cir.* 196. He defends his Quartodeciman Easter by the example of St. John, and of the apostle Philip (compare Extract XIII).

Titus Flavius Clemens (b. *cir.* 150) studied philosophy under sundry teachers before he came to rest in Christianity. He succeeded Pantaenus as head of the catechetical school at Alexandria, but left the city (*cir.* 202) during the persecution of Severus. We find him some years later in Cilicia or Cappadocia; and he seems to have been dead *cir.* 216.

Extract XXX gives his view of the double preparation of the world for Christ—the Jews by the law, the Gentiles by philosophy. Extracts XXXI and XXXII show his relation to the Gnostics, and his conception of the ideal Christian character. Extract XXXIII opens out the whole question of the mode of interpreting Scripture, which the school of Alexandria did so much to clear up.

Quintus Septimius Florens Tertullianus (b. *cir.* 155 at Carthage) was the son of a centurion, and practised as a lawyer. He was converted to Christianity before 197, and became presbyter at Carthage. Between 202 and 207 he joined the Montanists, and died as one of them *cir.* 225.

Extracts XXXIV-XXXVIII are taken from his *Apology*. Extract XXXIV is a review of the persecutions, coloured by Christian unwillingness to believe that good emperors really did persecute. Extract XXXV is the rough sketch of his treatise *de Testimonio animae naturaliter Christianae*—the proof of Christianity from its correspondence with the nature of man. In Extract XXXVI (compare Extract XXXVIII) the empire is presented as the restraining power which delays the end of the world. Extract

Introductory Notes.

XXXVII is his famous boast of the numbers of the Christians; which, however, he gives not as a proof of Christianity; only as a reason for toleration. Extract XXXVIII is a general account of the Christian assemblies like Justin's (Extract XVII), but specially contrasts them with the disorderly heathen clubs. Extract XXXVIII a shows us the development of the ceremonial of Baptism since Justin's time; the Lord's Supper (now in the morning and called *sacramentum*) upon occasion including a commemoration of the dead, and of martyrs on the day of their passion ('birth'). Prayer *standing* on Sundays and after Easter (as Canon 20 of Nicaea, Extract LXXIV). Care of common food, and of the elements, and constant sign of the cross.

The next three Extracts (XXXIX-XLI) are from his 'most plausible and most mischievous book' (Hort) *de Praescriptionibus*. Extract XXXIX is to show that heretics deal with philosophical questions and borrow the answers of the philosophers. In Extract XL we have his argument from Tradition. As we cannot confute heretics by Scripture, we refuse to meet them on that ground, and simply answer that Churches once founded by the apostles must necessarily be still the possessors of the truth—an argument as good for Leo XIII as it ever was for Pope Victor. Extract XLI is a satirical account of the disorderly worship of heretics, probably Marcionites.

Extract XLII comments on the 'edict' (as if he were a magistrate) of Callistus (note ironical titles) which offered pardon (on penance) to some gross offenders, and (according to Montanists) made the Church a partaker of their sin. Extract XLIII is a vivid picture of the difficulties of Christian life in heathen society. Extract XLIV is another Montanist complaint, that Praxeas was not only unsound in the faith, but had persuaded the bishop of Rome (Victor or Zephyrinus) to revoke his sanction of Montanist prophecy. In Extract XLV Tertullian gives his objections to infant Baptism—prudential objections, for he has no idea of any apostolic command on the other side.

Hippolytus was a disciple of Irenaeus, and a bishop—of what city, Eusebius did not know. According to some, he was bishop of

Portus or of the foreigners in Portus; but more likely he claimed to be bishop of Rome in opposition to Callistus. In 235 he was exiled to Sardinia, and seems to have died there. Book I of his great work *Against all Heresies* was ascribed to Origen, till the discovery in 1842 of Books IV–X in a MS. on Mount Athos.

Extract XXIV gives his account of the Montanists and their prophetesses. Extract XLVI is a difficult passage, but its chief burden is the change made by Callistus in Church law, by recognizing unequal marriages which the State did not.

Origenes Adamantius (b. 185 or 186) was the son of Christian parents at Alexandria. His father Leonides was put to death in the persecution of Severus (202), and Origen soon afterwards (aged 18) succeeded Clement as head of the catechetical school. There he laboured with splendid success for nearly thirty years, till his ordination (231) in Palestine (with other causes) gave offence to Demetrius of Alexandria. Origen betook himself to Caesarea, and laboured there. He was tortured in the Decian persecution, and died of the effects *cir.* 254.

Extract XLVII (from Eusebius) shows Origen's wide conception of a liberal education. Extract XLVIII gives some idea of his principle of interpretation, that every passage of Scripture has a spiritual meaning, commonly more important than the literal; and in Extract LIII we have the answer of Porphyry from the heathen side, that allegorical interpretations are a mere subterfuge. Extracts XLIX–LI are taken from Origen's answer to Celsus. In Extract XLIX the heathen replies to our Lord's miracles, that they were done by magic; and indeed the mediums and spiritualists of this time were as skilful as our own. In Extract L Celsus disputes the evidence of our Lord's resurrection quite in the style of Renan or *Supernatural Religion.* In Extract LI comes Origen's answer to the charge that the Gospel is only meant for fools. Extracts LI a and LI b are intended to show the *modern* character of Origen's opinions on the inspiration and interpretation of Scripture. Extract LII is given as a sample of Origen's width of view and tendency to Universalism. In Extract LIV we have his conclusions on the authorship of the Epistle to the Hebrews.

Introductory Notes.

Extract LIV a is one of the certificates given to Christians who sacrificed in the Decian persecution. It shows how systematic the procedure was.

Dionysius of Alexandria was a disciple of Origen. He succeeded Heracles in 232 as head of the catechetical school, and again (247-8) as bishop. He went into hiding, like Cyprian, in the persecution of Decius (249-251), but in that of Valerian (257) escaped with exile. He returned (260) under Gallienus, and died in 265. We have only fragments of his works, mostly preserved by Eusebius.

Extract LV is intended to give a general view of the controversy with Novatian. In Extract LXIII his discussion of the authorship of the Apocalypse is a piece of criticism unsurpassed in ancient times.

Thascius Caecilius Cyprianus, b. *cir.* 200; teacher of rhetoric in Carthage; converted by presbyter Caecilius; very soon bishop of Carthage (*cir.* 248); went into hiding during the Decian persecution (249-251); executed in that of Valerian (258).

Extract LVI states Cyprian's theory of the Church, and his doctrine that there is no salvation outside it. Extract LVII gives his position against Novatus and against the confessors who misused their power of intercession for offenders. Extract LVIII shows the method of appointing bishops, and glances at his parallel of the Christian ministry with the Jewish priesthood. In Extracts LIX and LX we have his position against Stephen of Rome, that heretical or schismatical Baptism is worthless. Extract LXI is from Firmilian of Cappadocia, writing to Cyprian against Stephen. He makes short work of Roman claims. Note one of the first references to 2 Peter. Extract LXII is Cyprian's report of Valerian's Edict. It should be compared with Diocletian's in Extract LXVI.

Arnobius was a teacher of rhetoric at Sicca in Africa, and a recent convert when he wrote his *Adversus Nationes*, apparently during the persecution of Diocletian, which began in 303.

Extract LXVII is from his discussion of our Lord's miracles, and may be taken as a reply to the argument of Celsus (Extract XLIX) that they were works of magic.

L. Caelius Firmianus Lactantius (b. *cir.* 260 in Africa) was a disciple of Arnobius, and became Professor of Rhetoric at Nicomedia *cir.* 290, but had to lay down his office when the persecution broke out. He is said to have settled afterwards in Gaul, and become tutor to Constantine's son Crispus.

Extract LXVIII is from his chief work, the *Divinae Institutiones*, and gives his criticism of his predecessors, Minucius Felix, Tertullian, and Cyprian. The other extracts are taken from his bitter pamphlet *de Mortibus Persecutorum*. Extract LXIX is a hostile and unfair account of Diocletian's government. Extract LXX is the first edict of toleration, issued by Galerius from his deathbed in the spring of 311, while Extract LXXI is an Eastern reissue of the Edict of Milan issued by Constantine and Licinius about November 312. The reason given by Galerius is that every god is entitled to the worship of his own people, while the Edict of Milan allows every man to practice whatever worship he thinks fit.

Eusebius (b. *cir.* 265) was presbyter and (from soon after 313) bishop of Caesarea in Palestine. The most learned man of his time. His *Ecclesiastical History* contains carefully selected quotations from some fifty different authors. At Nicene Council 325; wrote his *Life of Constantine* after the emperor's death in 337, and himself died 339.

We have taken about twenty extracts from Eusebius, and discussed many of them already. There remain:—

Extracts XI and XII together give us a fair view of the Canon of the New Testament as acknowledged by Eusebius. He recognizes certain doubts about five Catholic Epistles, and himself leans against the Apocalypse: otherwise it is the same as our own. In Extract XI it must be noted that Eusebius does not undertake to tell us of writers who used undisputed books. In Extract XII the word *spurious* refers not so much to the question of authorship as to that of canonicity.

Extract LXIV is the rescript of Gallienus (260-268) extending to Egypt the toleration he had already established in quieter parts of the empire. In Extract LXV is the first application to an emperor to settle a Church dispute—Aurelian's test of orthodoxy is communion with the bishops of Italy and Rome. Extract LXVI gives the first three edicts of Diocletian. New lines of policy in the demolition of the Churches and the burnings of the Scriptures:

Introductory Notes. xxi

special measures against the clergy since Maximin (235-238). Extract LXXII is the famous story of Constantine's cross, as told to Eusebius by the emperor himself. The event took place as he was marching against Maxentius in 312. Extract LXXIII is the letter of Eusebius to his people at Caesarea, in which he relates the proceedings of the Nicene Council, and tells them how he overcame his objections to the Creed. The heterodox passage in brackets is omitted by Socrates.

Extract LXXIV consists of Canons selected from those of—

(1) Elvira. Date 306? These Canons are Spanish, and do not necessarily represent other parts of Christendom. *Can.* 6 is ambiguous in Latin as in the English; but usage settles that *ut* introduces the command, not the error. Contrast *Laod.* 29. *Can.* 33 is the first prohibition of marriage to the clergy: at Nicaea a similar proposal was rejected. *Can.* 36 is the first trace of picture-worship among Christians, and *Can.* 49 forbids a strange superstition of calling Jews as well as clergy to bless the crops. *Can.* 60 refuses the rank of martyrs to lawless destroyers of idols. The Spanish martyrs seem to have tended to fanaticism of that sort.

(2) Nicaea. Date 325. *Can.* 6 (prefaced by a notorious Roman forgery) settles the affairs of Egypt. *Can.* 19 orders the rebaptism of the followers of Paul of Samosata: which the Church of Rome construed as implying that ordinary heretics were *not* to be baptized. *Can.* 3 deals with a gross scandal of the time (the *subintroductae*). The interest of *Can.* 17 and *Can.* 20 is their difference from modern ideas. *Can.* 17 forbids the clergy to lend at interest, and *Can.* 20 forbids the faithful to kneel in prayer on Sundays or between Easter and Pentecost.

(3) Laodicea. Date 325-381. *Can.* 11 raises the questions, who these πρεσβύτιδες are, and whether their appointment or only their ordination is forbidden. *Can.* 13 along with Extract LVIII indicates the narrowing of the old election of bishops by their churches. *Can.* 28 marks the decay of the *agapé*. *Can.* 29 notes the duty (and the occasional impossibility) of ceasing work on Sundays.

Extract LXXV (untranslated) consists of fragments bearing on the religion of Rome. Its fundamental law is given from the Twelve Tables, and its unspiritual character comes out in

the extract from Cicero. The policy of the Empire is given on its conservative side by the advice of Maecenas to Augustus, and on its constructive side by the inscription referring to the official worship of Rome and Augustus at Lyons: and the second inscription mentions some of the Eastern worships which overspread the empire. Of the three intermediate passages, the first two refer to the persecution of converts by Septimius Severus and the tolerance of Severus Alexander. The third gives extracts from the Manichaean edict of Diocletian in 296. Note the burning of the books, and the comparative moderation of the first edict against the Christians.

SELECTIONS

FROM

EARLY CHRISTIAN WRITERS

I.

Ergo abolendo rumori Nero subdidit reos et quaesitissimis poenis adfecit, quos per flagitia invisos vulgus Christianos appellabat. Auctor nominis eius Christus Tiberio imperitante per procuratorem Pontium Pilatum
5 supplicio adfectus erat; repressaque in praesens exitiabilis superstitio rursum erumpebat, non modo per Iudaeam, originem eius mali, sed per urbem etiam, quo cuncta undique atrocia aut pudenda confluunt celebranturque. Igitur primum correpti qui fatebantur, inde indicio eorum
10 multitudo ingens haud perinde in crimine incendii quam odio humani generis convicti sunt. Et pereuntibus addita ludibria, ut ferarum tergis contecti, laniatu canum interirent aut crucibus adfixi, aut flammandi, atque[1] ubi defecisset dies, in usum nocturni luminis urerentur. Hortos suos
15 ei spectaculo Nero obtulerat et circense ludicrum edebat, habitu aurigae permixtus plebi vel curriculo insistens. Unde quamquam adversus sontes et novissima exempla meritos miseratio oriebatur, tamquam non utilitate publica sed in saevitiam unius absumerentur.

Tacitus, *Ann.* xv. 44.

II.

20 Διὰ τὰς αἰφνιδίους καὶ ἐπαλλήλους γενομένας[2] ἡμῖν συμφορὰς καὶ περιπτώσεις, ἀδελφοί, βράδιον νομίζομεν ἐπιστροφὴν πεποιῆσθαι περὶ τῶν ἐπιζητουμένων παρ' ὑμῖν

---

[1] adfixi, aut flammandi, atque] *adfixi sunt flammandi, utque* Franklin Arnold.   [2] ... ενας A; γενομένας CL; γινομένας S.

The Neronian Persecution (*Tacitus*).

So to stifle the report, Nero put in his own place as culprits and punished with every refinement of cruelty the men whom the common people hated for their secret crimes. They called them Christians. Christ, from whom the name was given, had been put to death in the reign of Tiberius by the procurator Pontius Pilate, and the pestilent superstition checked for awhile. Afterwards it began to break out afresh, not only in Judaea, where the mischief first arose, but also at Rome, where all sorts of murder and filthy shame meet together and become fashionable. In the first place then some were seized and made to confess; then on their information a vast multitude was convicted not so much of arson as of hatred for the human race. And they were not only put to death, but put to death with insult, in that they were either dressed up in the skins of beasts to perish by the worrying of dogs or else put on crosses to be set on fire, and when the daylight failed, to be burnt for use as lights by night. Nero had thrown open his gardens for that spectacle, and was giving a circus exhibition, mingling with the people in a jockey's dress, or driving a chariot. Hence commiseration arose, though it was for men of the worst character and deserving of the severest punishment, on the ground that they were not destroyed for the good of the state, but to satisfy the cruelty of an individual.

Opening of Clement's Letter to the Corinthians.

By reason of the sudden and repeated calamities and reverses which are befalling us, brethren, we consider that we have been somewhat tardy in giving heed to the

πραγμάτων, ἀγαπητοί, τῆς τε ἀλλοτρίας καὶ ξένης τοῖς ἐκλεκτοῖς τοῦ Θεοῦ, μιαρᾶς καὶ ἀνοσίου στάσεως, ἣν ὀλίγα πρόσωπα προπετῆ καὶ αὐθάδη ὑπάρχοντα εἰς τοσοῦτον ἀπονοίας ἐξέκαυσαν, ὥστε τὸ σεμνὸν καὶ περιβόητον καὶ πᾶσιν ἀνθρώποις ἀξιαγάπητον ὄνομα ὑμῶν μεγάλως βλασφημηθῆναι. τίς γὰρ παρεπιδημήσας πρὸς ὑμᾶς τὴν πανάρετον καὶ βεβαίαν ὑμῶν πίστιν οὐκ ἐδοκίμασεν; τήν τε σώφρονα καὶ ἐπιεικῆ ἐν Χριστῷ εὐσέβειαν οὐκ ἐθαύμασεν; καὶ τὸ μεγαλοπρεπὲς τῆς φιλοξενίας ὑμῶν ἦθος οὐκ ἐκήρυξεν; καὶ τὴν τελείαν καὶ ἀσφαλῆ γνῶσιν οὐκ ἐμακάρισεν; ἀπροσωπολήμπτως γὰρ πάντα ἐποιεῖτε, καὶ τοῖς νομίμοις[1] τοῦ Θεοῦ ἐπορεύεσθε, ὑποτασσόμενοι τοῖς ἡγουμένοις ὑμῶν καὶ τιμὴν τὴν καθήκουσαν ἀπονέμοντες τοῖς παρ᾽ ὑμῖν πρεσβυτέροις· νέοις τε μέτρια καὶ σεμνὰ νοεῖν ἐπετρέπετε· γυναιξίν τε ἐν ἀμώμῳ καὶ σεμνῇ καὶ ἁγνῇ συνειδήσει πάντα ἐπιτελεῖν παρηγγέλλετε, στεργούσας καθηκόντως τοὺς ἄνδρας ἑαυτῶν· ἔν τε τῷ κανόνι τῆς ὑποταγῆς ὑπαρχούσας τὰ κατὰ τὸν οἶκον σεμνῶς οἰκουργεῖν ἐδιδάσκετε, πάνυ σωφρονούσας.

CLEMENS ROMANUS, Ad Cor. i.

III.

Ἀλλ᾽ ἵνα τῶν ἀρχαίων ὑποδειγμάτων παυσώμεθα, ἔλθωμεν ἐπὶ τοὺς ἔγγιστα γενομένους ἀθλητάς· λάβωμεν τῆς γενεᾶς ἡμῶν τὰ γενναῖα ὑποδείγματα. διὰ ζῆλον καὶ φθόνον οἱ μέγιστοι καὶ δικαιότατοι στύλοι ἐδιώχθησαν καὶ ἕως θανάτου ἤθλησαν. λάβωμεν πρὸ ὀφθαλμῶν ἡμῶν τοὺς ἀγαθοὺς ἀποστόλους· Πέτρον, ὃς διὰ ζῆλον ἄδικον οὐχ ἕνα οὐδὲ δύο ἀλλὰ πλείονας ὑπήνεγκεν πόνους, καὶ οὕτω μαρτυρήσας ἐπορεύθη εἰς τὸν ὀφειλόμενον τόπον τῆς δόξης. διὰ ζῆλον καὶ ἔριν Παῦλος ὑπομονῆς βραβεῖον

[1] τοῖς νομίμοις] Clem. Alex., τοῖς νόμοις AC; *in lege* S.

matters of dispute that have arisen among you, dearly
beloved, and to the detestable and unholy sedition, so
alien and strange to the elect of God, which a few head-
strong and self-willed persons have kindled to such
a pitch of madness that your name, once revered and
renowned and lovely in the sight of all men, hath been
greatly reviled. For who that had sojourned among you
did not approve your most virtuous and steadfast faith?
Who did not admire your sober and forbearing piety in
Christ? Who did not publish abroad your magnificent
disposition of hospitality? Who did not congratulate
you on your perfect and sound knowledge? For ye did
all things without respect of persons, and ye walked after
the ordinances of God, submitting yourselves to your
rulers and rendering to the older men among you the
honour which is their due. On the young too ye enjoined
modest and seemly thoughts: and the women ye charged
to perform all their duties in a blameless and seemly and
pure conscience, cherishing their own husbands, as is
meet; and ye taught them to keep in the rule of obedience,
and to manage the affairs of their household in seemliness,
with all discretion.   L.

The Neronian Persecution (Clement).

BUT, to pass from the examples of ancient days, let us
come to those champions who lived nearest to our time.
Let us set before us the noble examples which belong to our
generation. By reason of jealousy and envy the greatest
and most righteous pillars of the Church were persecuted,
and contended even unto death. Let us set before our
eyes the good Apostles. There was Peter who by reason
of unrighteous jealousy endured not one nor two but
many labours, and thus having borne his testimony went
to his appointed place of glory. By reason of jealousy
and strife Paul by his example pointed out the prize of

ὑπέδειξεν, ἑπτάκις δεσμὰ φορέσας, φυγαδευθείς, λιθασ-
θείς, κῆρυξ γενόμενος ἔν τε τῇ ἀνατολῇ καὶ ἐν τῇ δύσει,
τὸ γενναῖον τῆς πίστεως αὐτοῦ κλέος ἔλαβεν, δικαιοσύνην
διδάξας ὅλον τὸν κόσμον καὶ ἐπὶ τὸ τέρμα τῆς δύσεως
5 ἐλθών· καὶ μαρτυρήσας ἐπὶ τῶν ἡγουμένων, οὕτως ἀπηλ-
λάγη τοῦ κόσμου καὶ εἰς τὸν ἅγιον τόπον ἐπορεύθη,
ὑπομονῆς γενόμενος μέγιστος ὑπογραμμός.

Τούτοις τοῖς ἀνδράσιν ὁσίως πολιτευσαμένοις συνη-
θροίσθη πολὺ πλῆθος ἐκλεκτῶν, οἵτινες πολλαῖς αἰκίαις
10 καὶ βασάνοις, διὰ ζῆλος παθόντες, ὑπόδειγμα κάλλιστον
ἐγένοντο ἐν ἡμῖν. διὰ ζῆλος διωχθεῖσαι γυναῖκες, Δαναΐδες καὶ Δίρκαι¹, αἰκίσματα δεινὰ καὶ ἀνόσια παθοῦσαι,
ἐπὶ τὸν τῆς πίστεως βέβαιον δρόμον κατήντησαν καὶ
ἔλαβον γέρας γενναῖον αἱ ἀσθενεῖς τῷ σώματι.

Ibid. v, vi.

IV.

15 Προδήλων οὖν ἡμῖν ὄντων τούτων, καὶ ἐγκεκυφότες
εἰς τὰ βάθη τῆς θείας γνώσεως, πάντα τάξει ποιεῖν
ὀφείλομεν ὅσα ὁ δεσπότης ἐπιτελεῖν ἐκέλευσεν κατὰ
καιροὺς τεταγμένους· τάς τε προσφορὰς καὶ λειτουργίας
ἐπιμελῶς ἐπιτελεῖσθαι καὶ οὐκ εἰκῆ ἢ ἀτάκτως ἐκέλευσεν
20 γίνεσθαι, ἀλλ᾽ ὡρισμένοις καιροῖς καὶ ὥραις· ποῦ τε καὶ
διὰ τίνων ἐπιτελεῖσθαι θέλει, αὐτὸς ὥρισεν τῇ ὑπερτάτῳ
αὐτοῦ βουλήσει· ἵν᾽ ὁσίως πάντα γινόμενα ἐν εὐδοκήσει
εὐπρόσδεκτα εἴη τῷ θελήματι αὐτοῦ· οἱ οὖν τοῖς προσ-
τεταγμένοις καιροῖς ποιοῦντες τὰς προσφορὰς αὐτῶν εὐ-
25 πρόσδεκτοί τε καὶ μακάριοι, τοῖς γὰρ νομίμοις τοῦ δεσπότου
ἀκολουθοῦντες οὐ διαμαρτάνουσιν. τῷ γὰρ ἀρχιερεῖ ἴδιαι
λειτουργίαι δεδομέναι εἰσίν, καὶ τοῖς ἱερεῦσιν ἴδιος ὁ τόπος

¹ Δαναΐδες καὶ Δίρκαι] ACS; νεάνιδες παιδίσκαι coni. Wordsworth.

patient endurance. After that he had been seven times in bonds, had been driven into exile, had been stoned, had preached in the East and in the West, he won the noble renown which was the reward of his faith, having taught righteousness unto the whole world and having reached the farthest bounds of the West; and when he had borne his testimony before the rulers, so he departed from the world and went unto the holy place, having been found a notable pattern of patient endurance.

Unto these men of holy lives was gathered a vast multitude of the elect, who through many indignities and tortures, being the victims of jealousy, set a brave example among ourselves. By reason of jealousy women being persecuted after they had suffered cruel and unholy insults as Danaids and Dircae, safely reached the goal in the race of faith, and received a noble reward, feeble though they were in body. L.

Arrangements settled by the Apostles.

FORASMUCH then as these things are manifest beforehand, and we have searched into the depths of the Divine knowledge, we ought to do all things in order, as many as the Master hath commanded us to perform at their appointed seasons. Now the offerings and ministrations He commanded to be performed with care, and not to be done rashly or in disorder, but at fixed times and seasons. And where and by whom He would have them performed, He Himself fixed by His supreme will: that all things being done with piety according to His good pleasure might be acceptable to His will. They therefore that make their offerings at the appointed seasons are acceptable and blessed: for while they follow the institutions of the Master they cannot go wrong. For unto the highpriest his proper services have been assigned, and to the priests their proper office is appointed, and upon the

προστέτακται, καὶ λευΐταις ἴδιαι διακονίαι ἐπίκεινται· ὁ
λαϊκὸς ἄνθρωπος τοῖς λαϊκοῖς προστάγμασιν δέδεται.

Ἕκαστος ὑμῶν, ἀδελφοί, ἐν τῷ ἰδίῳ τάγματι εὐχαρισ-
τείτω Θεῷ ἐν ἀγαθῇ συνειδήσει ὑπάρχων, μὴ παρεκ-
βαίνων τὸν ὡρισμένον τῆς λειτουργίας αὐτοῦ κανόνα, ἐν
σεμνότητι. οὐ πανταχοῦ, ἀδελφοί, προσφέρονται θυσίαι
ἐνδελεχισμοῦ ἢ εὐχῶν ἢ περὶ ἁμαρτίας καὶ πλημμελείας,
ἀλλ᾽ ἢ ἐν Ἱερουσαλὴμ μόνῃ· κἀκεῖ δὲ οὐκ ἐν παντὶ τόπῳ
προσφέρεται, ἀλλ᾽ ἔμπροσθεν τοῦ ναοῦ πρὸς τὸ θυσιαστή-
ριον, μωμοσκοπηθὲν τὸ προσφερόμενον διὰ τοῦ ἀρχιερέως
καὶ τῶν προειρημένων λειτουργῶν. οἱ οὖν παρὰ τὸ καθῆκον
τῆς βουλήσεως αὐτοῦ ποιοῦντές τι θάνατον τὸ πρόστιμον
ἔχουσιν. ὁρᾶτε, ἀδελφοί, ὅσῳ πλείονος κατηξιώθημεν
γνώσεως, τοσούτῳ μᾶλλον ὑποκείμεθα κινδύνῳ.

Οἱ ἀπόστολοι ἡμῖν εὐηγγελίσθησαν ἀπὸ τοῦ Κυρίου
Ἰησοῦ Χριστοῦ, Ἰησοῦς ὁ Χριστὸς ἀπὸ τοῦ Θεοῦ ἐξ-
επέμφθη. ὁ Χριστὸς οὖν ἀπὸ τοῦ Θεοῦ, καὶ οἱ ἀπόστολοι ἀπὸ τοῦ Χριστοῦ· ἐγένοντο οὖν ἀμφότερα εὐτάκτως
ἐκ θελήματος Θεοῦ. παραγγελίας οὖν λαβόντες καὶ
πληροφορηθέντες διὰ τῆς ἀναστάσεως τοῦ Κυρίου ἡμῶν
Ἰησοῦ Χριστοῦ καὶ πιστωθέντες ἐν τῷ λόγῳ τοῦ Θεοῦ
μετὰ πληροφορίας πνεύματος ἁγίου ἐξῆλθον, εὐαγγελιζόμε-
νοι τὴν βασιλείαν τοῦ Θεοῦ μέλλειν ἔρχεσθαι. κατὰ χώρας
οὖν καὶ πόλεις κηρύσσοντες καθίστανον τὰς ἀπαρχὰς
αὐτῶν, δοκιμάσαντες τῷ πνεύματι, εἰς ἐπισκόπους καὶ
διακόνους τῶν μελλόντων πιστεύειν. καὶ τοῦτο οὐ καινῶς,
ἐκ γὰρ δὴ πολλῶν χρόνων ἐγέγραπτο περὶ ἐπισκόπων καὶ
διακόνων· οὕτως γάρ που λέγει ἡ γραφή· Καταστήσω
τοὺς ἐπισκόπους αὐτῶν ἐν δικαιοσύνῃ καὶ τοὺς διακόνους
αὐτῶν ἐν πίστει.

* * * * * * *

Καὶ οἱ ἀπόστολοι ἡμῶν ἔγνωσαν διὰ τοῦ Κυρίου ἡμῶν
Ἰησοῦ Χριστοῦ ὅτι ἔρις ἔσται ἐπὶ τοῦ ὀνόματος τῆς

levites their proper ministrations are laid. The layman is bound by the layman's ordinances.

Let each of you, brethren, in his own order give thanks unto God, maintaining a good conscience and not transgressing the appointed rule of His service, but acting with all seemliness. Not in every place, brethren, are the continual daily sacrifices offered, or the freewill offerings, or the sin offerings and the trespass offerings, but in Jerusalem alone. And even there the offering is not made in every place, but before the sanctuary in the court of the altar; and this too through the high-priest and the aforesaid ministers, after that the victim to be offered hath been inspected for blemishes. They therefore who do any thing contrary to the seemly ordinance of His will receive death as the penalty. Ye see, brethren, in proportion as greater knowledge hath been vouchsafed unto us, so much the more are we exposed to danger.

The Apostles received the Gospel for us from the Lord Jesus Christ; Jesus Christ was sent forth from God. So then Christ is from God, and the Apostles are from Christ. Both therefore came of the will of God in the appointed order. Having therefore received a charge, and having been fully assured through the resurrection of our Lord Jesus Christ and confirmed in the word of God with full assurance of the Holy Ghost, they went forth with the glad tidings that the kingdom of God should come. So preaching everywhere in country and town, they appointed their first-fruits, when they had proved them by the Spirit, to be bishops and deacons unto them that should believe. And this they did in no new fashion; for indeed it had been written concerning bishops and deacons from very ancient times; for thus saith the scripture in a certain place, I will appoint their bishops in righteousness and their deacons in faith.

* * * * * * *

And our Apostles knew through our Lord Jesus Christ that there would be strife over the name of the bishop's

ἐπισκοπῆς. διὰ ταύτην οὖν τὴν αἰτίαν πρόγνωσιν εἰληφότες τελείαν κατέστησαν τοὺς προειρημένους, καὶ μεταξὺ ἐπιμονὴν[1] δεδώκασιν ὅπως, ἐὰν κοιμηθῶσιν, διαδέξωνται ἕτεροι δεδοκιμασμένοι ἄνδρες τὴν λειτουργίαν αὐτῶν. τοὺς οὖν κατασταθέντας ὑπ' ἐκείνων ἢ μεταξὺ ὑφ' ἑτέρων ἐλλογίμων ἀνδρῶν, συνευδοκησάσης τῆς ἐκκλησίας πάσης, καὶ λειτουργήσαντας ἀμέμπτως τῷ ποιμνίῳ τοῦ Χριστοῦ μετὰ ταπεινοφροσύνης ἡσύχως καὶ ἀβαναύσως. μεμαρτυρημένους τε πολλοῖς χρόνοις ὑπὸ πάντων, τούτους οὐ δικαίως νομίζομεν ἀποβάλλεσθαι τῆς λειτουργίας. ἁμαρτία γὰρ οὐ μικρὰ ἡμῖν ἔσται, ἐὰν τοὺς ἀμέμπτως καὶ ὁσίως προσενεγκόντας τὰ δῶρα τῆς ἐπισκοπῆς ἀποβάλωμεν. μακάριοι οἱ προοδοιπορήσαντες πρεσβύτεροι, οἵτινες ἔγκαρπον καὶ τελείαν ἔσχον τὴν ἀνάλυσιν· οὐ γὰρ εὐλαβοῦνται μή τις αὐτοὺς μεταστήσῃ ἀπὸ τοῦ ἱδρυμένου αὐτοῖς τόπου. ὁρῶμεν γὰρ ὅτι ἐνίους ὑμεῖς μετηγάγετε καλῶς πολιτευομένους ἐκ τῆς ἀμέμπτως αὐτοῖς τετιμημένης λειτουργίας.

Ibid. xl–xlii, xliv.

IV A.

Κἀν τῷ αὐτῷ ἔτει ἄλλους τε πολλοὺς καὶ τὸν Φλαούιον Κλήμεντα ὑπατεύοντα, καίπερ ἀνεψιὸν ὄντα καὶ γυναῖκα καὶ αὐτὴν συγγενῆ ἑαυτοῦ Φλαουίαν Δομιτίλλαν ἔχοντα, κατέσφαξεν ὁ Δομιτιανός. ἐπηνέχθη δὲ ἀμφοῖν ἔγκλημα ἀθεότητος, ὑφ' ἧς καὶ ἄλλοι ἐς τὰ τῶν Ἰουδαίων ἔθη ἐξοκέλλοντες πολλοὶ κατεδικάσθησαν, καὶ οἱ μὲν ἀπέθανον, οἱ δὲ τῶν γοῦν οὐσιῶν ἐστερήθησαν· ἡ δὲ Δομιτίλλα ὑπερωρίσθη μόνον ἐς Πανδατερίαν. τὸν δὲ δὴ Γλαβρίωνα τὸν μετὰ τοῦ Τραιανοῦ ἄρξαντα, κατηγορηθέντα τά τε ἄλλα καὶ οἷα οἱ πολλοὶ καὶ ὅτι θηρίοις ἐμάχετο, ἀπέκτεινεν.

DIO CASSIUS, *Epitome*, lxvii. 14.

[1] ἐπιμονὴν] coni. Turner; ἐπινομὴν A; ἐπιδομὴν C; super probatione [ἐπὶ δοκιμῇ] S.

office. For this cause therefore, having received complete foreknowledge, they appointed the aforesaid persons, and afterwards they provided a continuance, that if these should fall asleep, other approved men should succeed to their ministration. Those therefore who were appointed by them, or afterward by other men of repute with the consent of the whole Church, and have ministered unblameably to the flock of Christ in lowliness of mind, peacefully and with all modesty, and for long time have borne a good report with all—these men we consider to be unjustly thrust out from their ministration. For it will be no light sin for us, if we thrust out those who have offered the gifts of the bishop's office unblameably and holily. Blessed are those presbyters who have gone before, seeing that their departure was fruitful and ripe: for they have no fear lest any one should remove them from their appointed place. For we see that ye have displaced certain persons, though they were living honourably, from the ministration which had been respected by them blamelessly.

L.

The Persecution of Domitian.

AND in the same year Domitian slew amongst many others Flavius Clemens in his consulship, though he was his cousin and had to wife his own kinswoman, Flavia Domitilla. Against them both was brought a charge of atheism: and on this many others who made shipwreck on Jewish customs were condemned, of whom some were put to death, while others were at the least deprived of their property; but Domitilla was only banished to Pandateria. Glabrio, however, who had been consul with Trajan, he also slew, partly on the same charges as the rest, and partly because he fought with beasts.

V.

Πάντες τῷ ἐπισκόπῳ ἀκολουθεῖτε, ὡς Ἰησοῦς Χριστὸς τῷ πατρί, καὶ τῷ πρεσβυτερίῳ ὡς τοῖς ἀποστόλοις· τοὺς δὲ διακόνους ἐντρέπεσθε ὡς Θεοῦ ἐντολήν. μηδεὶς χωρὶς ἐπισκόπου τι πρασσέτω τῶν ἀνηκόντων εἰς τὴν ἐκκλη-
5 σίαν. ἐκείνη βεβαία εὐχαριστία ἡγείσθω ἡ ὑπὸ τὸν ἐπίσκοπον οὖσα, ἢ ᾧ ἂν αὐτὸς ἐπιτρέψῃ. ὅπου ἂν φανῇ ὁ ἐπίσκοπος, ἐκεῖ τὸ πλῆθος ἔστω, ὥσπερ ὅπου ἂν ᾖ Χριστὸς Ἰησοῦς, ἐκεῖ ἡ καθολικὴ ἐκκλησία. οὐκ ἐξόν ἐστιν χωρὶς τοῦ ἐπισκόπου οὔτε βαπτίζειν οὔτε ἀγάπην
10 ποιεῖν· ἀλλ' ὃ ἂν ἐκεῖνος δοκιμάσῃ, τοῦτο καὶ τῷ Θεῷ εὐάρεστον, ἵνα ἀσφαλὲς ᾖ καὶ βέβαιον πᾶν ὃ πράσσετε.

IGNATIUS, *Ad Smyrn.* viii.

VI.

Κωφώθητε οὖν, ὅταν ὑμῖν χωρὶς Ἰησοῦ Χριστοῦ λαλῇ τις, τοῦ ἐκ γένους Δαυείδ, τοῦ ἐκ Μαρίας, ὃς ἀληθῶς ἐγεννήθη, ἔφαγέν τε καὶ ἔπιεν, ἀληθῶς ἐδιώχθη ἐπὶ
15 Ποντίου Πιλάτου, ἀληθῶς ἐσταυρώθη καὶ ἀπέθανεν, βλεπόντων [τῶν] ἐπουρανίων καὶ ἐπιγείων καὶ ὑποχθονίων· ὃς καὶ ἀληθῶς ἠγέρθη ἀπὸ νεκρῶν, ἐγείραντος αὐτὸν τοῦ πατρὸς αὐτοῦ, κατὰ τὸ ὁμοίωμα ὃς καὶ ἡμᾶς τοὺς πιστεύοντας αὐτῷ οὕτως ἐγερεῖ ὁ πατὴρ αὐτοῦ ἐν Χριστῷ
20 Ἰησοῦ, οὗ χωρὶς τὸ ἀληθινὸν ζῆν οὐκ ἔχομεν.

Εἰ δέ, ὥσπερ τινες ἄθεοι ὄντες, τουτέστιν ἄπιστοι, λέγουσιν τὸ δοκεῖν πεπονθέναι αὐτόν, αὐτοὶ ὄντες τὸ δοκεῖν, ἐγὼ τί δέδεμαι; τί δὲ καὶ εὔχομαι θηριομαχῆσαι; δωρεὰν οὖν ἀποθνήσκω. ἄρα οὖν καταψεύδομαι τοῦ Κυρίου.

Ibid. ix, x.

VII.

25 Χριστιανοὶ γὰρ οὔτε γῇ οὔτε φωνῇ οὔτε ἔθεσι διακεκριμένοι τῶν λοιπῶν εἰσὶν ἀνθρώπων. οὔτε γάρ που πόλεις ἰδίας κατοικοῦσιν οὔτε διαλέκτῳ τινὶ παρηλλαγ-

Ignatius on Episcopacy.

Do ye all follow your bishop, as Jesus Christ followed the Father, and the presbytery as the Apostles; and to the deacons pay respect, as to God's commandment. Let no man do aught of things pertaining to the Church apart from the bishop. Let that be held a valid eucharist which is under the bishop or one to whom he shall have committed it. Wheresoever the bishop shall appear, there let the people be; even as where Jesus Christ may be, there is the universal Church. It is not lawful apart from the bishop either to baptize or to hold a love-feast; but whatsoever he shall approve, this is well-pleasing also to God; that everything which ye do may be sure and valid.

L.

Ignatius on Docetism.

BE ye deaf therefore, when any man speaketh to you apart from Jesus Christ, who was of the race of David, who was the Son of Mary, who was truly born and ate and drank, was truly persecuted under Pontius Pilate, was truly crucified and died in the sight of those in heaven and those on earth and those under the earth; who moreover was truly raised from the dead, His Father having raised Him, who in the like fashion will so raise us also who believe on Him—His Father, I say, will raise us—in Christ Jesus, apart from whom we have not true life.

But if it were as certain persons who are godless, that is unbelievers, say, that He suffered only in semblance, being themselves mere semblance, why am I in bonds? And why also do I desire to fight with wild beasts? So I die in vain. Truly then I lie against the Lord.

L.

The Christians in the World.

FOR Christians are not distinguished from the rest of mankind either in locality or in speech or in customs. For they dwell not somewhere in cities of their own, neither do they use some different language, nor practise

μένῃ χρῶνται οὔτε βίον παράσημον ἀσκοῦσιν. οὐ μὴν ἐπινοίᾳ τινὶ καὶ φροντίδι πολυπραγμόνων ἀνθρώπων μάθημα τοιοῦτ᾽ αὐτοῖς ἐστὶν εὑρημένον, οὐδὲ δόγματος ἀνθρωπίνου προεστᾶσιν, ὥσπερ ἔνιοι. κατοικοῦντες δὲ πόλεις Ἑλλη-
5 νίδας τε καὶ βαρβάρους ὡς ἕκαστος ἐκληρώθη, καὶ τοῖς ἐγχωρίοις ἔθεσιν ἀκολουθοῦντες ἔν τε ἐσθῆτι καὶ διαίτῃ καὶ τῷ λοιπῷ βίῳ, θαυμαστὴν καὶ ὁμολογουμένως παράδοξον ἐνδείκνυνται τὴν κατάστασιν τῆς ἑαυτῶν πολιτείας. πατρίδας οἰκοῦσιν ἰδίας, ἀλλ᾽ ὡς πάροικοι·
10 μετέχουσι πάντων ὡς πολῖται, καὶ πάνθ᾽ ὑπομένουσιν ὡς ξένοι· πᾶσα ξένη πατρίς ἐστιν αὐτῶν, καὶ πᾶσα πατρὶς ξένη. γαμοῦσιν ὡς πάντες, τεκνογονοῦσιν· ἀλλ᾽ οὐ ῥίπτουσι τὰ γεννώμενα. τράπεζαν κοινὴν παρατίθενται, ἀλλ᾽ οὐ κοίτην. ἐν σαρκὶ τυγχάνουσιν, ἀλλ᾽ οὐ
15 κατὰ σάρκα ζῶσιν. ἐπὶ γῆς διατρίβουσιν, ἀλλ᾽ ἐν οὐρανῷ πολιτεύονται. πείθονται τοῖς ὡρισμένοις νόμοις, καὶ τοῖς ἰδίοις βίοις νικῶσι τοὺς νόμους. ἀγαπῶσι πάντας, καὶ ὑπὸ πάντων διώκονται. ἀγνοοῦνται, καὶ κατακρίνονται· θανατοῦνται, καὶ ζωοποιοῦνται. πτωχεύουσι, καὶ
20 πλουτίζουσι πολλούς· πάντων ὑστεροῦνται, καὶ ἐν πᾶσι περισσεύουσιν. ἀτιμοῦνται, καὶ ἐν ταῖς ἀτιμίαις δοξάζονται· βλασφημοῦνται, καὶ δικαιοῦνται. λοιδοροῦνται, καὶ εὐλογοῦσιν· ὑβρίζονται καὶ τιμῶσιν. ἀγαθοποιοῦντες ὡς κακοὶ κολάζονται· κολαζόμενοι χαίρουσιν ὡς ζωοποιού-
25 μενοι. ὑπὸ Ἰουδαίων ὡς ἀλλόφυλοι πολεμοῦνται καὶ ὑπὸ Ἑλλήνων διώκονται· καὶ τὴν αἰτίαν τῆς ἔχθρας εἰπεῖν οἱ μισοῦντες οὐκ ἔχουσιν.

Ἁπλῶς δ᾽ εἰπεῖν, ὅπερ ἐστὶν ἐν σώματι ψυχή, τοῦτ᾽ εἰσὶν ἐν κόσμῳ Χριστιανοί. ἔσπαρται κατὰ πάντων
30 τῶν τοῦ σώματος μελῶν ἡ ψυχή, καὶ Χριστιανοὶ κατὰ τὰς τοῦ κόσμου πόλεις. οἰκεῖ μὲν ἐν τῷ σώματι ψυχή, οὐκ ἔστι δὲ ἐκ τοῦ σώματος· καὶ Χριστιανοὶ ἐν κόσμῳ οἰκοῦσιν, οὐκ εἰσὶ δὲ ἐκ τοῦ κόσμου. ἀόρατος ἡ ψυχὴ ἐν ὁρατῷ φρουρεῖται τῷ σώματι· καὶ Χριστιανοὶ γινώ-
35 σκονται μὲν ὄντες ἐν τῷ κόσμῳ ἀόρατος δὲ αὐτῶν ἡ θεο-

an extraordinary kind of life. Nor again do they possess any invention discovered by any intelligence or study of ingenious men, nor are they masters of any human dogma as some are. But while they dwell in cities of Greeks and barbarians as the lot of each is cast, and follow the native customs in dress and food and the other arrangements of life, yet the constitution of their own citizenship, which they set forth, is marvellous, and confessedly contradicts expectation. They dwell in their own countries, but only as sojourners; they bear their share in all things as citizens, and they endure all hardships as strangers. Every foreign country is a fatherland to them, and every fatherland is foreign. They marry like all other men and they beget children; but they do not cast away their offspring. They have their meals in common, but not their wives. They find themselves in the flesh, and yet they live not after the flesh. Their existence is on earth, but their citizenship is in heaven. They obey the established laws, and they surpass the laws in their own lives. They love all men, and they are persecuted by all. They are ignored, and yet they are condemned. They are put to death, and yet they are endued with life. They are in beggary, and yet they make many rich. They are in want of all things, and yet they abound in all things. They are dishonoured, and yet they are glorified in their dishonour. They are evil spoken of, and yet they are vindicated. They are reviled, and they bless; they are insulted, and they respect. Doing good they are punished as evil-doers; being punished they rejoice, as if they were thereby quickened by life. War is waged against them as aliens by the Jews, and persecution is carried on against them by the Greeks, and yet those that hate them cannot tell the reason of their hostility.

In a word, what the soul is in a body, this the Christians are in the world. The soul is spread through all the members of the body, and Christians through the divers cities of the world. The soul hath its abode in the body, and yet it is not of the body. So Christians have their abode in the world, and yet they are not of the world. The soul which is invisible is guarded in the body which is visible: so Christians are recognised as being in the world, and yet their religion remaineth

σέβεια μένει. μισεῖ τὴν ψυχὴν ἡ σὰρξ καὶ πολεμεῖ μηδὲν ἀδικουμένη, διότι ταῖς ἡδοναῖς κωλύεται χρῆσθαι· μισεῖ καὶ Χριστιανοὺς ὁ κόσμος μηδὲν ἀδικούμενος, ὅτι ταῖς ἡδοναῖς ἀντιτάσσονται. ἡ ψυχὴ τὴν μισοῦσαν
5 ἀγαπᾷ σάρκα καὶ τὰ μέλη· καὶ Χριστιανοὶ τοὺς μισοῦντας ἀγαπῶσιν. ἐγκέκλεισται μὲν ἡ ψυχὴ τῷ σώματι, συνέχει δὲ αὐτὴ τὸ σῶμα· καὶ Χριστιανοὶ κατέχονται μὲν ὡς ἐν φρουρᾷ τῷ κόσμῳ, αὐτοὶ δὲ συνέχουσι τὸν κόσμον. ἀθάνατος ἡ ψυχὴ ἐν θνητῷ σκηνώματι κατοικεῖ·
10 καὶ Χριστιανοὶ παροικοῦσιν ἐν φθαρτοῖς, τὴν ἐν οὐρανοῖς ἀφθαρσίαν προσδεχόμενοι. κακουργουμένη σιτίοις καὶ ποτοῖς ἡ ψυχὴ βελτιοῦται· καὶ Χριστιανοὶ κολαζόμενοι καθ' ἡμέραν πλεονάζουσι μᾶλλον. εἰς τοσαύτην αὐτοὺς τάξιν ἔθετο ὁ Θεός, ἣν οὐ θεμιτὸν αὐτοῖς παραιτήσασθαι.
15 Οὐ γὰρ ἐπίγειον, ὡς ἔφην, εὕρημα τοῦτ' αὐτοῖς παρεδόθη, οὐδὲ θνητὴν ἐπίνοιαν φυλάσσειν οὕτως ἀξιοῦσιν ἐπιμελῶς, οὐδὲ ἀνθρωπίνων οἰκονομίαν μυστηρίων πεπίστευνται. ἀλλ' αὐτὸς ἀληθῶς ὁ παντοκράτωρ καὶ παντοκτίστης καὶ ἀόρατος Θεός, αὐτὸς ἀπ' οὐρανῶν τὴν
20 ἀλήθειαν καὶ τὸν λόγον τὸν ἅγιον καὶ ἀπερινόητον ἀνθρώποις ἐνίδρυσε καὶ ἐγκατεστήριξε ταῖς καρδίαις αὐτῶν, οὐ καθάπερ ἄν τις εἰκάσειεν ἄνθρωπος, ὑπηρέτην τινὰ πέμψας ἢ ἄγγελον ἢ ἄρχοντα ἤ τινα τῶν διεπόντων τὰ ἐπίγεια ἤ τινα τῶν πεπιστευμένων τὰς ἐν οὐρανοῖς διοικήσεις, ἀλλ'
25 αὐτὸν τὸν τεχνίτην καὶ δημιουργὸν τῶν ὅλων, ᾧ τοὺς οὐρανοὺς ἔκτισεν, ᾧ τὴν θάλασσαν ἰδίοις ὅροις ἐνέκλεισεν, οὗ τὰ μυστήρια πιστῶς πάντα φυλάσσει τὰ στοιχεῖα, παρ' οὗ τὰ μέτρα τῶν τῆς ἡμέρας δρόμων [ἥλιος] εἴληφε φυλάσσειν, ᾧ πειθαρχεῖ σελήνη νυκτὶ φαίνειν κελεύοντι,

invisible. The flesh hateth the soul and wageth war with it, though it receiveth no wrong, because it is forbidden to indulge in pleasures; so the world hateth Christians, though it receiveth no wrong from them, because they set themselves against its pleasures. The soul loveth the flesh which hateth it, and the members: so Christians love those that hate them. The soul is enclosed in the body, and yet itself holdeth the body together; so Christians are kept in the world as in a prison-house, and yet they themselves hold the world together. The soul though itself immortal dwelleth in a mortal tabernacle; so Christians sojourn amidst perishable things, while they look for the imperishability which is in the heavens. The soul when hardly treated in the matter of meats and drinks is improved; and so Christians when punished increase more and more daily. So great is the office for which God hath appointed them, and which it is not lawful for them to decline.

For it is no earthly discovery, as I said, which was committed to them, neither do they care to guard so carefully any mortal invention, nor have they entrusted to them the dispensation of human mysteries. But truly the Almighty Creator of the Universe, the Invisible God Himself from heaven planted among men the truth and the holy teaching which surpasseth the wit of man, and fixed it firmly in their hearts, not as any man might imagine, by sending (to mankind) a subaltern, or angel, or ruler, or one of those that direct the affairs of earth, or one of those who have been entrusted with the dispensations in heaven, but the very Artificer and Creator of the Universe Himself, by Whom He made the heavens, by Whom He enclosed the sea in its proper bounds, Whose mysteries all the elements faithfully observe from Whom [the sun] hath received even the measure of the courses of the day to keep them, Whom the moon obeys as He bids

ᾧ πειθαρχεῖ τὰ ἄστρα τῷ τῆς σελήνης ἀκολουθοῦι τα δρόμῳ, ᾧ πάντα διατέτακται καὶ διώρισται καὶ ὑποτέτακται, οὐρανοὶ καὶ τὰ ἐν οὐρανοῖς, γῆ καὶ τὰ ἐν γῇ, θάλασσα καὶ τὰ ἐν τῇ θαλάσσῃ, πῦρ, ἀήρ, ἄβυσσος, τὰ 5 ἐν ὕψεσι, τὰ ἐν βάθεσι, τὰ ἐν τῷ μεταξύ· τοῦτον πρὸς αὐτοὺς ἀπέστειλεν. ἆρά γε, ὡς ἀνθρώπων ἄν τις λογίσαιτο, ἐπὶ τυραννίδι καὶ φόβῳ καὶ καταπλήξει; οὐμενοῦν· ἀλλ᾽ ἐν ἐπιεικείᾳ [καὶ] πραΰτητι ὡς βασιλεὺς πέμπων υἱὸν βασιλέα ἔπεμψεν, ὡς Θεὸν ἔπεμψεν, ὡς 10 [ἄνθρωπον] πρὸς ἀνθρώπους ἔπεμψεν, ὡς σώζων ἔπεμψεν, ὡς πείθων, οὐ βιαζόμενος· βία γὰρ οὐ πρόσεστι τῷ Θεῷ. ἔπεμψεν ὡς καλῶν, οὐ διώκων· ἔπεμψεν ὡς ἀγαπῶν, οὐ κρίνων. πέμψει γὰρ αὐτὸν κρίνοντα, καὶ τίς αὐτοῦ τὴν παρουσίαν ὑποστήσεται; .... [οὐχ ὁρᾷς] παρα-
15 βαλλομένους θηρίοις, ἵνα ἀρνήσωνται τὸν Κύριον, καὶ μὴ νικωμένους; οὐχ ὁρᾷς ὅσῳ πλείονες κολάζονται, τοσούτῳ πλεονάζοντας ἄλλους; ταῦτα ἀνθρώπου οὐ δοκεῖ τὰ ἔργα, ταῦτα δύναμίς ἐστι Θεοῦ· ταῦτα τῆς παρουσίας αὐτοῦ δείγματα.

AUCT. *Ad Diognetum*, 5-7.

VIII.

20 7. Περὶ δὲ τοῦ βαπτίσματος, οὕτω βαπτίσατε· ταῦτα πάντα προειπόντες βαπτίσατε εἰς τὸ ὄνομα τοῦ Πατρὸς καὶ τοῦ Υἱοῦ καὶ τοῦ ἁγίου Πνεύματος ἐν ὕδατι ζῶντι. ἐὰν δὲ μὴ ἔχῃς ὕδωρ ζῶν, εἰς ἄλλο ὕδωρ βάπτισον· εἰ δ᾽ οὐ δύνασαι ἐν ψυχρῷ, ἐν θερμῷ. ἐὰν δὲ ἀμφό-
25 τερα μὴ ἔχῃς, ἔκχεον εἰς τὴν κεφαλὴν τρὶς ὕδωρ εἰς ὄνομα Πατρὸς καὶ Υἱοῦ καὶ ἁγίου Πνεύματος. πρὸ δὲ τοῦ βαπτίσματος προνηστευσάτω ὁ βαπτίζων καὶ ὁ βαπτιζόμενος καὶ εἴ τινες ἄλλοι δύνανται. κελεύεις δὲ νηστεῦσαι τὸν βαπτιζόμενον πρὸ μιᾶς ἢ δύο.

30 8. Αἱ δὲ νηστεῖαι ὑμῶν μὴ ἔστωσαν μετὰ τῶν ὑποκριτῶν·

her shine by night, Whom the stars obey as they follow the course of the moon, by Whom all things are ordered and bounded and placed in subjection, the heavens and the things that are in the heavens, the earth and the things that are in the earth, the sea and the things that are in the sea, fire, air, abyss, the things that are in the heights, the things that are in the depths, the things that are between the two. Him He sent unto them. Was He sent, think you, as any man might suppose, to establish a sovereignty, to inspire fear and terror? Not so. But in gentleness [and] meekness has He sent Him, as a king might send his son who is a king. He sent Him, as sending God; He sent Him, as [a man] unto men; He sent Him, as Saviour, as using persuasion, not force: for force is no attribute of God. He sent Him, as summoning, not as persecuting; He sent Him, as loving, not as judging. For He will send Him in judgement, and who shall endure His presence?... [Dost thou not see] them thrown to wild beasts that so they may deny the Lord, and yet not overcome? Dost thou not see that the more of them are punished, just so many others abound? These look not like the works of a man; they are the power of God; they are proofs of His presence.

L.

Church order of the Didaché.

BUT concerning baptism, thus shall ye baptize. Having first recited all these things, baptize in the name of the Father and of the Son and of the Holy Spirit in living (running) water. But if thou hast not living water, then baptize in other water, and if thou art not able in cold, then in warm. But if thou hast neither, then pour water on the head thrice in the name of the Father and of the Son and of the Holy Spirit. But before the baptism let him that baptizeth and him that is baptized fast, and any others also who are able; and thou shalt order him that is baptized to fast a day or two before.

And let not your fastings be with the hypocrites, for

νηστεύουσι γὰρ δευτέρᾳ σαββάτων καὶ πέμπτῃ· ὑμεῖς δὲ νηστεύσατε τετράδα καὶ παρασκευήν. μηδὲ προσεύχεσθε ὡς οἱ ὑποκριταί, ἀλλ᾽ ὡς ἐκέλευσεν ὁ Κύριος ἐν τῷ εὐαγγελίῳ αὐτοῦ, οὕτως προσεύχεσθε· Πάτερ ἡμῶν
5 ὁ ἐν τῷ οὐρανῷ, ἁγιασθήτω τὸ ὄνομά σου, ἐλθέτω ἡ βασιλεία σου, γενηθήτω τὸ θέλημά σου ὡς ἐν οὐρανῷ καὶ ἐπὶ γῆς· τὸν ἄρτον ἡμῶν τὸν ἐπιούσιον δὸς ἡμῖν σήμερον, καὶ ἄφες ἡμῖν τὴν ὀφειλὴν ἡμῶν ὡς καὶ ἡμεῖς ἀφίεμεν τοῖς ὀφειλέταις ἡμῶν, καὶ μὴ εἰσενέγκῃς ἡμᾶς εἰς πειρασ-
10 μόν, ἀλλὰ ῥῦσαι ἡμᾶς ἀπὸ τοῦ πονηροῦ· ὅτι σοῦ ἐστὶν ἡ δύναμις καὶ ἡ δόξα εἰς τοὺς αἰῶνας. τρὶς τῆς ἡμέρας οὕτω προσεύχεσθε.

9. Περὶ δὲ τῆς εὐχαριστίας, οὕτω εὐχαριστήσατε· πρῶτον περὶ τοῦ ποτηρίου· Εὐχαριστοῦμέν σοι, Πάτερ ἡμῶν,
15 ὑπὲρ τῆς ἁγίας ἀμπέλου Δαυεὶδ τοῦ παιδός σου, ἧς ἐγνώρισας ἡμῖν διὰ Ἰησοῦ τοῦ παιδός σου· σοὶ ἡ δόξα εἰς τοὺς αἰῶνας. περὶ δὲ τοῦ κλάσματος· Εὐχαριστοῦμέν σοι, Πάτερ ἡμῶν, ὑπὲρ τῆς ζωῆς καὶ γνώσεως, ἧς ἐγνώρισας ἡμῖν διὰ Ἰησοῦ τοῦ παιδός σου· σοὶ ἡ δόξα
20 εἰς τοὺς αἰῶνας. ὥσπερ ἦν τοῦτο τὸ κλάσμα διεσκορπισμένον ἐπάνω τῶν ὀρέων καὶ συναχθὲν ἐγένετο ἕν, οὕτω συναχθήτω σου ἡ ἐκκλησία ἀπὸ τῶν περάτων τῆς γῆς εἰς τὴν σὴν βασιλείαν· ὅτι σοῦ ἐστὶν ἡ δόξα καὶ ἡ δύναμις διὰ Ἰησοῦ Χριστοῦ εἰς τοὺς αἰῶνας. μηδεὶς δὲ
25 φαγέτω μηδὲ πιέτω ἀπὸ τῆς εὐχαριστίας ὑμῶν, ἀλλ᾽ οἱ βαπτισθέντες εἰς ὄνομα Κυρίου. καὶ γὰρ περὶ τούτου εἴρηκεν ὁ Κύριος· Μὴ δῶτε τὸ ἅγιον τοῖς κυσί.

10. Μετὰ δὲ τὸ ἐμπλησθῆναι οὕτως εὐχαριστήσατε· Εὐχαριστοῦμέν σοι, Πάτερ ἅγιε, ὑπὲρ τοῦ ἁγίου ὀνόματός
30 σου, οὗ κατεσκήνωσας ἐν ταῖς καρδίαις ἡμῶν, καὶ ὑπὲρ τῆς γνώσεως καὶ πίστεως καὶ ἀθανασίας, ἧς ἐγνώρισας ἡμῖν διὰ Ἰησοῦ τοῦ παιδός σου· σοὶ ἡ δόξα εἰς τοὺς αἰῶνας. σύ, δέσποτα παντοκράτορ, ἔκτισας τὰ πάντα

they fast on the second and the fifth day of the week; but do ye keep your fast on the fourth and on the preparation (the sixth) day. Neither pray ye as the hypocrites, but as the Lord commanded in His Gospel, thus pray ye: Our Father, which art in heaven, hallowed be Thy name; Thy kingdom come; Thy will be done, as in heaven, so also on earth; give us this day our daily bread; and forgive us our debt, as we also forgive our debtors; and lead us not into temptation, but deliver us from the Evil One; for Thine is the power and the glory for ever and ever. Three times in the day pray ye so.

But, as touching the eucharistic thanksgiving, give ye thanks thus. First, as regards the cup: We give Thee thanks, O our Father, for the holy vine of Thy son David, which Thou madest known unto us through Thy Son Jesus; Thine is the glory for ever and ever. Then as regards the broken bread: We give Thee thanks, O our Father, for the life and knowledge which Thou didst make known unto us through Thy Son Jesus; Thine is the glory for ever and ever. As this broken bread was scattered upon the mountains and being gathered together became one, so may Thy Church be gathered together from the ends of the earth into Thy kingdom; for Thine is the glory and the power through Jesus Christ for ever and ever. But let no one eat or drink of this eucharistic thanksgiving, but they that have been baptized into the name of the Lord; for concerning this also the Lord hath said: Give not that which is holy to the dogs.

And after ye are satisfied thus give ye thanks: We give Thee thanks, Holy Father, for Thy holy name, which Thou hast made to tabernacle in our hearts, and for the knowledge and faith and immortality, which Thou hast made known unto us through Thy Son Jesus; Thine is the glory for ever and ever. Thou, Almighty Master, didst create all things for Thy name's sake, and didst

ἕνεκεν τοῦ ὀνόματός σου, τροφήν τε καὶ ποτὸν ἔδωκας
τοῖς ἀνθρώποις εἰς ἀπόλαυσιν ἵνα σοι εὐχαριστήσωσιν,
ἡμῖν δὲ ἐχαρίσω πνευματικὴν τροφὴν καὶ ποτὸν καὶ ζωὴν
αἰώνιον διὰ τοῦ παιδός σου. πρὸ πάντων εὐχαρισ-
5 τοῦμέν σοι ὅτι δυνατὸς εἶ σύ· σοὶ ἡ δόξα εἰς τοὺς αἰῶνας.
μνήσθητι, Κύριε, τῆς ἐκκλησίας σου τοῦ ῥύσασθαι
αὐτὴν ἀπὸ παντὸς πονηροῦ καὶ τελειῶσαι αὐτὴν ἐν τῇ
ἀγάπῃ σου, καὶ σύναξον αὐτὴν ἀπὸ τῶν τεσσάρων ἀνέμων,
τὴν ἁγιασθεῖσαν εἰς τὴν σὴν βασιλείαν, ἣν ἡτοίμασας
10 αὐτῇ· ὅτι σοῦ ἐστὶν ἡ δύναμις καὶ ἡ δόξα εἰς τοὺς
αἰῶνας. ἐλθέτω χάρις καὶ παρελθέτω ὁ κόσμος οὗτος.
ὡσαννὰ τῷ θεῷ Δαυείδ. εἴ τις ἅγιός ἐστιν, ἐρχέσθω·
εἴ τις οὐκ ἐστί, μετανοείτω. μαρὰν ἀθά. ἀμήν. τοῖς
δὲ προφήταις ἐπιτρέπετε εὐχαριστεῖν ὅσα θέλουσιν.
15 11. Ὃς ἂν οὖν ἐλθὼν διδάξῃ ὑμᾶς ταῦτα πάντα τὰ
προειρημένα, δέξασθε αὐτόν· ἐὰν δὲ αὐτὸς ὁ διδάσκων στρα-
φεὶς διδάσκῃ ἄλλην διδαχὴν εἰς τὸ καταλῦσαι, μὴ αὐτοῦ
ἀκούσητε· εἰς δὲ τὸ προσθεῖναι δικαιοσύνην καὶ γνῶσιν
Κυρίου, δέξασθε αὐτὸν ὡς Κύριον. περὶ δὲ τῶν ἀπο-
20 στόλων καὶ προφητῶν κατὰ τὸ δόγμα τοῦ εὐαγγελίου
οὕτως ποιήσατε. πᾶς δὲ ἀπόστολος ἐρχόμενος πρὸς
ὑμᾶς δεχθήτω ὡς Κύριος· οὐ μενεῖ δὲ εἰ μὴ ἡμέραν
μίαν· ἐὰν δὲ ᾖ χρεία, καὶ τὴν ἄλλην· τρεῖς δὲ ἐὰν
μείνῃ, ψευδοπροφήτης ἐστίν· ἐξερχόμενος δὲ ὁ ἀπόστολος
25 μηδὲν λαμβανέτω εἰ μὴ ἄρτον, ἕως οὗ αὐλισθῇ· ἐὰν
δὲ ἀργύριον αἰτῇ, ψευδοπροφήτης ἐστί. καὶ πάντα
προφήτην λαλοῦντα ἐν πνεύματι οὐ πειράσετε οὐδὲ δια-
κρινεῖτε· πᾶσα γὰρ ἁμαρτία ἀφεθήσεται, αὕτη δὲ ἡ
ἁμαρτία οὐκ ἀφεθήσεται. οὐ πᾶς δὲ ὁ λαλῶν ἐν
30 πνεύματι προφήτης ἐστίν, ἀλλ᾽ ἐὰν ἔχῃ τοὺς τρόπους
Κυρίου. ἀπὸ οὖν τῶν τρόπων γνωσθήσεται ὁ ψευδοπροφήτης καὶ ὁ προφήτης. καὶ πᾶς προφήτης ὁρίζων

give food and drink unto men for enjoyment, that they might render thanks to Thee; but didst bestow upon us spiritual food and drink and eternal life through Thy Son. Before all things we give Thee thanks that Thou art powerful; Thine is the glory for ever and ever. Remember, Lord, Thy Church to deliver it from all evil and to perfect it in Thy love; and gather it together from the four winds—even the Church which has been sanctified—into Thy kingdom which Thou hast prepared for it; for Thine is the power and the glory for ever and ever. May grace come and may this world pass away. Hosanna to the God of David. If any man is holy, let him come; if any man is not, let him repent. Maran Atha. Amen.

But permit the prophets to offer thanksgiving as much as they desire.

Whosoever therefore shall come and teach you all these things that have been said before, receive him; but if the teacher himself be perverted and teach a different doctrine to the destruction thereof, hear him not; but if to the increase of righteousness and the knowledge of the Lord, receive him as the Lord.

But concerning the apostles and prophets, so do ye according to the ordinance of the Gospel. Let every apostle, when he cometh to you, be received as the Lord; but he shall not abide more than a single day, or if there be need, a second likewise; but if he abide three days, he is a false prophet. And when he departeth let the apostle receive nothing save bread, until he findeth shelter; but if he ask money, he is a false prophet. And any prophet speaking in the Spirit ye shall not try neither discern; for every sin shall be forgiven, but this sin shall not be forgiven. Yet not every one that speaketh in the Spirit is a prophet, but only if he have the ways of the Lord. From his ways therefore the false prophet and the prophet shall be recognized. And no prophet when

τράπεζαν ἐν πνεύματι οὐ φάγεται ἀπ' αὐτῆς· εἰ δὲ μήγε, ψευδοπροφήτης ἐστίν. πᾶς δὲ προφήτης διδάσκων τὴν ἀλήθειαν εἰ ἃ διδάσκει οὐ ποιεῖ, ψευδοπροφήτης ἐστίν. πᾶς δὲ προφήτης δεδοκιμασμένος ἀληθινὸς ποιῶν εἰς 5 μυστήριον κοσμικὸν ἐκκλησίας, μὴ διδάσκων δὲ ποιεῖν ὅσα αὐτὸς ποιεῖ, οὐ κριθήσεται ἐφ' ὑμῶν· μετὰ Θεοῦ γὰρ ἔχει τὴν κρίσιν· ὡσαύτως γὰρ ἐποίησαν καὶ οἱ ἀρχαῖοι προφῆται. ὃς δ' ἂν εἴπῃ ἐν πνεύματι· Δός μοι ἀργύρια ἢ ἕτερά τινα, οὐκ ἀκούσεσθε αὐτοῦ· ἐὰν δὲ περὶ ἄλλων 10 ὑστερούντων εἴπῃ δοῦναι, μηδεὶς αὐτὸν κρινέτω.

12. Πᾶς δὲ ὁ ἐρχόμενος ἐν ὀνόματι Κυρίου δεχθήτω· ἔπειτα δὲ δοκιμάσαντες αὐτὸν γνώσεσθε. σύνεσιν γὰρ ἕξετε δεξιὰν καὶ ἀριστεράν. εἰ μὲν παρόδιός ἐστιν ὁ ἐρχόμενος, βοηθεῖτε αὐτῷ ὅσον δύνασθε· οὐ μενεῖ δὲ πρὸς 15 ὑμᾶς εἰ μὴ δύο ἢ τρεῖς ἡμέρας, ἐὰν ᾖ ἀνάγκη. εἰ δὲ θέλει πρὸς ὑμᾶς καθῆσθαι, τεχνίτης ὤν, ἐργαζέσθω καὶ φαγέτω. εἰ δὲ οὐκ ἔχει τέχνην, κατὰ τὴν σύνεσιν ὑμῶν προνοήσατε, πῶς μὴ ἀργὸς μεθ' ὑμῶν ζήσεται Χριστιανός. εἰ δ' οὐ θέλει οὕτω ποιεῖν, χριστέμπορός 20 ἐστιν· προσέχετε ἀπὸ τῶν τοιούτων.

13. Πᾶς δὲ προφήτης ἀληθινὸς θέλων καθῆσθαι πρὸς ὑμᾶς ἄξιός ἐστιν τῆς τροφῆς αὐτοῦ. ὡσαύτως διδάσκαλος ἀληθινός ἐστιν ἄξιος καὶ αὐτός, ὥσπερ ὁ ἐργάτης, τῆς τροφῆς αὐτοῦ. πᾶσαν οὖν ἀπαρχὴν γεννημάτων ληνοῦ 25 καὶ ἅλωνος, βοῶν τε καὶ προβάτων λαβὼν δώσεις τὴν ἀπαρχὴν τοῖς προφήταις· αὐτοὶ γάρ εἰσιν οἱ ἀρχιερεῖς ὑμῶν. ἐὰν δὲ μὴ ἔχητε προφήτην, δότε τοῖς πτωχοῖς. ἐὰν σιτίαν ποιῇς, τὴν ἀπαρχὴν λαβὼν δὸς κατὰ τὴν ἐντολήν. ὡσαύτως κεράμιον οἴνου ἢ ἐλαίου ἀνοίξας τὴν 30 ἀπαρχὴν λαβὼν δὸς τοῖς προφήταις· ἀργυρίου δὲ καὶ ἱματισμοῦ καὶ παντὸς κτήματος λαβὼν τὴν ἀπαρχήν, ὡς ἄν σοι δόξῃ, δὸς κατὰ τὴν ἐντολήν.

he ordereth a table in the Spirit shall eat of it; otherwise
he is a false prophet. And every prophet teaching the
truth, if he doeth not what he teacheth, is a false prophet.
And every prophet approved and found true, if he doeth
ought as an outward mystery typical of the Church, and
yet teacheth you not to do all that he himself doeth, shall
not be judged before you; he hath his judgement in the
presence of God; for in like manner also did the prophets
of old time. And whosoever shall say in the Spirit, Give
me silver or anything else, ye shall not listen to him; but
if he tell you to give on behalf of others that are in want,
let no man judge him.

But let every one that cometh in the name of the Lord
be received; and that when ye have tested him ye shall
know him, for ye shall have understanding on the right
hand and on the left. If the comer is a traveller, assist
him, so far as ye are able; but he shall not stay with you
more than two or three days, if it be necessary. But if he
wishes to settle with you, being a craftsman, let him work
for and eat his bread. But if he has no craft, according
to your wisdom provide how he shall live as a Christian
among you, but not in idleness. If he will not do this, he
is trafficking upon Christ. Beware of such men.

But every true prophet desiring to settle among you is
worthy of his food. In like manner a true teacher is also
worthy, like the workman, of his food. Every firstfruit
then of the produce of the wine-vat and of the threshing-
floor, of thy oxen and of thy sheep, thou shalt take and
give as the firstfruit to the prophets; for they are your
chief-priests. But if ye have not a prophet, give them to
the poor. If thou makest bread, take the firstfruit and
give according to the commandment. In like manner,
when thou openest a jar of wine or of oil, take the firstfruit
and give to the prophets; yea and of money and raiment
and every possession take the firstfruit, as shall seem
good to thee, and give according to the commandment.

14. Κατὰ κυριακὴν δὲ Κυρίου συναχθέντες κλάσατε ἄρτον καὶ εὐχαριστήσατε προεξομολογησάμενοι τὰ παραπτώματα ὑμῶν, ὅπως καθαρὰ ἡ θυσία ὑμῶν ᾖ. πᾶς δὲ ἔχων τὴν ἀμφιβολίαν μετὰ τοῦ ἑταίρου αὐτοῦ μὴ συνελ-
5 θέτω ὑμῖν, ἕως οὗ διαλλαγῶσιν, ἵνα μὴ κοινωθῇ ἡ θυσία ὑμῶν. αὕτη γάρ ἐστιν ἡ ῥηθεῖσα ὑπὸ Κυρίου· Ἐν παντὶ τόπῳ καὶ χρόνῳ προσφέρειν μοι θυσίαν καθαράν· ὅτι βασιλεὺς μέγας εἰμί, λέγει Κύριος, καὶ τὸ ὄνομά μου θαυμαστὸν ἐν τοῖς ἔθνεσι.

10 15. Χειροτονήσατε οὖν ἑαυτοῖς ἐπισκόπους καὶ διακόνους ἀξίους τοῦ Κυρίου, ἄνδρας πραεῖς καὶ ἀφιλαργύρους καὶ ἀληθεῖς καὶ δεδοκιμασμένους· ὑμῖν γὰρ λειτουργοῦσι καὶ αὐτοὶ τὴν λειτουργίαν τῶν προφητῶν καὶ διδασκάλων. μὴ οὖν ὑπερίδητε αὐτούς· αὐτοὶ γάρ εἰσιν οἱ τετιμημένοι
15 ὑμῶν μετὰ τῶν προφητῶν καὶ διδασκάλων.

Doctrina Apost. 7-15.

IX.
Plinius Traiano.

SOLLEMNE est mihi, domine, omnia de quibus dubito ad te referre. Quis enim potest melius vel cunctationem meam regere vel ignorantiam instruere? Cognitionibus de Christianis interfui numquam: ideo nescio quid et qua-
20 tenus aut puniri soleat aut quaeri. Nec mediocriter haesitavi, sitne aliquod discrimen aetatum, an quamlibet teneri nihil a robustioribus differant, detur paenitentiae venia, an ei qui omnino Christianus fuit desisse non prosit, nomen ipsum, si flagitiis careat, an flagitia cohaerentia
25 nomini puniantur. Interim in iis qui ad me tamquam Christiani deferebantur hunc sum secutus modum. Interrogavi ipsos an essent Christiani: confitentes iterum ac tertio interrogavi supplicium minatus: perseverantes duci iussi. Neque enim dubitabam, qualecumque esset
30 quod faterentur, pertinaciam certe et inflexibilem obstinationem debere puniri. Fuerunt alii similis amentiae, quos,

And on the Lord's own day gather yourselves together
and break bread and give thanks, first confessing your
transgressions, that your sacrifice may be pure. And let
no man, having his dispute with his fellow, join your
assembly until they have been reconciled, that your sacrifice may not be defiled; for this sacrifice it is that was
spoken of by the Lord; In every place and at every time
offer Me a pure sacrifice; for I am a great king, saith the
Lord, and My name is wonderful among the nations.

Appoint for yourselves therefore bishops and deacons
worthy of the Lord, men who are meek and not lovers of
money, and true and approved; for unto you they also
perform the service of the prophets and teachers. Therefore despise them not; for they are your honourable men
along with prophets and teachers.

Pliny's Correspondence with Trajan.
Pliny to Trajan.

IT is my custom, lord emperor, to refer to you all
questions whereof I am in doubt. Who can better guide
me when I am at a stand, or enlighten me if I am in
ignorance? In investigations of Christians I have never
taken part; hence I do not know what is the crime usually
punished or investigated, or what allowances are made.
So I have had no little uncertainty whether there is any
distinction of age, or whether the very weakest offenders
are treated exactly like the stronger; whether pardon is
given to those who repent, or whether nobody who has
ever been a Christian at all gains anything by having
ceased to be such; whether punishment attaches to the
mere name apart from secret crimes, or to the secret
crimes connected with the name. Meantime this is the
course I have taken with those who were accused before
me as Christians. I asked at their own lips whether they
were Christians, and if they confessed, I asked them a
second and third time with threats of punishment. If they
kept to it, I ordered them for execution; for I held no
question that whatever it was that they admitted, in any
case obstinacy and unbending perversity deserve to be
punished. There were others of the like insanity; but as

quia cives Romani erant, adnotavi in urbem remittendos.
Mox ipso tractatu, ut fieri solet, diffundente se crimine
plures species inciderunt. Propositus est libellus sine
auctore multorum nomina continens. Qui negabant esse
5 se Christianos aut fuisse, cum praeeunte me deos appel-
larent et imagini tuae, quam propter hoc iusseram cum
simulacris numinum adferri, ture ac vino supplicarent,
praeterea male dicerent Christo, quorum nihil posse cogi
dicuntur qui sunt re vera Christiani, dimittendos esse
10 putavi. Alii ab indice nominati esse se Christianos dixerunt
et mox negaverunt; fuisse quidem, sed desisse, quidam
ante triennium, quidam ante plures annos, non nemo
etiam ante viginti. Hi quoque omnes et imaginem tuam
deorumque simulacra venerati sunt et Christo male dixe-
15 runt. Adfirmabant autem hanc fuisse summam vel culpae
suae vel erroris, quod essent soliti stato die ante lucem
convenire carmenque Christo quasi deo dicere secum
invicem seque sacramento non in scelus aliquod ob-
stringere, sed ne furta, ne latrocinia, ne adulteria com-
20 mitterent, ne fidem fallerent, ne depositum appellati
abnegarent: quibus peractis morem sibi discedendi
fuisse, rursusque coeundi ad capiendum cibum, promis-
cuum tamen et innoxium; quod ipsum facere desisse post
edictum meum, quo secundum mandata tua hetaerias esse
25 vetueram. Quo magis necessarium credidi ex duabus
ancillis, quae ministrae dicebantur, quid esset veri et per
tormenta quaerere. Nihil aliud inveni quam supersti-
tionem pravam immodicam. Ideo dilata cognitione ad

these were Roman citizens, I noted them down to be sent
to Rome. Before long, as is often the case, the mere
fact that the charge was taken notice of made it commoner,
and several distinct cases arose. An unsigned paper was
presented, which gave the names of many. As for those
who said that they neither were nor ever had been
Christians, I thought it right to let them go, since they
recited a prayer to the gods at my dictation, made sup-
plication with incense and wine to your statue, which
I had ordered to be brought into court for the purpose
together with the images of the gods, and moreover
cursed Christ—not one of which things (so it is said) those
who are really Christians can be made to do. Others
who were named by the informer said that they were
Christians and then denied it, explaining that they had
been, but had ceased to be such, some three years ago, some
a good many years, and a few as many as twenty. All
these too not only worshipped your statue and the images
of the gods, but cursed Christ. They maintained, however,
that the amount of their fault or error had been this, that
it was their habit on a fixed day to assemble before daylight
and sing by turns a hymn to Christ as a god; and that
they bound themselves with an oath, not for any crime,
but not to commit theft or robbery or adultery, not to
break their word, and not to deny a deposit when de-
manded. After this was done, their custom was to depart,
and meet together again to take food, but ordinary and
harmless food; and even this (they said) they had given
up doing after the issue of my edict, by which in accordance with your commands I had forbidden the existence
of clubs. On this I considered it the more necessary
to find out from two maid-servants who were called
deaconesses, and that by torments, how far this was true:
but I discovered nothing else than a wicked and arrogant
superstition. I therefore adjourned the case and hastened

consulendum te decucurri. Visa est enim mihi res digna consultatione, maxime propter periclitantium numerum. Multi enim omnis aetatis, omnis ordinis, utriusque sexus etiam, vocantur in periculum et vocabuntur. Neque civi-
5 tates tantum sed vicos etiam atque agros superstitionis istius contagio pervagata est; quae videtur sisti et corrigi posse. Certe satis constat prope iam desolata templa coepisse celebrari et sacra sollemnia diu intermissa repeti pastumque venire victimarum, cuius adhuc rarissimus
10 emptor inveniebatur. Ex quo facile est opinari, quae turba hominum emendari possit, si sit paenitentiae locus.

Traianus Plinio.

Actum quem debuisti, mi Secunde, in excutiendis causis eorum qui Christiani ad te delati fuerant secutus es. Neque enim in universum aliquid quod quasi certam
15 formam habeat constitui potest. Conquirendi non sunt: si deferantur et arguantur, puniendi sunt, ita tamen ut qui negaverit se Christianum esse idque re ipsa manifestum fecerit, id est supplicando dis nostris, quamvis suspectus in praeteritum, veniam ex paenitentia impetret. Sine
20 auctore vero propositi libelli in nullo crimine locum habere debent. Nam et pessimi exempli nec nostri saeculi est.

PLINY, *Epp.* x. 96, 97.

X.

Ταύτῃ γοῦν οὗτος θεομάχος ἐν τοῖς μάλιστα πρῶτος ἀνακηρυχθείς, ἐπὶ τὰς κατὰ τῶν ἀποστόλων ἐπήρθη σφαγάς. Παῦλος δὴ οὖν ἐπ' αὐτῆς Ῥώμης τὴν κεφαλὴν
25 ἀποτμηθῆναι, καὶ Πέτρος ὡσαύτως ἀνασκολοπισθῆναι

to consult you. The matter seemed to me worth deliberation, especially on account of the number of those in danger; for many of all ages and every rank, and even of both sexes are brought into present or future danger. The contagion of that superstition has penetrated not the cities only, but the villages and country; yet it seems possible to stop it and set it right. At any rate it is certain enough that the almost deserted temples begin to be resorted to, that long disused ceremonies of religion are restored, and that fodder for victims finds a market, whereas buyers till now were very few. From this it may easily be supposed, what a multitude of men can be reclaimed, if there be a place of repentance.

Trajan to Pliny.

You have followed, my dear Secundus, the process you should have done in examining the cases of those who were accused to you as Christians, for indeed nothing can be laid down as a general law involving something like a definite rule of action. They are not to be sought out; but if they are accused and convicted, they must be punished—yet on this condition, that whoso denies himself to be a Christian, and makes the fact plain by his action, that is, by worshipping our gods, shall obtain pardon on his repentance, however suspicious his past conduct may be. Papers, however, which are presented unsigned ought not to be admitted in any charge, for they are a very bad example and unworthy of our time.

The Neronian Persecution (Eusebius).

IN this way then declaring himself the first of God's chief enemies, [Nero] was stirred up to the slaughter of the Apostles. It is recorded then that Paul was beheaded at Rome itself, and that Peter likewise was crucified in his

κατ' αὐτὸν ἱστοροῦνται. καὶ πιστοῦταί γε τὴν ἱστορίαν
ἡ Πέτρου καὶ Παύλου εἰς δεῦρο κρατήσασα ἐπὶ τῶν
αὐτόθι κοιμητηρίων πρόσρησις. οὐδὲν δ' ἧττον καὶ
ἐκκλησιαστικὸς ἀνὴρ Γάϊος ὄνομα, κατὰ Ζεφυρῖνον Ῥω-
5 μαίων γεγονὼς ἐπίσκοπον· ὃς δὴ Πρόκλῳ τῆς κατὰ
Φρύγας προϊσταμένῳ γνώμης ἐγγράφως διαλεχθείς, αὐτὰ
δὴ ταῦτα περὶ τῶν τόπων ἔνθα τῶν εἰρημένων ἀποστόλων
τὰ ἱερὰ σκηνώματα κατατέθειται, φησίν·
Ἐγὼ δὲ τὰ τρόπαια τῶν ἀποστόλων ἔχω δεῖξαι. ἐὰν
10 γὰρ θελήσῃς ἀπελθεῖν ἐπὶ τὸν Βατικανόν, ἢ ἐπὶ τὴν
ὁδὸν τὴν Ὠστίαν, εὑρήσεις τὰ τρόπαια τῶν ταύτην ἱδρυ-
σαμένων τὴν ἐκκλησίαν.

Ὡς δὲ κατὰ τὸν αὐτὸν ἄμφω καιρὸν ἐμαρτύρησαν,
Κορινθίων ἐπίσκοπος Διονύσιος ἐγγράφως Ῥωμαίοις
15 ὁμιλῶν, ὧδέ πως παρίστησιν·

Ταῦτα καὶ ὑμεῖς διὰ τῆς τοσαύτης νουθεσίας τὴν ἀπὸ
Πέτρου καὶ Παύλου φυτείαν γενηθεῖσαν Ῥωμαίων τε καὶ
Κορινθίων συνεκεράσατε. καὶ γὰρ ἄμφω καὶ εἰς τὴν
ἡμετέραν Κόρινθον φυτεύσαντες ἡμᾶς, ὁμοίως ἐδίδαξαν·
20 ὁμοίως δὲ καὶ εἰς τὴν Ἰταλίαν ὁμόσε διδάξαντες, ἐμαρτύρησαν κατὰ τὸν αὐτὸν καιρόν.

EUSEBIUS, *Hist. Eccles.* ii. 25.

XI.

Πέτρου μὲν οὖν Ἐπιστολὴ μία ἡ λεγομένη αὐτοῦ
προτέρα ἀνωμολόγηται· ταύτῃ δὲ καὶ οἱ πάλαι πρεσβύτεροι ὡς ἀναμφιλέκτῳ ἐν τοῖς σφῶν αὐτῶν κατακέχρηνται
25 συγγράμμασι. τὴν δὲ φερομένην αὐτοῦ δευτέραν, οὐκ
ἐνδιάθηκον μὲν εἶναι παρειλήφαμεν. ὅμως δὲ πολλοῖς
χρήσιμος φανεῖσα, μετὰ τῶν ἄλλων ἐσπουδάσθη γραφῶν.
τό γε μὴν τῶν ἐπικεκλημένων αὐτοῦ Πράξεων, καὶ τὸ
κατ' αὐτὸν ὠνομασμένον Εὐαγγέλιον, τό τε λεγόμενον
30 αὐτοῦ Κήρυγμα, καὶ τὴν καλουμένην Ἀποκάλυψιν, οὐδ'

time; and the story is confirmed by the attachment (usual even now) of their names to the cemeteries at Rome. It is also confirmed by an ecclesiastical writer, Gaius by name, who lived in the time of Zephyrinus bishop of Rome. He in his written dialogue with Proclus, a champion of the Phrygian heresy, speaks thus of the places where the holy corpses of the aforesaid Apostles are laid:—

'But I can show the trophies of the Apostles. For if thou wilt go to the Vatican, or to the Ostian road, thou wilt find the trophies of those who founded this Church.'

And that they were both martyred at the same time is shown by Dionysius, the Bishop of Corinth, who writes to the Romans thus:—

'In this way by such an admonition you too joined together the plantings of Peter and Paul at Rome and Corinth. For they both together in Corinth here planted us and taught alike; and both together in Italy taught alike, and then were martyred at the same time.'

Of the Canonical Epistles.

OF Peter then one Epistle, his so-called Former, is fully acknowledged; and of this even the ancient elders have made constant use in their writings as undisputed. But as for the current Second Epistle, we have understood that it is not canonical: yet as it seemed useful to many, it was studied along with the other writings. The Acts, however, which bear his name, and the Gospel inscribed 'according to Peter,' and his so-called Preaching and so-called Apocalypse we know have not been handed down

ὅλως ἐν καθολικοῖς ἴσμεν παραδεδομένα, ὅτι μήτε ἀρχαίων μήτε τῶν καθ' ἡμᾶς τις ἐκκλησιαστικὸς συγγραφεὺς ταῖς ἐξ αὐτῶν συνεχρήσατο μαρτυρίαις. προϊούσης δὲ τῆς ἱστορίας, προὔργου ποιήσομαι σὺν ταῖς
5 διαδοχαῖς ὑποσημήνασθαι, τίνες τῶν κατὰ χρόνους ἐκκλησιαστικῶν συγγραφέων ὁποίαις κέχρηνται τῶν ἀντιλεγομένων, τίνα τε περὶ τῶν ἐνδιαθήκων καὶ ὁμολογουμένων γραφῶν, καὶ ὅσα περὶ τῶν μὴ τοιούτων αὐτοῖς εἴρηται. ἀλλὰ τὰ μὲν ὀνομαζόμενα Πέτρου, ὧν μόνην μίαν
10 γνησίαν ἔγνων ἐπιστολήν, καὶ παρὰ τοῖς πάλαι πρεσβυτέροις ὁμολογουμένην, τοσαῦτα. τοῦ δὲ Παύλου πρόδηλοι καὶ σαφεῖς αἱ δεκατέσσαρες. ὅτι γε μὴν τινες ἠθετήκασι τὴν πρὸς Ἑβραίους, πρὸς τῆς Ῥωμαίων ἐκκλησίας ὡς μὴ Παύλου οὖσαν αὐτὴν ἀντιλέγεσθαι φήσαντες, οὐ
15 δίκαιον ἀγνοεῖν. καὶ τὰ περὶ ταύτης δὲ τοῖς πρὸ ἡμῶν εἰρημένα κατὰ καιρὸν παραθήσομαι. οὐδὲ μὴν τὰς λεγομένας αὐτοῦ Πράξεις ἐν ἀναμφιλέκτοις παρείληφα. ἐπεὶ δὲ ὁ αὐτὸς ἀπόστολος, ἐν ταῖς ἐπὶ τέλει προσρήσεσι τῆς πρὸς Ῥωμαίους, μνήμην πεποίηται μετὰ τῶν ἄλλων
20 καὶ Ἑρμᾶ, οὗ φασιν ὑπάρχειν τὸ τοῦ Ποιμένος βιβλίον, ἰστέον ὡς καὶ τοῦτο πρὸς μὲν τινῶν ἀντιλέλεκται, δι' οὓς οὐκ ἂν ἐν ὁμολογουμένοις τεθείη, ὑφ' ἑτέρων δὲ ἀναγκαιότατον οἷς μάλιστα δεῖ στοιχειώσεως εἰσαγωγικῆς, κέκριται. ὅθεν ἤδη καὶ ἐν ἐκκλησίαις ἴσμεν αὐτὸ δεδημοσιευμένον,
25 καὶ τῶν παλαιοτάτων δὲ συγγραφέων κεχρημένους τινὰς αὐτῷ κατείληφα. ταῦτα εἰς παράστασιν τῶν τε ἀναντιρρήτων καὶ τῶν μὴ παρὰ πᾶσιν ὁμολογοιμένων θείων γραμμάτων εἰρήσθω.

Ibid. iii. 3.

XII.

Εὔλογον δ' ἐνταῦθα γενομένους ἀνακεφαλαιώσασθαι
30 τὰς δηλωθείσας τῆς καινῆς Διαθήκης γραφάς. καὶ δὴ

at all among canonical books, because no ecclesiastical writer, either of the ancients or of our own time, ever made general use of testimonies from them. But, as my history goes on, I shall do my diligence to signify along with the successions, who of the ecclesiastical writers from time to time used disputed books, and which of them they used, and also what they have said concerning the canonical and acknowledged books, and all that they have said concerning those that are not such. But so many are the writings that bear the name of Peter; and of them I recognize one single Epistle as genuine and acknowledged by the ancient elders. Of Paul the fourteen are manifest and clear. It is not indeed right to ignore the fact that some have rejected that to the Hebrews, saying that it is disputed by the Roman Church as not being Paul's; but I will set out at suitable opportunities what has been said by our predecessors concerning this Epistle too. The so-called Acts however of Paul I have not understood to be among the undisputed books. But whereas the same Apostle in the final salutations of the Epistle to the Romans mentions among others Hermas, whose work the so-called *Shepherd* is said to be, it ought to be known that this too has been disputed by some, and on their account must not be set down among the acknowledged books, but by others it has been judged indispensable for those who specially need elementary instruction. Hence, as we know, it has actually been read in public in churches, and I have found some even of the oldest writers using it. Let this serve to show those of the divine writings which are undisputed, and those which are not acknowledged by all.

Of the Canon of the New Testament.

Now that we have reached this point, it is reasonable to sum up the writings of the New Testament already mentioned. Well, then, we must set in the first place the holy

τακτέον ἐν πρώτοις τὴν ἁγίαν τῶν Εὐαγγελίων τετρακτύν, οἶς ἕπεται ἡ τῶν Πράξεων τῶν ἀποστόλων γραφή. μετὰ δὲ ταύτην, τὰς Παύλου καταλεκτέον Ἐπιστολάς, αἶς ἑξῆς τὴν φερομένην Ἰωάννου προτέραν, καὶ ὁμοίως τὴν Πέτρου
5 κυρωτέον Ἐπιστολήν. ἐπὶ τούτοις τακτέον, εἴγε φανείη, τὴν Ἀποκάλυψιν Ἰωάννου, περὶ ἧς τὰ δόξαντα κατὰ καιρὸν ἐκθησόμεθα. καὶ ταῦτα μὲν ἐν ὁμολογουμένοις. τῶν δ᾽ ἀντιλεγομένων, γνωρίμων δ᾽ οὖν ὅμως τοῖς πολλοῖς, ἡ λεγομένη Ἰακώβου φέρεται καὶ ἡ Ἰούδα, ἥ τε Πέτρου
10 δευτέρα Ἐπιστολή, καὶ ἡ ὀνομαζομένη δευτέρα καὶ τρίτη Ἰωάννου, εἴτε τοῦ εὐαγγελιστοῦ τυγχάνουσαι, εἴτε καὶ ἑτέρου ὁμωνύμου ἐκείνῳ. ἐν τοῖς νόθοις κατατετάχθω καὶ τῶν Παύλου Πράξεων ἡ γραφή, ὅ τε λεγόμενος Ποιμήν, καὶ ἡ Ἀποκάλυψις Πέτρου. καὶ πρὸς τούτοις,
15 ἡ φερομένη Βαρνάβα ἐπιστολή, καὶ τῶν ἀποστόλων αἱ λεγόμεναι Διδαχαί· ἔτι τε, ὡς ἔφην, ἡ Ἰωάννου Ἀποκάλυψις, εἰ φανείη, ἥν τινες, ὡς ἔφην, ἀθετοῦσιν, ἕτεροι δὲ ἐγκρίνουσι τοῖς ὁμολογουμένοις. ἤδη δ᾽ ἐν τούτοις τινὲς καὶ τὸ καθ᾽ Ἑβραίους Εὐαγγέλιον κατέλεξαν, ᾧ μάλιστα
20 Ἑβραίων οἱ τὸν Χριστὸν παραδεξάμενοι χαίρουσι. ταῦτα μὲν πάντα τῶν ἀντιλεγομένων ἂν εἴη. ἀναγκαίως δὲ καὶ τούτων ὅμως τὸν κατάλογον πεποιήμεθα, διακρίναντες τάς τε κατὰ τὴν ἐκκλησιαστικὴν παράδοσιν ἀληθεῖς καὶ ἀπλάστους καὶ ἀνωμολογημένας γραφάς, καὶ τὰς ἄλλας
25 παρὰ ταύτας, οὐκ ἐνδιαθήκους μέν, ἀλλὰ καὶ ἀντιλεγομένας, ὅμως δὲ παρὰ πλείστοις τῶν ἐκκλησιαστικῶν γιγνωσκομένας, ἵν᾽ εἰδέναι ἔχοιμεν αὐτάς τε ταύτας, καὶ τὰς ὀνόματι τῶν ἀποστόλων πρὸς τῶν αἱρετικῶν προφερομένας, ἤτοι ὡς Πέτρου καὶ Θωμᾶ καὶ Ματθία, ἢ καί
30 τινων παρὰ τούτους ἄλλων εὐαγγέλια περιεχούσας, ὡς Ἀνδρέου καὶ Ἰωάννου καὶ τῶν ἄλλων ἀποστόλων πράξεις, ὧν οὐδὲν οὐδαμῶς ἐν συγγράμματι τῶν κατὰ τὰς

quaternion of the Gospels, which are followed by the writing of the Acts of the Apostles. After this we have to place on the list the Epistles of Paul ; and next to these we must maintain the current Former Epistle of John, and likewise that of Peter. In addition to these we must set down, if it do seem right, the Apocalypse of John ; but the opinions which have been held concerning this book we will set forth in due course. And these are counted as acknowledged. But of the disputed books, which are nevertheless familiar to most [writers], the so-called Epistle of James is current, and that of Jude; also the Second of Peter, and those called Second and Third of John, whether they be the work of the Evangelist, or possibly of some other John. Among the spurious we must set down the writing of the Acts of Paul, and the so-called *Shepherd*, and the Apocalypse of Peter; and in addition to these the current Epistle of Barnabas, and the so called Teachings of the Apostles, and, moreover, as I said, the Apocalypse of John if it seem good; though some, as I said, reject it, while others include it in the acknowledged books. Some moreover have also counted in this class the Gospel according to the Hebrews, which is in especial honour with those of the Hebrews who have received the Christ. Now all these will belong to the disputed books. We have been obliged to include these also in our list notwithstanding [the doubts about them], distinguishing the writings which according to orthodox tradition are true and genuine and fully acknowledged, from the others outside their number, which are not canonical but disputed, yet recognized by most orthodox [writers], that we might be able to mark these books, and those put forward by the heretics in the name of the Apostles, whether as containing Gospels of Peter and Thomas and Matthias or also of others beside them, or as Acts of Andrew and John and the other Apostles—books of which no one of the succession of ecclesiastical

διαδοχὰς ἐκκλησιαστικῶν τις ἀνὴρ εἰς μνήμην ἀγαγεῖν ἠξίωσεν. πόρρω δέ που καὶ ὁ τῆς φράσεως παρὰ τὸ ἦθος τὸ ἀποστολικὸν ἐναλλάττει χαρακτήρ· ἥ τε γνώμη καὶ ἡ τῶν ἐν αὐτοῖς φερομένων προαίρεσις, πλεῖστον ὅσον 5 τῆς ἀληθοῦς ὀρθοδοξίας ἀπᾴδουσα, ὅτι δὴ αἱρετικῶν ἀνδρῶν ἀναπλάσματα τυγχάνει, σαφῶς παρίστησιν· ὅθεν οὐδ' ἐν νόθοις αὐτὰ κατατακτέον, ἀλλ' ὡς ἄτοπα πάντη καὶ δυσσεβῆ παραιτητέον. *Ibid.* iii. 25.

XIII.

Τοῦ δὲ Παπία συγγράμματα πέντε τὸν ἀριθμὸν φέρε-
10 ται, ἃ καὶ ἐπιγέγραπται, 'Λογίων Κυριακῶν Ἐξηγήσεις.' τούτων καὶ Εἰρηναῖος ὡς μόνων αὐτῷ γραφέντων μνημονεύει, ὧδέ πως λέγων· Ταῦτα δὲ καὶ Παπίας ὁ Ἰωάννου μὲν ἀκουστής, Πολυκάρπου δὲ ἑταῖρος γεγονώς, ἀρχαῖος ἀνήρ, ἐγγράφως ἐπιμαρτυρεῖ ἐν τῇ τετάρτῃ τῶν ἑαυτοῦ
15 βιβλίων. ἔστι γὰρ αὐτῷ πέντε βιβλία συντεταγμένα.

Καὶ ὁ μὲν Εἰρηναῖος ταῦτα. αὐτός γε μὴν ὁ Παπίας κατὰ τὸ προοίμιον τῶν αὐτοῦ λόγων ἀκροατὴν μὲν καὶ αὐτόπτην οὐδαμῶς ἑαυτὸν γενέσθαι τῶν ἱερῶν ἀποστόλων ἐμφαίνει, παρειληφέναι δὲ τὰ τῆς πίστεως παρὰ τῶν
20 ἐκείνοις γνωρίμων διδάσκει δι' ὧν φησι λέξεων·

Οὐκ ὀκνήσω δέ σοι καὶ ὅσα ποτε παρὰ τῶν πρεσβυτέρων καλῶς ἔμαθον καὶ καλῶς ἐμνημόνευσα, συγκατατάξαι ταῖς ἑρμηνείαις, διαβεβαιούμενος ὑπὲρ αὐτῶν ἀλήθειαν. οὐ γὰρ τοῖς τὰ πολλὰ λέγουσιν ἔχαιρον ὥσπερ οἱ πολλοί,
25 ἀλλὰ τοῖς τἀληθῆ διδάσκουσιν, οὐδὲ τοῖς τὰς ἀλλοτρίας ἐντολὰς μνημονεύουσιν, ἀλλὰ τοῖς τὰς παρὰ τοῦ Κυρίου τῇ πίστει δεδομένας καὶ ἀπ' αὐτῆς παραγινομένας τῆς ἀληθείας. εἰ δέ που καὶ παρηκολουθηκώς τις τοῖς πρεσβυτέροις ἔλθοι, τοὺς τῶν πρεσβυτέρων ἀνέκρινον
30 λόγους· τί Ἀνδρέας ἢ τί Πέτρος εἶπεν ἢ τί Φίλιππος ἢ τί Θωμᾶς ἢ Ἰάκωβος ἢ τί Ἰωάννης ἢ Ματθαῖος ἤ τις

[writers] ever condescended to make any mention in his writings. Moreover, the character of their language differs greatly from the apostolic spirit, and the sentiment and purpose of their contents, which is in the highest degree discordant with true orthodoxy, plainly shows that they are forgeries of heretics; so that we must not count them even among the spurious books, but reject them as in every way monstrous and impious.

Papias.

FIVE books of Papias are extant, which bear the title Expositions of Oracles of the Lord. Of these Irenaeus also makes mention as the only works written by him, in the following words: 'These things Papias, who was a hearer of John and a companion of Polycarp, an ancient worthy, witnesseth in writing in the fourth of his books. For there are five books composed by him.' So far Irenaeus.

Yet Papias himself, in the preface to his discourses, certainly does not declare that he himself was a hearer and eye-witness of the holy Apostles, but he shows, by the language which he uses, that he received the matters of the faith from those who were their friends:—

But I will not scruple also to give a place for you along with my interpretations to everything that I learnt carefully and remembered carefully in time past from the elders, guaranteeing its truth. For, unlike the many, I did not take pleasure in those who have so very much to say, but in those who teach the truth; nor in those who relate foreign commandments, but in those [who record] such as were given from the Lord to the Faith, and are derived from the Truth itself. And again, on any occasion when a person came [in my way] who had been a follower of the Elders, I would inquire about the discourses of the elders —what was said by Andrew, or by Peter, or by Philip, or by Thomas or James, or by John or Matthew or any other

ἕτερος τῶν τοῦ Κυρίου μαθητῶν, ἅ τε Ἀριστίων καὶ ὁ πρεσβύτερος Ἰωάννης, οἱ τοῦ Κυρίου μαθηταί, λέγουσιν. οὐ γὰρ τὰ ἐκ τῶν βιβλίων τοσοῦτόν με ὠφελεῖν ὑπελάμβανον, ὅσον τὰ παρὰ ζώσης φωνῆς καὶ μενούσης.

5 Ἔνθα καὶ ἐπιστῆσαι ἄξιον δὶς καταριθμοῦντι αὐτῷ τὸ Ἰωάννου ὄνομα, ὧν τὸν μὲν πρότερον Πέτρῳ καὶ Ἰακώβῳ καὶ Ματθαίῳ καὶ τοῖς λοιποῖς ἀποστόλοις συγκαταλέγει, σαφῶς δηλῶν τὸν εὐαγγελιστήν, τὸν δ' ἕτερον Ἰωάννην διαστείλας τὸν λόγον ἑτέροις παρὰ τὸν τῶν ἀποστόλων
10 ἀριθμὸν κατατάσσει, προτάξας αὐτοῦ τὸν Ἀριστίωνα, σαφῶς τε αὐτὸν πρεσβύτερον ὀνομάζει. ὡς καὶ διὰ τούτων ἀποδείκνυσθαι τὴν ἱστορίαν ἀληθῆ τῶν δύο κατὰ τὴν Ἀσίαν ὁμωνυμίᾳ κεχρῆσθαι εἰρηκότων, δύο τε ἐν Ἐφέσῳ γενέσθαι μνήματα καὶ ἑκάτερον Ἰωάννου ἔτι νῦν λέγεσθαι.
15 οἷς καὶ ἀναγκαῖον προσέχειν τὸν νοῦν· εἰκὸς γὰρ τὸν δεύτερον, εἰ μή τις ἐθέλοι τὸν πρῶτον, τὴν ἐπ' ὀνόματος φερομένην Ἰωάννου Ἀποκάλυψιν ἑωρακέναι. καὶ ὁ νῦν δὲ ἡμῖν δηλούμενος Παπίας τοὺς μὲν τῶν ἀποστόλων λόγους παρὰ τῶν αὐτοῖς παρηκολουθηκότων ὁμολογεῖ
20 παρειληφέναι, Ἀριστίωνος δὲ καὶ τοῦ πρεσβυτέρου Ἰωάννου αὐτήκοον ἑαυτόν φησι γενέσθαι. ὀνομαστὶ γοῦν πολλάκις αὐτῶν μνημονεύσας, ἐν τοῖς αὐτοῦ συγγράμμασι τίθησιν αὐτῶν καὶ παραδόσεις. καὶ ταῦτα δ' ἡμῖν οὐκ εἰς τὸ ἄχρηστον εἰρήσθω.

25 Ἄξιον δὲ ταῖς ἀποδοθείσαις τοῦ Παπία φωναῖς προσάψαι λέξεις ἑτέρας αὐτοῦ, δι' ὧν παράδοξά τινα ἱστορεῖ καὶ ἄλλα, ὡσὰν ἐκ παραδόσεως εἰς αὐτὸν ἐλθόντα. τὸ μὲν οὖν κατὰ τὴν Ἱεράπολιν Φίλιππον τὸν ἀπόστολον ἅμα ταῖς θυγατράσι διατρῖψαι, διὰ τῶν πρόσθεν δεδή-
30 λωται, ὡς δὲ κατὰ τοὺς αὐτοὺς ὁ Παπίας γενόμενος διήγησιν παρειληφέναι θαυμασίαν ὑπὸ τῶν τοῦ Φιλίππου θυγατέρων μνημονεύει, τὰ νῦν σημειωτέον. νεκροῦ γὰρ ἀνάστασιν κατ' αὐτὸν γεγονυῖαν ἱστορεῖ, καὶ αὖ πάλιν

of the Lord's disciples, and what Aristion and the Elder John, the disciples of the Lord, say. For I did not think that I could get so much profit from the contents of books as from the utterances of a living and abiding voice.

Here it is worth while to observe that he twice enumerates the name of John. The first he mentions in connexion with Peter and James and Matthew and the rest of the Apostles, evidently meaning the Evangelist, but the other John he mentions after an interval and classes with others outside the number of the Apostles, placing Aristion before him, and he distinctly calls him an Elder. So that he hereby makes it quite evident that their statement is true who say that there were two persons of that name in Asia, and that there are two tombs in Ephesus, each of which even now is called [the tomb] of John. And it is important to notice this; for it is probable that it was the second, if one will not admit that it was the first, who saw the Revelation which is ascribed by name to John. And Papias, of whom we are now speaking, confesses that he had received the words of the Apostles from those who had followed them, but says that he was himself a hearer of Aristion and the Elder John. At all events he mentions them frequently by name, and besides records their traditions in his writings. So much for these points which I trust have not been uselessly adduced.

It is worth while however to add to the words of Papias given above other passages from him, in which he records some other wonderful events likewise, as having come down to him by tradition. That Philip the Apostle resided in Hierapolis with his daughters has been already stated; but how Papias, their contemporary, relates that he had heard a marvellous tale from the daughters of Philip, must be noted here. For he relates that in his time a man rose from the dead, and again he gives another

ἕτερον παράδοξον περὶ Ἰοῦστον τὸν ἐπικληθέντα Βαρσαββᾶν γεγονός, ὡς δηλητήριον φάρμακον ἐμπιόντος καὶ μηδὲν ἀηδὲς διὰ τὴν τοῦ Κυρίου χάριν ὑπομείναντος. τοῦτον δὲ τὸν Ἰοῦστον μετὰ τὴν τοῦ Σωτῆρος ἀνάληψιν τοὺς ἱεροὺς ἀποστόλους μετὰ Ματθία στῆσαί τε καὶ ἐπεύξασθαι ἀντὶ τοῦ προδότου Ἰούδα ἐπὶ τὸν κλῆρον τῆς ἀναπληρώσεως τοῦ αὐτῶν ἀριθμοῦ, ἡ τῶν πράξεων ὧδέ πως ἱστορεῖ γραφή· Καὶ ἔστησαν δύο, Ἰωσὴφ τὸν καλούμενον Βαρσαββᾶν, ὃς ἐπεκλήθη Ἰοῦστος, καὶ Ματθίαν· καὶ προσευξάμενοι εἶπαν. καὶ ἄλλα δὲ ὁ αὐτὸς ὡσὰν ἐκ παραδόσεως ἀγράφου εἰς αὐτὸν ἥκοντα παρατέθειται, ξένας τέ τινας παραβολὰς τοῦ Σωτῆρος καὶ διδασκαλίας αὐτοῦ, καί τινα ἄλλα μυθικώτερα. ἐν οἷς καὶ χιλιάδα τινά φησιν ἐτῶν ἔσεσθαι μετὰ τὴν ἐκ νεκρῶν ἀνάστασιν, σωματικῶς τῆς Χριστοῦ βασιλείας ἐπὶ ταυτησὶ τῆς γῆς ὑποστησομένης. ἃ καὶ ἡγοῦμαι τὰς ἀποστολικὰς παρεκδεξάμενον διηγήσεις ὑπολαβεῖν, τὰ ἐν ὑποδείγμασι πρὸς αὐτῶν μυστικῶς εἰρημένα μὴ συνεωρακότα. σφόδρα γάρ τοι σμικρὸς ὢν τὸν νοῦν, ὡσὰν ἐκ τῶν αὐτοῦ λόγων τεκμηράμενον εἰπεῖν, φαίνεται· πλὴν καὶ τοῖς μετ' αὐτὸν πλείστοις ὅσοις τῶν ἐκκλησιαστικῶν τῆς ὁμοίας αὐτῷ δόξης παραίτιος γέγονε, τὴν ἀρχαιότητα τἀνδρὸς προβεβλημένοις, ὥσπερ οὖν Εἰρηναίῳ, καὶ εἴ τις ἄλλος τὰ ὅμοια φρονῶν ἀναπέφηνεν. καὶ ἄλλας δὲ τῇ ἑαυτοῦ γραφῇ παραδίδωσιν Ἀριστίωνος τοῦ πρόσθεν δεδηλωμένου τῶν τοῦ Κυρίου λόγων διηγήσεις καὶ τοῦ πρεσβυτέρου Ἰωάννου παραδόσεις, ἐφ' ἃς τοὺς φιλομαθεῖς ἀναπέμψαντες, ἀναγκαίως νῦν προσθήσομεν ταῖς προεκτεθείσαις αὐτοῦ φωναῖς παράδοσιν, ἣν περὶ Μάρκου τοῦ τὸ εὐαγγέλιον γεγραφότος ἐκτέθειται διὰ τούτων·

Καὶ τοῦτο ὁ πρεσβύτερος ἔλεγε· Μάρκος μὲν ἑρμηνευτὴς Πέτρου γενόμενος, ὅσα ἐμνημόνευσεν, ἀκριβῶς ἔγραψεν, οὐ μέντοι τάξει, τὰ ὑπὸ τοῦ Χριστοῦ ἢ λεχθέντα

wonderful story about Justus who was surnamed Barsabas, how that he drank a deadly poison, and yet, by the grace of the Lord, suffered no inconvenience. Of this Justus the Book of the Acts records that after the ascension of the Saviour the holy Apostles put him forward with Matthias, and prayed for the [right] choice, in place of the traitor Judas, that should make their number complete. The passage is somewhat as follows: 'And they put forward two, Joseph, called Barsabas, who was surnamed Justus, and Matthias; and they prayed, and said.' The same writer has recorded other notices as having come down to him from oral tradition, certain strange parables of the Saviour and teachings of His, and some other statements of a rather mythical character. Among which he says that there will be a period of about a thousand years after the resurrection, and that the kingdom of Christ will be set up in material form on this earth. These ideas I suppose he got through a misunderstanding of the apostolic accounts, not perceiving that the things recorded there in figures were spoken by them mystically. For he evidently was a man of very mean capacity, as one may say judging from his own statements: yet it was owing to him that so many church fathers after him adopted a like opinion, urging in their own support the antiquity of the man, as for instance Irenaeus and whoever else they were who declared that they held like views. Papias also gives in his own work other accounts of the words of the Lord on the authority of Aristion who has been mentioned above, and traditions of the Elder John. To these we refer the curious, and for our present purpose we will merely add to his words, which have been quoted above, a tradition, which has been set forth through these sources concerning Mark who wrote the Gospel:—

And the Elder said this also: Mark, having become the interpreter of Peter, wrote down accurately everything that he remembered, without however recording in order what was either said or done by Christ. For neither did

ἢ πραχθέντα. οὔτε γὰρ ἤκουσε τοῦ Κυρίου, οὔτε παρηκολούθησεν αὐτῷ, ὕστερον δέ, ὡς ἔφην, Πέτρῳ, ὃς πρὸς τὰς χρείας ἐποιεῖτο τὰς διδασκαλίας, ἀλλ' οὐχ ὥσπερ σύνταξιν τῶν κυριακῶν ποιούμενος λογίων, ὥστε οὐδὲν
5 ἥμαρτε Μάρκος, οὕτως ἔνια γράψας ὡς ἀπεμνημόνευσεν. ἑνὸς γὰρ ἐποιήσατο πρόνοιαν, τοῦ μηδὲν ὧν ἤκουσε παραλιπεῖν ἢ ψεύσασθαί τι ἐν αὐτοῖς.

Ταῦτα μὲν οὖν ἱστόρηται τῷ Παπίᾳ περὶ τοῦ Μάρκου. περὶ δὲ τοῦ Ματθαίου ταῦτ' εἴρηται·
10 Ματθαῖος μὲν οὖν Ἑβραΐδι διαλέκτῳ τὰ λόγια συνεγράψατο, ἡρμήνευσε δ' αὐτὰ ὡς ἦν δυνατὸς ἕκαστος.

Κέχρηται δ' αὐτὸς μαρτυρίαις ἀπὸ τῆς Ἰωάννου προτέρας ἐπιστολῆς καὶ ἀπὸ τῆς Πέτρου ὁμοίως. ἐκτέθειται δὲ καὶ ἄλλην ἱστορίαν περὶ γυναικὸς ἐπὶ πολλαῖς ἁμαρτί-
15 αις διαβληθείσης ἐπὶ τοῦ Κυρίου, ἣν τὸ κατ' Ἑβραίους εὐαγγέλιον περιέχει. καὶ ταῦτα δ' ἡμῖν ἀναγκαίως πρὸς τοῖς ἐκτεθεῖσιν ἐπιτετηρήσθω.

Ibid. iii. 39.

XIV.

Τοῦ δὲ Σωτῆρος ἡμῶν τὰ ἔργα ἀεὶ παρῆν· ἀληθῆ γὰρ ἦν· οἱ θεραπευθέντες, οἱ ἀναστάντες ἐκ νεκρῶν, οἳ οὐκ
20 ὤφθησαν μόνον θεραπευόμενοι καὶ ἀνιστάμενοι, ἀλλὰ καὶ ἀεὶ παρόντες· οὐδὲ ἐπιδημοῦντος μόνον τοῦ Σωτῆρος, ἀλλὰ καὶ ἀπαλλαγέντος, ἦσαν ἐπὶ χρόνον ἱκανόν, ὥστε καὶ εἰς τοὺς ἡμετέρους χρόνους τινὲς αὐτῶν ἀφίκοντο.

QUADRATUS: *ibid.* iv. 3.

XIV A.

Imperatori Hadriano Caesari et Aristide philosopho
25 Atheniensi.

* * * * * * *

Καὶ οὗτοί εἰσιν οἱ ὑπὲρ πάντα τὰ ἔθνη τῆς γῆς εὑρόντες τὴν ἀλήθειαν· γινώσκουσι γὰρ τὸν Θεόν, κτίστην

he hear the Lord, nor did he follow Him; but afterwards, as I said, [attended] Peter, who adapted his instructions to the needs [of his hearers] but had no design of giving a connected account of the Lord's oracles. So then Mark made no mistake, while he thus wrote down some things as he remembered them; for he made it his one care not to omit anything that he heard, or to set down any false statement therein.

Such then is the account given by Papias concerning Mark. But concerning Matthew, the following statement is made [by him]:

So then Matthew composed the oracles in the Hebrew language, and each one interpreted them as he could.

The same writer employed testimonies from the First Epistle of John, and likewise from that of Peter. And he has related another story about a woman accused of many sins before the Lord, which the Gospel according to the Hebrews contains.
L.

Quadratus on our Lord's Miracles.

BUT our Saviour's works were always present, for they were true,—even the men who were healed, who rose from the dead,—who were seen not only while healed or rising, but always present, and that not only during the Saviour's stay on earth, but also after His departure they remained for a long time, so that some of them came down even to our own times.

The Apology of Aristides.

. . . Caesar Titus Hadrianus Antoninus, Worshipful and Clement, from Marcianus Aristides, philosopher of Athens[1].

* * * * * * *

And these are they who more than all the nations of the

---

[1] This mutilated inscription is given from the Syriac: the Latin opposite is translated from the Armenian.

καὶ δημιουργὸν τῶν ἀπάντων ἐν Υἱῷ μονογενεῖ καὶ Πνεύματι ἁγίῳ, καὶ ἄλλον θεὸν πλὴν τούτου οὐ σέβονται. Ἔχουσι τὰς ἐντολὰς αὐτοῦ τοῦ Κυρίου Ἰησοῦ Χριστοῦ ἐν ταῖς καρδίαις κεχαραγμένας, καὶ ταύτας φυλάττουσι, προσδοκῶντες ἀνάστασιν νεκρῶν καὶ ζωὴν τοῦ μέλλοντος αἰῶνος. Οὐ μοιχεύουσιν, οὐ πορνεύουσιν, οὐ ψευδομαρτυροῦσιν, οὐκ ἐπιθυμοῦσι τὰ ἀλλότρια, τιμῶσι πατέρα καὶ μητέρα, καὶ τοὺς πλησίον φιλοῦσι, δίκαια κρίνουσιν, ὅσα οὐ θέλουσιν αὐτοῖς γίνεσθαι ἑτέρῳ οὐ ποιοῦσι, τοὺς ἀδικοῦντας αὐτοὺς παρακαλοῦσι καὶ προσφιλεῖς αὐτοὺς ἑαυτοῖς ποιοῦσι, τοὺς ἐχθροὺς εὐεργετεῖν σπουδάζουσι, πραεῖς εἰσι καὶ ἐπιεικεῖς, ἀπὸ πάσης συνουσίας ἀνόμου καὶ ἀπὸ πάσης ἀκαθαρσίας ἐγκρατεύονται, χήραν οὐχ ὑπερορῶσιν, ὀρφανὸν οὐ λυποῦσιν· ὁ ἔχων τῷ μὴ ἔχοντι ἀφθόνως ἐπιχορηγεῖ· ξένον ἐὰν ἴδωσιν, ὑπὸ στέγην εἰσάγουσι, καὶ χαίρουσιν ἐπ' αὐτῷ ὡς ἐπὶ ἀδελφῷ ἀληθινῷ· οὐ γὰρ κατὰ σάρκα ἀδελφοὺς ἑαυτοὺς καλοῦσιν, ἀλλὰ κατὰ πνεῦμα. Ἕτοιμοί εἰσιν ὑπὲρ Χριστοῦ τὰς ψυχὰς αὐτῶν προέσθαι· τὰ γὰρ προστάγματα αὐτοῦ ἀσφαλῶς φυλάττουσιν, ὁσίως καὶ δικαίως ζῶντες, καθὼς Κύριος ὁ Θεὸς αὐτοῖς προέταξεν, εὐχαριστοῦντες αὐτῷ κατὰ πᾶσαν ὥραν ἐν παντὶ βρώματι καὶ ποτῷ καὶ τοῖς λοιποῖς ἀγαθοῖς. Ὄντως οὖν αὕτη ἐστὶν ἡ ὁδὸς τῆς ἀληθείας ἥτις τοὺς ὁδεύοντας αὐτὴν εἰς τὴν αἰώνιον χειραγωγεῖ βασιλείαν, τὴν ἐπηγγελμένην παρὰ Χριστοῦ ἐν τῇ μελλούσῃ ζωῇ.

Vita Barlaam et Joasaph, p. 252.

XV.

Τί δὴ οὖν τοῦτ' ἂν εἴη; Ἐφ' ἡμῶν ὑπισχνουμένων μηδὲν ἀδικεῖν μηδὲ τὰ ἄθεα ταῦτα δοξάζειν, οὐ κρίσεις ἐξετάζετε, ἀλλ' ἀλόγῳ πάθει καὶ μάστιγι δαιμόνων φαύλων ἐξελαυνόμενοι ἀκρίτως κολάζετε μὴ φροντίζοντες.

earth have found the truth, for they know God the maker and creator in His only Son and Holy Spirit, and other god than Him they worship not. For they have the commands of the Lord Himself, even Jesus Christ, written in their hearts, and these they keep, looking for the resurrection of the dead and life of the age to come. They commit no adultery or fornication, they bear no false witness, they covet not other men's goods, they honour father and mother and love their neighbours, they judge righteously, and whatsoever things they would not have done to themselves they do not to another. They exhort them that do them wrong, and make them friendly to themselves, they strive to do good to their enemies, are meek and moderate, restrain themselves from all unlawful intercourse and from all uncleanness, they despise not a widow, and an orphan they grieve not. He that hath giveth help ungrudgingly to him that hath not. If they see a stranger, they bring him under their roof, and rejoice over him as over a brother of their own, for they call not themselves brethren after the flesh, but after the spirit. They are ready to give up their lives for Christ, for they keep His commands firmly, living holily and righteously as the Lord God commanded them, giving thanks to Him every hour at all meat and drink and all other good things.

Heathenism the work of demons.

WHAT does this mean? In our case, though we profess to do no man wrong and to reject these godless opinions, you do not examine charges, but are driven by unreasoning passion and the scourge of evil demons to punish us without investigation or consideration. For the truth

εἰρήσεται γὰρ τἀληθές· ἐπεὶ τὸ παλαιὸν δαίμονες φαῦλοι, ἐπιφανείας ποιησάμενοι, καὶ γυναῖκας ἐμοίχευσαν καὶ παῖδας διέφθειραν καὶ φόβητρα ἀνθρώποις ἔδειξαν, ὡς καταπλαγῆναι τοὺς οἳ λόγῳ τὰς γινομένας πράξεις οὐκ ἔκρινον, ἀλλὰ δέει συνηρπασμένοι καὶ μὴ ἐπιστάμενοι, δαίμονας εἶναι φαύλους, θεοὺς προσωνόμαζον καὶ ὀνόματι ἕκαστον προσηγόρευον, ὅπερ ἕκαστος αὑτῷ τῶν δαιμόνων ἐτίθετο. ὅτε δὲ Σωκράτης λόγῳ ἀληθεῖ καὶ ἐξεταστικῶς ταῦτα εἰς φανερὸν ἐπειρᾶτο φέρειν καὶ ἀπάγειν τῶν δαιμόνων τοὺς ἀνθρώπους, καὶ αὐτοὶ οἱ δαίμονες διὰ τῶν χαιρόντων τῇ κακίᾳ ἀνθρώπων ἐνήργησαν ὡς ἄθεον καὶ ἀσεβῆ ἀποκτεῖναι, λέγοντες καινὰ εἰσφέρειν αὐτὸν δαιμόνια. καὶ ὁμοίως ἐφ᾽ ἡμῶν τὸ αὐτὸ ἐνεργοῦσιν· οὐ γὰρ μόνον ἐν Ἕλλησι διὰ Σωκράτους ὑπὸ λόγου ἠλέγχθη ταῦτα, ἀλλὰ καὶ ἐν βαρβάροις ὑπ᾽ αὐτοῦ τοῦ λόγου μορφωθέντος καὶ ἀνθρώπου γενομένου καὶ Ἰησοῦ Χριστοῦ κληθέντος, ᾧ πεισθέντες ἡμεῖς τοὺς ταῦτα πράξαντας δαίμονας οὐ μόνον μὴ ὀρθοὺς εἶναί φαμεν, ἀλλὰ κακοὺς καὶ ἀνοσίους δαίμονας, οἳ οὐδὲ τοῖς ἀρετὴν ποθοῦσιν ἀνθρώποις τὰς πράξεις ὁμοίας ἔχουσι.

JUSTIN, *Apol.* i. 5.

XVI.

Ἵνα δὲ μή τινες ἀλογισταίνοντες εἰς ἀποτροπὴν τῶν δεδιδαγμένων ὑφ᾽ ἡμῶν εἴπωσι, πρὸ ἐτῶν ἑκατὸν πεντήκοντα γεγεννῆσθαι τὸν Χριστὸν λέγειν ἡμᾶς ἐπὶ Κυρηνίου, δεδιδαχέναι δὲ ἃ φαμεν διδάξαι αὐτὸν ὕστερον χρόνοις ἐπὶ Ποντίου Πιλάτου, καὶ ἐπικαλῶσιν, ὡς ἀνευθύνων ὄντων τῶν προγεγενημένων πάντων ἀνθρώπων, φθάσαντες τὴν ἀπορίαν λυσώμεθα. τὸν Χριστὸν πρωτότοκον τοῦ Θεοῦ εἶναι ἐδιδάχθημεν καὶ προεμηνύσαμεν λόγον ὄντα, οὗ πᾶν γένος ἀνθρώπων μετέσχε. καὶ οἱ μετὰ λόγου βιώσαντες Χριστιανοί εἰσι, κἂν ἄθεοι ἐνομίσθησαν,

shall be told. It is because evil demons of old made
apparitions, and defiled women and corrupted boys, and
showed to men such horrors that those were struck with
terror who did not judge by reason the acts performed,
but were carried away by fear, and in their ignorance
that these were evil demons called them gods, and addressed each of them by name according as each demon
styled himself. But when Socrates essayed by true reason
and examination to bring these things to the light and
lead men away from the demons, then these same demons
by means of men who rejoiced in iniquity caused them to
slay him as a godless and impious man, saying that he
was introducing new divinities—and the same likewise
they cause to be done in our case. For not among the
Greeks alone were these things through Socrates condemned by reason, but among the barbarians also by the
Reason himself taking shape and made man and called
Jesus Christ; and at His persuasion we hold that the
demons who did these things are not only not good, but
wicked and unholy demons, whose acts are not like even
those of men who long for virtue.

Christianity before Christ.

But that some may not in reply to our teachings unreasonably say that according to us Christ was born 150
years ago in the time of Cyrenius, and taught what we
assert Him to have taught at a later time under Pontius
Pilate, and so object that all men who lived before Him
were irresponsible, let us solve the difficulty in advance.
We were taught that Christ is the firstborn of God, and
we have already signified that He is the reason, in which
every race of men did share. Thus those who lived with
reason are Christians even if they were counted godless,

οἷον ἐν Ἕλλησι μὲν Σωκράτης καὶ Ἡράκλειτος καὶ οἱ ὅμοιοι αὐτοῖς, ἐν βαρβάροις δὲ Ἀβραὰμ καὶ Ἀνανίας καὶ Ἀζαρίας καὶ Μισαὴλ καὶ Ἠλίας καὶ ἄλλοι πολλοί, ὧν τὰς πράξεις ἢ τὰ ὀνόματα καταλέγειν μακρὸν εἶναι 5 ἐπιστάμενοι τανῦν παραιτούμεθα.

Ibid. i. 46.

XVII.

61. Ὃν τρόπον δὲ καὶ ἀνεθήκαμεν ἑαυτοὺς τῷ Θεῷ καινοποιηθέντες διὰ τοῦ Χριστοῦ, ἐξηγησόμεθα, ὅπως μὴ τοῦτο παραλιπόντες δόξωμεν πονηρεύειν τι ἐν τῇ ἐξηγήσει. ὅσοι ἂν πεισθῶσι καὶ πιστεύωσιν ἀληθῆ ταῦτα τὰ ὑφ᾽ 10 ἡμῶν διδασκόμενα καὶ λεγόμενα εἶναι, καὶ βιοῦν οὕτως δύνασθαι ὑπισχνῶνται, εὔχεσθαί τε καὶ αἰτεῖν νηστεύοντες παρὰ τοῦ Θεοῦ τῶν προημαρτημένων ἄφεσιν διδάσκονται, ἡμῶν συνευχομένων καὶ συννηστευόντων αὐτοῖς. ἔπειτα ἄγονται ὑφ᾽ ἡμῶν ἔνθα ὕδωρ ἐστί, καὶ τρόπον 15 ἀναγεννήσεως, ὃν καὶ ἡμεῖς αὐτοὶ ἀνεγεννήθημεν, ἀναγεννῶνται· ἐπ᾽ ὀνόματος γὰρ τοῦ πατρὸς τῶν ὅλων καὶ δεσπότου Θεοῦ καὶ τοῦ σωτῆρος ἡμῶν Ἰησοῦ Χριστοῦ καὶ Πνεύματος ἁγίου τὸ ἐν τῷ ὕδατι τότε λουτρὸν ποιοῦνται. καὶ γὰρ ὁ Χριστὸς εἶπεν· Ἂν μὴ ἀναγεννηθῆτε, οὐ μὴ 20 εἰσέλθητε εἰς τὴν βασιλείαν τῶν οὐρανῶν. ὅτι δὲ καὶ ἀδύνατον εἰς τὰς μήτρας τῶν τεκουσῶν τοὺς ἅπαξ γεννωμένους ἐμβῆναι, φανερὸν πᾶσίν ἐστι.... καλεῖται δὲ τοῦτο τὸ λουτρὸν φωτισμός, ὡς φωτιζομένων τὴν διάνοιαν τῶν ταῦτα μανθανόντων....

65. 25 Ἡμεῖς δὲ μετὰ τὸ οὕτως λοῦσαι τὸν πεπεισμένον καὶ συγκατατεθειμένον ἐπὶ τοὺς λεγομένους ἀδελφοὺς ἄγομεν, ἔνθα συνηγμένοι εἰσί, κοινὰς εὐχὰς ποιησόμενοι ὑπέρ τε ἑαυτῶν καὶ τοῦ φωτισθέντος καὶ ἄλλων πανταχοῦ πάντων εὐτόνως, ὅπως καταξιωθῶμεν τὰ ἀληθῆ μαθόντες καὶ δι᾽ 30 ἔργων ἀγαθοὶ πολιτευταὶ καὶ φύλακες τῶν ἐντεταλμένων

as of the Greeks, Socrates, Heraclitus and others like them, and of the barbarians Abraham, Hananiah, Azariah, Mishael, Elijah, and many others, whose names and acts we decline to set down here, knowing that they would be long to tell.

Christian Worship.

But I will explain how we also dedicated ourselves to God when we were made new through Christ, lest by passing it over I should seem in any way unfair in my explanation. As many as are persuaded and believe that the things are true which are taught by us and said to be true, and promise that they can live accordingly—they are taught to pray and to ask of God with fasting forgiveness of their former sins, and we pray and fast together with them. Then they are brought by us to a place where there is water, and born again with a new birth even as we ourselves were born again. For in the name of God the Father and Lord of the universe, and of our Saviour Jesus Christ and the Holy Spirit do they then receive the washing in water. For Christ said, Except ye be born again, ye shall not enter into the kingdom of heaven. But that it is impossible for those once born to enter into the wombs of their mothers is manifest to all. . . . And this washing is called Enlightenment, because those who learn these things have their understanding enlightened. . . .

But after having thus washed him that is persuaded and has given his assent, we bring him to where the brethren as they are called are gathered together, to make earnest prayers in common for ourselves and for the newly enlightened, and for all others everywhere, that we may be counted worthy after we have learned the truth, by our works also to be found right livers and keepers of the commandments, that we may be saved with

εὑρεθῆναι, ὅπως τὴν αἰώνιον σωτηρίαν σωθῶμεν. ἀλλήλους φιλήματι ἀσπαζόμεθα παυσάμενοι τῶν εὐχῶν. ἔπειτα προσφέρεται τῷ προεστῶτι τῶν ἀδελφῶν ἄρτος καὶ ποτήριον ὕδατος καὶ κράματος, καὶ οὗτος λαβὼν
5 αἶνον καὶ δόξαν τῷ Πατρὶ τῶν ὅλων διὰ τοῦ ὀνόματος τοῦ Υἱοῦ καὶ τοῦ Πνεύματος τοῦ ἁγίου ἀναπέμπει καὶ εὐχαριστίαν ὑπὲρ τοῦ κατηξιῶσθαι τούτων παρ᾽ αὐτοῦ ἐπὶ πολὺ ποιεῖται· οὗ συντελέσαντος τὰς εὐχὰς καὶ τὴν εὐχαριστίαν πᾶς ὁ παρὼν λαὸς ἐπευφημεῖ λέγων· Ἀμήν. τὸ δὲ ἀμὴν
10 τῇ Ἑβραΐδι φωνῇ τὸ γένοιτο σημαίνει. εὐχαριστήσαντος δὲ τοῦ προεστῶτος καὶ ἐπευφημήσαντος παντὸς τοῦ λαοῦ οἱ καλούμενοι παρ᾽ ἡμῖν διάκονοι διδόασιν ἑκάστῳ τῶν παρόντων μεταλαβεῖν ἀπὸ τοῦ εὐχαριστηθέντος ἄρτου καὶ οἴνου καὶ ὕδατος καὶ τοῖς οὐ παροῦσιν ἀποφέρουσι.

66.15 Καὶ ἡ τροφὴ αὕτη καλεῖται παρ᾽ ἡμῖν εὐχαριστία, ἧς οὐδενὶ ἄλλῳ μετασχεῖν ἐξόν ἐστιν, ἢ τῷ πιστεύοντι ἀληθῆ εἶναι τὰ δεδιδαγμένα ὑφ᾽ ἡμῶν καὶ λουσαμένῳ τὸ ὑπὲρ ἀφέσεως ἁμαρτιῶν καὶ εἰς ἀναγέννησιν λουτρόν καὶ οὕτως βιοῦντι ὡς ὁ Χριστὸς παρέδωκεν. οὐ γὰρ ὡς κοινὸν
20 ἄρτον οὐδὲ κοινὸν πόμα ταῦτα λαμβάνομεν, ἀλλ᾽ ὃν τρόπον διὰ λόγου Θεοῦ σαρκοποιηθεὶς Ἰησοῦς Χριστὸς ὁ σωτὴρ ἡμῶν καὶ σάρκα καὶ αἷμα ὑπὲρ σωτηρίας ἡμῶν ἔσχεν, οὕτως καὶ τὴν δι᾽ εὐχῆς λόγου τοῦ παρ᾽ αὐτοῦ εὐχαριστηθεῖσαν τροφήν, ἐξ ἧς αἷμα καὶ σάρκες κατὰ
25 μεταβολὴν τρέφονται ἡμῶν, ἐκείνου τοῦ σαρκοποιηθέντος Ἰησοῦ καὶ σάρκα καὶ αἷμα ἐδιδάχθημεν εἶναι. οἱ γὰρ ἀπόστολοι ἐν τοῖς γενομένοις ὑπ᾽ αὐτῶν ἀπομνημονεύμασιν, ἃ καλεῖται εὐαγγέλια, οὕτως παρέδωκαν ἐντετάλθαι αὐτοῖς· τὸν Ἰησοῦν, λαβόντα ἄρτον εὐχαριστήσαντα
30 εἰπεῖν· Τοῦτο ποιεῖτε εἰς τὴν ἀνάμνησίν μου, τοῦτό ἐστι τὸ σῶμά μου· καὶ τὸ ποτήριον ὁμοίως λαβόντα καὶ εὐχαριστήσαντα εἰπεῖν· Τοῦτό ἐστι αἷμά μου, καὶ μόνοις αὐτοῖς μεταδοῦναι. ὅπερ καὶ ἐν τοῖς τοῦ Μίθρα μυστη-

the eternal salvation. We salute each other with a kiss when our prayers are ended. Afterwards is brought to the president of the brethren bread and a cup of water and [mixed] wine, and he takes it and offers up praise and glory to the Father of the universe through the name of the Son and the Holy Spirit, and gives thanks at length, that we have received these favours from Him; and at the end of his prayers and thanksgiving the whole people present responds, saying Amen. Now the word Amen in the Hebrew language signifies So be it. Then after the president has given thanks and all the people responded, the deacons as we call them allow every one of those present to partake of the bread and wine and water for which thanks have been given; and for those absent they take away a portion.

And this food is called by us Eucharist, and it is not lawful for any man to partake of it but he who believes our teaching to be true, and has been washed with the washing which is for the forgiveness of sins and unto a new birth, and is so living as Christ commanded. For not as common bread and common drink do we receive these; but like as Jesus Christ our Saviour being made flesh through the word of God took both flesh and blood for our salvation, so also were we taught that the food for which thanks are given by the word of prayer that comes from him—food by which blood and flesh by conversion are nourished, is both flesh and blood of that Jesus who was made flesh. For the Apostles in the memoirs which they composed, which are called Gospels, thus delivered that command was given them—that Jesus took bread and gave thanks and said, This do in remembrance of me, this is my body; and that He likewise took the cup, and after He had given thanks said, This is my blood, and gave of it only to them. Which the evil demons imitated, commanding it to be done also in the mysteries of Mithras;

ρίοις παρέδωκαν γίνεσθαι μιμησάμενοι οἱ πονηροὶ δαίμονες· ὅτι γὰρ ἄρτος καὶ ποτήριον ὕδατος τίθεται ἐν ταῖς τοῦ μυουμένου τελεταῖς μετ' ἐπιλόγων τινῶν, ἢ ἐπίστασθε ἢ μαθεῖν δύνασθε.

67. 5 Ἡμεῖς δὲ μετὰ ταῦτα λοιπὸν ἀεὶ τούτων ἀλλήλους ἀναμιμνῄσκομεν· καὶ οἱ ἔχοντες τοῖς λειπομένοις πᾶσιν ἐπικουροῦμεν, καὶ σύνεσμεν ἀλλήλοις ἀεί. ἐπὶ πᾶσί τε οἷς προσφερόμεθα εὐλογοῦμεν τὸν ποιητὴν τῶν πάντων διὰ τοῦ Υἱοῦ αὐτοῦ Ἰησοῦ Χριστοῦ καὶ διὰ Πνεύματος τοῦ
10 ἁγίου. καὶ τῇ τοῦ ἡλίου λεγομένῃ ἡμέρᾳ πάντων κατὰ πόλεις ἢ ἀγροὺς μενόντων ἐπὶ τὸ αὐτὸ συνέλευσις γίνεται, καὶ τὰ ἀπομνημονεύματα τῶν ἀποστόλων ἢ τὰ συγγράμματα τῶν προφητῶν ἀναγινώσκεται μέχρις ἐγχωρεῖ. εἶτα παυσαμένου τοῦ ἀναγινώσκοντος ὁ προεστὼς διὰ
15 λόγου τὴν νουθεσίαν καὶ πρόκλησιν τῆς τῶν καλῶν τούτων μιμήσεως ποιεῖται. ἔπειτα ἀνιστάμεθα κοινῇ πάντες καὶ εὐχὰς πέμπομεν. καί, ὡς προέφημεν, παυσαμένων ἡμῶν τῆς εὐχῆς ἄρτος προσφέρεται καὶ οἶνος καὶ ὕδωρ, καὶ ὁ προεστὼς εὐχὰς ὁμοίως καὶ εὐχαριστίας, ὅση δύναμις
20 αὐτῷ, ἀναπέμπει καὶ ὁ λαὸς ἐπευφημεῖ λέγων τὸ ἀμήν· καὶ ἡ διάδοσις καὶ ἡ μετάληψις ἀπὸ τῶν εὐχαριστηθέντων ἑκάστῳ γίνεται καὶ τοῖς οὐ παροῦσι διὰ τῶν διακόνων πέμπεται. οἱ εὐποροῦντες δὲ καὶ βουλόμενοι κατὰ προαίρεσιν ἕκαστος τὴν ἑαυτοῦ ὃ βούλεται δίδωσι, καὶ τὸ
25 συλλεγόμενον παρὰ τῷ προεστῶτι ἀποτίθεται, καὶ αὐτὸς ἐπικουρεῖ ὀρφανοῖς τε καὶ χήραις, καὶ τοῖς διὰ νόσον ἢ δι' ἄλλην αἰτίαν λειπομένοις, καὶ τοῖς ἐν δεσμοῖς οὖσι, καὶ τοῖς παρεπιδήμοις οὖσι ξένοις, καὶ ἁπλῶς πᾶσι τοῖς ἐν χρείᾳ οὖσι κηδεμὼν γίνεται. τὴν δὲ τοῦ ἡλίου ἡμέραν
30 κοινῇ πάντες τὴν συνέλευσιν ποιούμεθα, ἐπειδὴ πρώτη ἐστὶν ἡμέρα, ἐν ᾗ ὁ Θεὸς τὸ σκότος καὶ τὴν ὕλην τρέψας κόσμον ἐποίησε, καὶ Ἰησοῦς Χριστὸς ὁ ἡμέτερος σωτὴρ τῇ αὐτῇ ἡμέρᾳ ἐκ νεκρῶν ἀνέστη· τῇ γὰρ πρὸ τῆς

for that bread and a cup of water are set forth with
certain formulae in the ceremonial of initiation, you
either know or can learn.

But we afterwards henceforth continually put each other
in mind of these things, and those of us who are wealthy
help all that are in want, and we always remain together.
And for all things that we eat we bless the Maker of all
through His Son Jesus Christ, and through the Holy
Spirit. And on the so-called day of the Sun there is a
meeting of all of us who live in cities or the country, and
the memoirs of the Apostles or the writings of the prophets
are read, as long as time allows. Then when the reader
has ceased, the president gives by word of mouth his
admonition and exhortation to follow these excellent
things. Afterwards we all rise at once and offer prayers;
and as I said, when we have ceased to pray, bread is
brought and wine and water, and the president likewise
offers up prayers and thanksgivings to the best of his
power, and the people responds with its Amen. Then
follows the distribution to each and the partaking of that
for which thanks were given; and to them that are absent
a portion is sent by the hand of the deacons. Of those
that are well to do and willing, every one gives what he
will according to his own purpose, and the collection is
deposited with the president, and he it is that succours
orphans and widows, and those that are in want through
sickness or any other cause, and those that are in bonds,
and the strangers that are sojourning, and in short he has
the care of all that are in need. Now we all hold our
common meeting on the day of the Sun, because it is the
first day, on which God changed the darkness and matter
in His making of the world, and Jesus Christ our Saviour
on the same day rose from the dead. For on the day

Κρονικῆς ἐσταύρωσαν αὐτὸν καὶ τῇ μετὰ τὴν Κρονικήν, ἥτις ἐστὶν ἡλίου ἡμέρα, φανεὶς τοῖς ἀποστόλοις αὐτοῦ καὶ μαθηταῖς ἐδίδαξε ταῦτα, ἅπερ εἰς ἐπίσκεψιν καὶ ὑμῖν ἀνεδώκαμεν. *Ibid.* i. 61, 65-67.

XVIII.

Καὶ ὁ Τρύφων ἀπεκρίνατο· Ἡ γραφὴ οὐκ ἔχει· Ἰδοὺ ἡ παρθένος ἐν γαστρὶ λήψεται καὶ τέξεται υἱόν, ἀλλ'· Ἰδοὺ ἡ νεᾶνις ἐν γαστρὶ λήψεται καὶ τέξεται υἱόν, καὶ τὰ ἑξῆς λοιπὰ ὡς ἔφης. ἔστι δὲ ἡ πᾶσα προφητεία λελεγμένη εἰς Ἐζεκίαν, εἰς ὃν καὶ ἀποδείκνυται ἀποβάντα κατὰ τὴν προφητείαν ταύτην. ἐν δὲ τοῖς τῶν λεγομένων Ἑλλήνων μύθοις λέλεκται ὅτι Περσεὺς ἐκ Δανάης, παρθένου οὔσης, ἐν χρυσοῦ μορφῇ ῥεύσαντος ἐπ' αὐτὴν τοῦ παρ' αὐτοῖς Διὸς καλουμένου, γεγέννηται· καὶ ὑμεῖς τὰ αὐτὰ ἐκείνοις λέγοντες αἰδεῖσθαι ὀφείλετε, καὶ μᾶλλον ἄνθρωπον ἐξ ἀνθρώπων γενόμενον λέγειν τὸν Ἰησοῦν τοῦτον, καί, ἐὰν ἀποδεικνύητε ἀπὸ τῶν γραφῶν ὅτι αὐτός ἐστιν ὁ Χριστός, διὰ τὸ ἐννόμως καὶ τελέως πολιτεύεσθαι αὐτὸν κατηξιῶσθαι τοῦ ἐκλεγῆναι εἰς Χριστόν, ἀλλὰ μὴ τερατολογεῖν τολμᾶτε, ὅπως μήτε ὁμοίως τοῖς Ἕλλησι μωραίνειν ἐλέγχησθε. Justin, *Dial.* 67.

XIX.

Ὅταν γὰρ ὡς υἱὸν ἀνθρώπου λέγῃ Δανιὴλ τὸν παραλαμβάνοντα τὴν αἰώνιον βασιλείαν, οὐκ αὐτὸ τοῦτο αἰνίσσεται; τὸ γὰρ ὡς υἱὸν ἀνθρώπου εἰπεῖν, φαινόμενον μὲν καὶ γενόμενον ἄνθρωπον μηνύει, οὐκ ἐξ ἀνθρωπίνου δὲ σπέρματος ὑπάρχοντα δηλοῖ. καὶ τὸ λίθον τοῦτον εἰπεῖν ἄνευ χειρῶν τμηθέντα, ἐν μυστηρίῳ τὸ αὐτὸ κέκραγε· τὸ γὰρ ἄνευ χειρῶν εἰπεῖν αὐτὸν ἐκτετμῆσθαι, ὅτι οὐκ ἔστιν ἀνθρώπινον ἔργον, ἀλλὰ τῆς βουλῆς τοῦ

before Saturn's they crucified Him ; and on the day after Saturn's, which is the day of the Sun, he appeared to His Apostles and disciples and taught them these things, which we have offered to you also for consideration.

The Jewish interpretation of Isa. vii. 14.

AND Trypho answered, The scripture has not Behold the virgin shall conceive and bear a son, but Behold the young woman shall conceive and bear a son, and the rest of it as you say. But the whole prophecy was spoken of Hezekiah, and in him it is proved that the things were fulfilled according to this prophecy. But in the legends of those who are called Greeks we read that Perseus was born of Danae, who was a virgin, and on whom he who is by them called Zeus came down in the form of a shower of gold ; and you ought to be ashamed of telling the same tale as they, and should rather say that this Jesus was a man born of men, and, if you prove from the Scriptures that he is the Christ, that he was counted worthy of being chosen for the Christ because he lived a perfect life and according to the law. But do not venture to tell romancing tales, lest you be convicted of making fools of yourselves like the Greeks.

The Christian interpretation of various passages.

WHEN Daniel says As a son of man [1] of him who receives the everlasting kingdom, is he not hinting this very thing? For the words, As a son of man, show that he seemed and became a man, but declare that he was not born of human seed. And in that he speaks of him as a stone cut without hands [2], he proclaims the same in a mystery, for the words Cut out without hands signify

---

[1] Dan. vii. 13.   [2] Dan. ii. 34.

προβάλλοντος αὐτὸν Πατρὸς τῶν ὅλων Θεοῦ. καὶ τὸ
Ἠσαΐαν φάναι· Τὴν γενεὰν αὐτοῦ τίς διηγήσεται;
ἀνεκδιήγητον ἔχοντα τὸ γένος αὐτὸν ἐδήλου· οὐδεὶς γάρ,
ἄνθρωπος ὢν ἐξ ἀνθρώπων, ἀνεκδιήγητον ἔχει τὸ γένος.
5 καὶ τὸ τὸν Μωσέα εἰπεῖν πλυνεῖν αὐτὸν τὴν στολὴν
αὐτοῦ ἐν αἵματι σταφυλῆς, οὐχ, ὃ καὶ ἤδη πολλάκις πρὸς
ὑμᾶς παρακεκαλυμμένως πεπροφητευκέναι αὐτὸν εἶπον,
ἐστίν; ὅτι αἷμα μὲν ἔχειν αὐτὸν προεμήνυεν, ἀλλ᾿ οὐκ ἐξ
ἀνθρώπων· ὃν τρόπον τὸ τῆς ἀμπέλου αἷμα οὐκ ἄνθρω-
10 πος ἐγέννησεν, ἀλλ᾿ ὁ Θεός. καὶ Ἠσαΐας δὲ μεγάλης
βουλῆς ἄγγελον αὐτὸν εἰπών, οὐχὶ τούτων, ὧνπερ ἐδίδαξεν
ἐλθών, διδάσκαλον αὐτὸν γεγενῆσθαι προεκήρυσσεν;
Ἃ γὰρ μεγάλα ἐβεβούλευτο ὁ Πατὴρ εἴς τε πάντας
τοὺς εὐαρέστους γενομένους αὐτῷ καὶ γενησομένους
15 ἀνθρώπους, καὶ τοὺς ἀποστάντας τῆς βουλῆς αὐτοῦ
ὁμοίως ἀνθρώπους ἢ ἀγγέλους, οὗτος μόνος ἀπαρακαλύπτως
ἐδίδαξεν.

Ibid. 76.

XIX A.

Ἤκμαζον δὲ ἐν τούτοις ἐπὶ τῆς ἐκκλησίας Ἡγήσιππός
τε ὃν ἴσμεν ἐκ τῶν προτέρων, καὶ Διονύσιος Κορινθίων
20 ἐπίσκοπος, Πινυτός τε ἄλλος τῶν ἐπὶ Κρήτης ἐπίσκοπος,
Φίλιππός τε ἐπὶ τούτοις, καὶ Ἀπολινάριος, καὶ Μελίτων,
Μουσανός τε καὶ Μόδεστος, καὶ ἐπὶ πᾶσιν Εἰρηναῖος· ὧν
καὶ εἰς ἡμᾶς τῆς ἀποστολικῆς παραδόσεως ἡ τῆς ὑγιοῦς
πίστεως ἔγγραφος κατῆλθεν ὀρθοδοξία.
25 Ὁ μὲν οὖν Ἡγήσιππος ἐν πέντε τοῖς εἰς ἡμᾶς ἐλθοῦσιν

that it is not a work of men, but of God the Father of the universe, who produces him. Again, when Isaiah said, Who shall declare his generation[1]? it was a plain proof that he had a generation which could not be declared, for none who is a man from men has a generation that cannot be declared. And in that Moses says that he washes his raiment in the blood of the grape[2], is not this the thing that I have often told you he prophesied obscurely, how he signified aforetime that he had blood, but not of men, even as it was not man but God that brought forth the blood of the vine? Again, when Isaiah called him Angel of mighty counsel[3], did he not foretell that he would be the teacher of the things which he taught when he came? For he alone taught openly the mighty works which the Father had counselled with regard to all men who ever were or shall be well-pleasing to him, and with regard to those who rebelled against his counsel, as well men as angels, saying [Matt. viii. 11, 12].

Hegesippus.

At that time there flourished in the church Hegesippus, whom we know from former passages, and Dionysius bishop of Corinth, and another bishop Pinytus in Crete, and beside these Philip, and Apolinarius and Melito, also Musanus and Modestus, and lastly Irenaeus. From these has come down to us in writing the true doctrine of sound faith received from the apostolic tradition.

Hegesippus then, in the five books of Memoirs which

---

[1] Isa. liii. 8.   [2] Gen. xlix. 11.   [3] Isa. ix. 6, LXX.

ὑπομνήμασι τῆς ἰδίας γνώμης πληρεστάτην μνήμην καταλέλοιπεν, ἐν οἷς δηλοῖ, ὡς πλείστοις ἐπισκόποις συμμίξειεν, ἀποδημίαν στειλάμενος μέχρι Ῥώμης, καὶ ὡς ὅτι τὴν αὐτὴν παρὰ πάντων παρείληφε διδασκαλίαν. Ἀκοῦσαι 5 γέτοι πάρεστι μετά τινα περὶ τῆς Κλήμεντος πρὸς Κορινθίους ἐπιστολῆς αὐτῷ εἰρημένα, ἐπιλέγοντος ταῦτα·

Καὶ ἐπέμενεν ἡ ἐκκλησία ἡ Κορινθίων ἐν τῷ ὀρθῷ λόγῳ, μέχρι Πρίμου ἐπισκοπεύοντος ἐν Κορίνθῳ· οἷς συνέμιξα πλέων εἰς Ῥώμην, καὶ συνδιέτριψα τοῖς Κοριν-
10 θίοις ἡμέρας ἱκανάς, ἐν αἷς συνανεπάημεν τῷ ὀρθῷ λόγῳ. Γενόμενος δὲ ἐν Ῥώμῃ, διαδοχὴν[1] ἐποιησάμην μέχρις Ἀνικήτου, οὗ διάκονος ἦν Ἐλεύθερος. Καὶ παρὰ Ἀνικήτου διαδέχεται Σωτήρ, μεθ᾽ ὃν Ἐλεύθερος. Ἐν ἑκάστῃ δὲ διαδοχῇ καὶ ἐν ἑκάστῃ πόλει οὕτως ἔχει, ὡς ὁ νόμος
15 κηρύσσει καὶ οἱ προφῆται καὶ ὁ Κύριος. . . . .

Καὶ ἕτερα δὲ πλεῖστα γράφει, ὧν ἐκ μέρους ἤδη πρότερον ἐμνημονεύσαμεν, οἰκείως τοῖς καιροῖς τὰς ἱστορίας παραθέμενοι. Ἔκ τε τοῦ καθ᾽ Ἑβραίους Εὐαγγελίου καὶ τοῦ Συριακοῦ, καὶ ἰδίως ἐκ τῆς Ἑβραΐδος διαλέκτου
20 τινὰ τίθησιν, ἐμφαίνων ἐξ Ἑβραίων ἑαυτὸν πεπιστευκέναι· καὶ ἄλλα δὲ ὡς ἂν ἐξ Ἰουδαϊκῆς ἀγράφου παραδόσεως μνημονεύει· οὐ μόνος δὲ οὗτος, ἀλλὰ καὶ Εἰρηναῖος καὶ ὁ πᾶς τῶν ἀρχαίων χορός, 'Πανάρετον Σοφίαν' τὰς Σολομῶνος Παροιμίας ἐκάλουν. Καὶ περὶ τῶν λεγομένων
25 δὲ Ἀποκρύφων διαλαμβάνων, ἐπὶ τῶν αὐτοῦ χρόνων πρός τινων αἱρετικῶν ἀναπεπλάσθαι τινὰ τούτων ἱστορεῖ.

EUSEBIUS, *Hist. Eccl.* iv. 21, 22.

[1] διαδοχὴν Codd. So Lft.: Harnack still prefers διατριβήν.

have come down to us, has left a very full record of his own opinion. In these he shows how he made acquaintance with a great many bishops when he made a journey as far as Rome, and that he received the same teaching from them all. At any rate, we can hear what he says after some words about the Epistle of Clement to the Corinthians. He goes on—'And the church of Corinth remained in the right faith till Primus was bishop in Corinth. I made acquaintance with them on my voyage to Rome, and stayed many days with the Corinthians, and together with them found refreshment in the right faith. And when I came to Rome I made a list of succession till the time of Anicetus, whose deacon was Eleutherus. Anicetus was succeeded by Soter, and after him Eleutherus. But in every succession and in every city things are ordered according to the preaching of the law and the prophets and the Lord.'

And he writes many other things, which we have in part already mentioned, setting forth the stories at their proper places. And from the Gospel according to the Hebrews and from the Syriac (Gospel), and in particular from (writings in) the Hebrew tongue, he sets down certain passages, showing that he was himself a convert from the Hebrews; and he mentions other things as coming from unwritten Jewish tradition. And not only he, but Irenaeus also and the whole company of the ancients called the Proverbs of Solomon All-virtuous Wisdom. And discoursing of the books called Apocryphal, he relates that some of these were composed in his own times by certain heretics.

XIX B.

Καὶ τοῦτο νῦν ἐξευρέθη παρ' αὐτοῖς, Τατιανοῦ τινὸς πρώτως ταύτην εἰσενέγκαντος τὴν βλασφημίαν· ὃς Ἰουστίνου ἀκροατὴς γεγονώς, ἐφ' ὅσον μὲν συνῆν ἐκείνῳ, οὐδὲν ἐξέφηνε τοιοῦτον, μετὰ δὲ τὴν ἐκείνου μαρτυρίαν
5 ἀποστὰς τῆς ἐκκλησίας, οἰήματι διδασκάλου ἐπαρθεὶς καὶ τυφωθεὶς ὡς διαφέρων τῶν λοιπῶν, ἴδιον χαρακτῆρα διδασκαλείου συνεστήσατο, αἰῶνάς τινας ἀοράτους ὁμοίως τοῖς ἀπὸ Οὐαλεντίνου μυθολογήσας, γάμον τε φθορὰν καὶ πορνείαν παραπλησίως Μαρκίωνι καὶ Σατορνίνῳ ἀναγο-
10 ρεύσας, τῇ δὲ τοῦ Ἀδὰμ σωτηρίᾳ παρ' ἑαυτοῦ τὴν αἰτιολογίαν ποιησάμενος. Ταῦτα μὲν ὁ Εἰρηναῖος . . . Ὁ μέντοι γε πρότερος αὐτῶν ἀρχηγὸς Τατιανὸς συνάφειάν τινα καὶ συναγωγὴν οὐκ οἶδ' ὅπως τῶν εὐαγγελίων συνθείς, τὸ "Διὰ τεσσάρων" τοῦτο προσωνόμασεν· ὃ καὶ
15 παρά τισιν εἰσέτι νῦν φέρεται.

Ibid. iv. 29.

XX.

Ἔτι τοῦ Διονυσίου καὶ "πρὸς Ῥωμαίους" ἐπιστολὴ φέρεται, ἐπισκόπῳ τῷ τότε Σωτῆρι προσφωνοῦσα. ἐξ ἧς οὐδὲν οἷον τὸ καὶ παραθέσθαι λέξεις, δι' ὧν τὸ μέχρι τοῦ καθ' ἡμᾶς διωγμοῦ φυλαχθὲν Ῥωμαίων ἔθος ἀποδεχό-
20 μενος, ταῦτα γράφει·

Ἐξ ἀρχῆς γὰρ ὑμῖν ἔθος ἐστὶ τοῦτο, πάντας μὲν ἀδελφοὺς ποικίλως εὐεργετεῖν, ἐκκλησίαις τε πολλαῖς ταῖς κατὰ πᾶσαν πόλιν ἐφόδια πέμπειν, ὧδε μὲν τὴν τῶν δεομένων πενίαν ἀναψύχοντας, ἐν μετάλλοις δὲ ἀδελφοῖς
25 ὑπάρχουσιν ἐπιχορηγοῦντας· δι' ὧν πέμπετε ἀρχῆθεν

The Encratites.

'AND this is a recent discovery of theirs, one Tatian being the chief introducer of the blasphemy. He was a hearer of Justin, and as long as he continued with him put forth no such doctrine: but after Justin's martyrdom he left the church, being lifted up with the reputation of a teacher, and puffed up with the idea that he was better than others. So he formed a peculiar school of his own, inventing some invisible aeons like the Valentinians, and like Marcion and Saturninus declaring marriage to be corruption and fornication, though his argument for the salvation of Adam was his own.' So far Irenaeus. . . . Their former leader, however, Tatian, put together somehow or other a kind of combination and collection of the Gospels, to which he gave the name of *Diatessaron*, which book is still used in some quarters.

Letter of Dionysius of Corinth to the Romans.

MOREOVER there is current an Epistle of Dionysius to the Romans, addressed to Soter who was then bishop. But there is nothing like quoting from it words in which he approves the custom of the Romans which was kept up till the persecution of our own time, writing thus, For you have from the beginning this custom of doing good in divers ways to all the brethren, and sending supplies to many churches in all the cities, in one place refreshing the poverty of them that need, in another helping brethren in the mines with the supplies which you have sent from

ἐφοδίων, πατροπαράδοτον ἔθος Ῥωμαίων Ῥωμαῖοι διαφυλάττοντες, ὃ οὐ μόνον διατετήρηκεν ὁ μακάριος ὑμῶν ἐπίσκοπος Σωτήρ, ἀλλὰ καὶ ἐπηύξηκεν, ἐπιχορηγῶν μὲν τὴν διαπεμπομένην δαψίλειαν τὴν εἰς τοὺς ἁγίους, λόγοις
5 δὲ μακαρίοις τοὺς ἀνιόντας ἀδελφούς, ὡς τέκνα πατὴρ φιλόστοργος, παρακαλῶν.

Ἐν αὐτῇ δὲ ταύτῃ καὶ τῆς Κλήμεντος πρὸς Κορινθίους μέμνηται ἐπιστολῆς, δηλῶν ἀνέκαθεν ἐξ ἀρχαίου ἔθους ἐπὶ τῆς ἐκκλησίας τὴν ἀνάγνωσιν αὐτῆς ποιεῖσθαι.
10 λέγει γοῦν·

Τὴν σήμερον οὖν Κυριακὴν ἁγίαν ἡμέραν διηγάγομεν, ἐν ᾗ ἀνέγνωμεν ὑμῶν τὴν ἐπιστολήν· ἣν ἕξομεν ἀεί ποτε ἀναγινώσκοντες νουθετεῖσθαι, ὡς καὶ τὴν προτέραν ἡμῖν διὰ Κλήμεντος γραφεῖσαν.
15 Ἔτι δὲ ὁ αὐτὸς καὶ περὶ τῶν ἰδίων ἐπιστολῶν ὡς ῥᾳδιουργηθεισῶν, ταῦτα φησίν·

Ἐπιστολὰς γὰρ ἀδελφῶν ἀξιωσάντων με γράψαι, ἔγραψα. καὶ ταύτας οἱ τοῦ διαβόλου ἀπόστολοι ζιζανίων γεγέμικαν, ἃ μὲν ἐξαιροῦντες, ἃ δὲ προστιθέντες.
20 οἷς τὸ οὐαὶ κεῖται. οὐ θαυμαστὸν ἄρα εἰ καὶ τῶν Κυριακῶν ῥᾳδιουργῆσαί τινες ἐπιβέβληνται γραφῶν, ὁπότε καὶ ταῖς οὐ τοιαύταις ἐπιβεβουλεύκασι.

Ibid. iv. 23.

XX A.

Περινοοῦντι δέ μοι τὰ σπουδαῖα συνέβη γραφαῖς τισιν ἐντυχεῖν βαρβαρικαῖς, πρεσβυτέραις μὲν ὡς πρὸς τὰ
25 Ἑλλήνων δόγματα, θειοτέραις δὲ ὡς πρὸς τὴν ἐκείνων πλάνην· καί μοι πεισθῆναι ταύταις συνέβη διά τε τῶν

the beginning, maintaining like Romans the traditional custom of the Romans, which your worthy bishop Soter has not only kept up but increased, helping the saints with the abundant supply he sends from time to time, and with blessed words exhorting, as a loving father his children, the brethren who come up to Rome. In this same Epistle he also mentions Clement's Epistle to the Corinthians, showing that from the first of ancient custom it was read before the Church. He says, To-day being the Lord's day we kept holy; and in it we read your letter, from the reading of which we shall always be able to obtain admonition, as from the former one written to us through Clement. Again, the same writer speaks of his own epistles as having been falsified, in these words, For when the brethren asked me to write letters, I wrote them; and these the apostles of the devil have filled with tares, taking away some things and adding others. For them the Woe is reserved. So it is no marvel if some have endeavoured to falsify even the dominical scriptures, when they have plotted also against writings of another sort.

Tatian's Conversion.

WHILE I was thinking over such weighty matters, I chanced to meet with certain barbarian writings, too old for comparison with the doctrines of the Greeks, and too divine for comparison with their error: and I chanced to be convinced by them, on account of the soberness of their language, the simplicity of the writers, their intelligible

λέξεων τὸ ἄτυφον καὶ τῶν εἰπόντων τὸ ἀνεπιτήδευτον
καὶ τῆς τοῦ παντὸς ποιήσεως τὸ εὐκατάληπτον καὶ τῶν
μελλόντων τὸ προγνωστικὸν καὶ τῶν παραγγελμάτων τὸ
ἐξαίσιον καὶ τῶν ὅλων τὸ μοναρχικόν. θεοδιδάκτου δέ
5 μου γενομένης τῆς ψυχῆς συνῆκα ὅτι τὰ μὲν καταδίκης
ἔχει τρόπον, τὰ δὲ ὅτι λύει τὴν ἐν κόσμῳ δουλείαν καὶ
ἀρχόντων μὲν πολλῶν καὶ μυρίων ἡμᾶς ἀποσπᾷ τυράννων,
δίδωσι δὲ ἡμῖν οὐχ ὅπερ μὴ ἐλάβομεν, ἀλλ' ὅπερ λαβόντες
ὑπὸ τῆς πλάνης ἔχειν ἐκωλύθημεν.

TATIAN, Ad Graecos, 29.

XXI.

10 Οἱ ἐν Βιέννῃ καὶ Λουγδούνῳ τῆς Γαλλίας παροικοῦντες
δοῦλοι Χριστοῦ, τοῖς κατὰ τὴν Ἀσίαν καὶ Φρυγίαν τὴν
αὐτὴν τῆς ἀπολυτρώσεως ἡμῖν πίστιν καὶ ἐλπίδα ἔχουσιν
ἀδελφοῖς, εἰρήνη καὶ χάρις καὶ δόξα ἀπὸ Θεοῦ Πατρὸς
καὶ Χριστοῦ Ἰησοῦ τοῦ Κυρίου ἡμῶν.
15 Τὸ μὲν οὖν μέγεθος τῆς ἐνθάδε θλίψεως, καὶ τὴν
τοσαύτην τῶν ἐθνῶν εἰς τοὺς ἁγίους ὀργήν, καὶ ὅσα
ὑπέμειναν οἱ μακάριοι μάρτυρες, ἐπ' ἀκριβὲς οὔθ' ἡμεῖς
εἰπεῖν ἱκανοί, οὔτε μὴν γραφῇ περιληφθῆναι δυνατόν.
παντὶ γὰρ σθένει ἐνέσκηψεν ὁ ἀντικείμενος, προοιμιαζό-
20 μενος ἤδη τὴν ἀδεῶς μέλλουσαν ἔσεσθαι παρουσίαν αὐτοῦ·
καὶ διὰ πάντων διῆλθεν, ἐθίζων τοὺς ἑαυτοῦ καὶ προ-
γυμνάζων κατὰ τῶν δούλων τοῦ Θεοῦ, ὥστε μὴ μόνον
οἰκιῶν καὶ βαλανείων καὶ ἀγορᾶς εἴργεσθαι, ἀλλὰ καὶ τὸ
καθόλου φαίνεσθαι ἡμῶν τινὰ αὐτοῖς ἀπειρῆσθαι ἐν ὁποίῳ
25 δήποτε τόπῳ. ἀντεστρατήγει δὴ ἡ χάρις τοῦ Θεοῦ, καὶ
τοὺς μὲν ἀσθενεῖς ἐρρύετο, ἀντιπαρέτασσε δὲ στύλους
ἑδραίους, δυναμένους διὰ τῆς ὑπομονῆς πᾶσαν τὴν ὁρμὴν

account of the creation, their prediction of the future, the reasonableness of their precepts, and their reference of the universe to a single ruler. And as my soul became taught of God I understood that the Greek doctrines lead to condemnation, while these destroy the slavery to which we are subject in the world and rescue us from many rulers and tyrants without number, though they give us not that which we never received before, but that wh'ch we did receive and were hindered by the error from keeping.

The Persecution at Lyons and Vienne.

THE servants of Christ residing at Vienne and Lyons, in Gaul, to the brethren throughout Asia and Phrygia, who hold the same faith and hope of redemption, peace and grace and glory from God the Father and Christ Jesus our Lord.

The greatness of the tribulation in this region, and the fury of the heathen against the saints, and the sufferings of the blessed witnesses, we cannot recount accurately, nor indeed could they possibly be recorded. For with all his might the adversary fell upon us, giving us a foretaste of his unbridled activity at his future coming. He endeavoured in every manner to practise and exercise his servants against the servants of God, not only shutting us out from houses and baths and markets, but forbidding any of us to be seen in any place whatever. But the grace of God led the conflict against him, and delivered the weak, and set them as firm pillars, able through patience to endure all the wrath of the Evil One. And

τοῦ πονηροῦ εἰς ἑαυτοὺς ἑλκύσαι· οἳ καὶ ὁμόσε ἐχώρουν
αὐτῷ, πᾶν εἶδος ὀνειδισμοῦ καὶ κολάσεως ἀνεχόμενοι, οἳ
καὶ τὰ πολλὰ ὀλίγα ἡγούμενοι ἔσπευδον πρὸς Χριστόν,
ὄντως ἐπιδεικνύμενοι, ὅτι "οὐκ ἄξια τὰ παθήματα τοῦ νῦν
5 καιροῦ, πρὸς τὴν μέλλουσαν δόξαν ἀποκαλυφθῆναι εἰς
ἡμᾶς." καὶ πρῶτον μὲν τὰ ἀπὸ τοῦ ὄχλου πανδημεὶ
σωρηδὸν ἐπιφερόμενα γενναίως ὑπέμενον, ἐπιβοήσεις, καὶ
πληγάς, καὶ συρμούς, καὶ διαρπαγάς, καὶ λίθων βολάς,
καὶ συγκλείσεις, καὶ πάνθ' ὅσα ἠγριωμένῳ πλήθει ὡς
10 πρὸς ἐχθροὺς καὶ πολεμίους φιλεῖ γίνεσθαι. καὶ δὴ
ἀναχθέντες εἰς τὴν ἀγορὰν ὑπό τε τοῦ χιλιάρχου καὶ τῶν
προεστηκότων τῆς πόλεως ἐξουσιῶν, ἐπὶ παντὸς τοῦ πλή-
θους ἀνακριθέντες καὶ ὁμολογήσαντες, συνεκλείσθησαν
εἰς τὴν εἱρκτὴν ἕως τῆς τοῦ ἡγεμόνος παρουσίας. . . . . .
15 Τότε δὴ οἱ πάντες μεγάλως ἐπτοήθημεν, διὰ τὸ ἄδηλον
τῆς ὁμολογίας, οὐ τὰς ἐπιφερομένας κολάσεις φοβού-
μενοι, ἀλλὰ τὸ τέλος ἀφορῶντες, καὶ τὸ ἀποπεσεῖν τινα
δεδιότες. συνελαμβάνοντο μέντοι καθ' ἑκάστην ἡμέραν
οἱ ἄξιοι, τὸν ἐκείνων ἀναπληροῦντες ἀριθμόν, ὥστε συλ-
20 λεγῆναι ἐκ τῶν δύο ἐκκλησιῶν πάντας τοὺς σπουδαίους,
καὶ δι' ὧν μάλιστα συνειστήκει τὰ ἐνθάδε. συνελαμβάνοντο δὲ καὶ ἐθνικοί τινες οἰκέται τῶν ἡμετέρων, ἐπεὶ
δημοσίᾳ ἐκέλευσεν ὁ ἡγεμὼν ἀναζητεῖσθαι πάντας ἡμᾶς·
οἳ καὶ κατ' ἐνέδραν τοῦ Σατανᾶ, φοβηθέντες τὰς βασά-
25 νους ἃς τοὺς ἁγίους ἔβλεπον πάσχοντας, τῶν στρατιωτῶν ἐπὶ τοῦτο παρορμώντων αὐτούς, κατεψεύσαντο ἡμῶν
Θυέστεια δεῖπνα, καὶ Οἰδιποδείους μίξεις, καὶ ὅσα μήτε
λαλεῖν μήτε νοεῖν θέμις ἡμῖν, ἀλλὰ μηδὲ πιστεύειν εἴ τι
τοιοῦτο πώποτε παρὰ ἀνθρώποις ἐγένετο. τούτων δὲ
30 φημισθέντων πάντες ἀπεθηριώθησαν εἰς ἡμᾶς, ὥστε καὶ
εἴ τινες τὸ πρότερον δι' οἰκειότητα ἐμετρίαζον, τότε μεγάλως ἐχαλέπαινον καὶ διεπρίοντο καθ' ἡμῶν. ἐπληροῦτο
δὲ τὸ ὑπὸ τοῦ Κυρίου ἡμῶν εἰρημένον, ὅτι "ἐλεύσεται

they joined battle with him, undergoing all kinds of shame and injury; and regarding their great sufferings as little, they hastened to Christ, manifesting truly that 'the sufferings of this present time are not worthy to be compared with the glory which shall be revealed to us-ward.' First of all, they endured nobly the injuries heaped upon them by the populace; clamours and blows and draggings and robberies and stonings and imprisonments, and all things which an infuriated mob delight in inflicting on enemies and adversaries. Then being taken to the forum by the chiliarch and the authorities of the city, they were examined in the presence of the whole multitude, and having confessed, they were imprisoned until the arrival of the governor.

Then all of us feared greatly on account of uncertainty as to their confession; not because we dreaded the sufferings to be endured, but because we looked to the end, and were afraid that some of them might fall away. But those who were worthy were seized day by day, filling up their number, so that all the zealous persons, and those through whom especially our affairs had been established, were collected together out of the two churches. And some of our heathen servants also were seized, as the governor had publicly commanded that all of us should be sought out. These, being ensnared by Satan, and fearing for themselves the tortures which they beheld the saints endure, and being also urged on by the soldiers, accused us falsely of Thyestean banquets and Oedipodean intercourse, and of deeds which are not only unlawful for us to speak of or to think, but which we cannot believe were ever done by men. When these accusations were reported, all the people raged like wild beasts against us, so that even if any had before been moderate on account of friendship, they were now exceedingly furious and gnashed

καιρός, ἐν ᾧ πᾶς ὁ ἀποκτείνας ὑμᾶς δόξει λατρείαν προσφέρειν τῷ Θεῷ." ἐνταῦθα λοιπὸν ὑπεράνω πάσης ἐξηγήσεως ὑπέμενον κολάσεις οἱ ἅγιοι μάρτυρες, φιλοτιμουμένου τοῦ Σατανᾶ καὶ δι' ἐκείνων ῥηθῆναί τι τῶν βλασφήμων.

Ὑπερβεβλημένως δὲ ἐνέσκηψεν ἡ ὀργὴ πᾶσα καὶ ὄχλου καὶ ἡγεμόνος καὶ στρατιωτῶν εἰς Σάγκτον διάκονον ἀπὸ Βιέννης, καὶ εἰς Μάτουρον νεοφώτιστον μέν, ἀλλὰ γενναῖον ἀγωνιστήν, καὶ εἰς Ἄτταλον Περγαμηνὸν τῷ γένει, "στῦλον καὶ ἑδραίωμα" τῶν ἐνταῦθα ἀεὶ γεγονότα, καὶ εἰς Βλανδίναν, δι' ἧς ἐπέδειξεν ὁ Χριστὸς ὅτι τὰ παρὰ ἀνθρώποις εὐτελῆ καὶ ἀειδῆ καὶ εὐκαταφρόνητα φαινόμενα μεγάλης καταξιοῦται παρὰ Θεῷ δόξης, διὰ τὴν πρὸς αὐτὸν ἀγάπην, τὴν ἐν δυνάμει δεικνυμένην, καὶ μὴ ἐν εἴδει καυχωμένην. ἡμῶν γὰρ πάντων δεδιότων, καὶ τῆς σαρκίνης δεσποίνης αὐτῆς, ἥτις ἦν καὶ αὐτὴ τῶν μαρτύρων μία ἀγωνίστρια, ἀγωνιώσης μὴ οὐδὲ τὴν ὁμολογίαν δυνήσεται παρρησιάσασθαι διὰ τὸ ἀσθενὲς τοῦ σώματος, ἡ Βλανδίνα τοσαύτης ἐπληρώθη δυνάμεως, ὥστε ἐκλυθῆναι καὶ παρεθῆναι τοὺς κατὰ διαδοχὰς παντὶ τρόπῳ βασανίζοντας αὐτὴν ἀπὸ ἑωθινῆς ἕως ἑσπέρας, καὶ αὐτοὺς ὁμολογοῦντας ὅτι νενίκηνται, μηδὲν ἔχοντες μηκέτι ὃ ποιήσουσιν αὐτῇ, καὶ θαυμάζειν ἐπὶ τῷ παραμένειν ἔμπνουν αὐτήν, παντὸς τοῦ σώματος περιερρωγότος καὶ ἠνεῳγμένου, καὶ μαρτυρεῖν, ὅτι ἓν εἶδος στρεβλώσεως ἱκανὸν ἦν πρὸς τὸ ἐξαγαγεῖν τὴν ψυχήν, οὐχ ὅτι γε τοιαῦτα καὶ τοσαῦτα. ἀλλ' ἡ μακαρία ὡς γενναῖος ἀθλητὴς ἀνενέαζεν ἐν τῇ ὁμολογίᾳ· καὶ ἦν αὐτῆς ἀνάληψις καὶ ἀνάπαυσις καὶ ἀναλγησία τῶν συμβαινόντων, τὸ λέγειν ὅτι "Χριστιανή εἰμι," καί, "παρ' ἡμῖν οὐδὲν φαῦλον γίνεται."

Ὁ δὲ Σάγκτος καὶ αὐτὸς ὑπερβεβλημένως καὶ ὑπὲρ πάντα ἄνθρωπον πάσας τὰς ἐξ ἀνθρώπων αἰκίας γενναίως

their teeth against us. And that which was spoken by our Lord was fulfilled: 'The time will come when whosoever killeth you will think that he doeth God service.' Then finally the holy witnesses endured sufferings beyond description, Satan striving earnestly that some of the slanders might be uttered by them also.

But the whole wrath of the populace, and governor, and soldiers was aroused exceedingly against Sanctus, the deacon from Vienne, and Maturus, a late convert, yet a noble combatant, and against Attalus, a native of Pergamos, where he had always been a pillar and foundation, and Blandina, through whom Christ showed that things which appear mean and obscure and despicable to men are with God of great glory, through love toward Him manifested in power, and not boasting in appearance. For while we all trembled, and her earthly mistress, who was herself also one of the witnesses, feared that on account of the weakness of her body, she would be unable to make bold confession, Blandina was filled with such power that the men were weary and faint who were torturing her by turns from morning till evening in every manner, so that they acknowledged that they were conquered, and could do nothing more to her. And they were astonished at her endurance, as her entire body was mangled and broken; and they testified that one of these forms of torture was sufficient to destroy life, not to speak of so many and so great sufferings. But the blessed woman, like a noble athlete, renewed her strength in her confession; and her comfort and recreation and relief from the pain of her sufferings was in exclaiming, 'I am a Christian, and there is nothing vile done by us.'

But Sanctus also endured marvellously and superhumanly all the outrages which he suffered. While the

ὑπομένων, τῶν ἀνόμων ἐλπιζόντων διὰ τὴν ἐπιμονὴν καὶ τὸ μέγεθος τῶν βασάνων ἀκούσεσθαί τι παρ' αὐτοῦ τῶν μὴ δεόντων, τοσαύτῃ ὑποστάσει ἀντιπαρετάξατο αὐτοῖς, ὥστε μηδὲ τὸ ἴδιον κατειπεῖν ὄνομα, μήτε ἔθνους, μήτε
5 πόλεως ὅθεν ἦν, μήτε εἰ δοῦλος ἢ ἐλεύθερος εἴη, ἀλλὰ πρὸς πάντα τὰ ἐπερωτώμενα ἀπεκρίνατο τῇ 'Ρωμαϊκῇ φωνῇ, "Χριστιανός εἰμι." τοῦτο καὶ ἀντὶ ὀνόματος, καὶ ἀντὶ πόλεως, καὶ ἀντὶ γένους, καὶ ἀντὶ παντὸς ἐπαλλήλως ὡμολόγει, ἄλλην δὲ φωνὴν οὐκ ἤκουσαν αὐτοῦ τὰ ἔθνη....
10 Μετὰ ταῦτα δὴ λοιπὸν εἰς πᾶν εἶδος διῃρεῖτο τὰ μαρτύρια τῆς ἐξόδου αὐτῶν. ἐκ διαφόρων γὰρ χρωμάτων καὶ παντοίων ἀνθῶν ἕνα πλέξαντες στέφανον, προσήνεγκαν τῷ Πατρί. ἐχρῆν γοῦν τοὺς γενναίους ἀθλητάς, ποικίλον ὑπομείναντας ἀγῶνα καὶ μεγάλως νικήσαντας,
15 ἀπολαβεῖν τὸν μέγαν τῆς ἀφθαρσίας στέφανον. ὁ μὲν οὖν Μάτουρος καὶ ὁ Σάγκτος καὶ ἡ Βλανδίνα καὶ Ἄτταλος ἤγοντο ἐπὶ τὰ θηρία εἰς τὸ δημόσιον, καὶ εἰς τὸ κοινὸν τῶν ἐθνῶν τῆς ἀπανθρωπίας θέαμα, ἐπίτηδες τῆς τῶν θηριομαχιῶν ἡμέρας διὰ τοὺς ἡμετέρους διδομένης.

20 Καὶ ὁ μὲν Μάτουρος καὶ ὁ Σάγκτος αὖθις διῄεσαν ἐν τῷ ἀμφιθεάτρῳ διὰ πάσης κολάσεως, ὡς μηδὲν ὅλως προπεπονθότες, μᾶλλον δὲ ὡς διὰ πλειόνων ἤδη κλήρων ἐκβεβιακότες τὸν ἀντίπαλον, καὶ περὶ τοῦ στεφάνου αὐτοῦ τὸν ἀγῶνα ἔχοντες, ὑπέφερον πάλιν τὰς διεξόδους τῶν
25 μαστίγων τὰς ἐκεῖσε εἰθισμένας, καὶ τοὺς ἀπὸ τῶν θηρίων ἑλκηθμούς, καὶ πάνθ' ὅσα μαινόμενος ὁ δῆμος ἄλλοι ἀλλαχόθεν ἐπεβόων καὶ ἐπεκελεύοντο, ἐπὶ πᾶσι τὴν σιδηρᾶν, ἐφ' ἧς τηγανιζόμενα τὰ σώματα κνίσσης αὐτοὺς ἐνεφόρει. οἱ δ' οὐδ' οὕτως ἔληγον, ἀλλ' ἔτι καὶ μᾶλλον
30 ἐξεμαίνοντο, βουλόμενοι νικῆσαι τὴν ἐκείνων ὑπομονήν. καὶ οὐδ' ὣς παρὰ Σάγκτου ἕτερόν τι εἰσήκουσαν, παρ' ἣν ἀπ' ἀρχῆς εἴθιστο λέγειν τῆς ὁμολογίας φωνήν. οὗτοι μὲν οὖν, δι' ἀγῶνος μεγάλου ἐπιπολὺ παραμενούσης

wicked men hoped, by the continuance and severity of his tortures to wring something from him which he ought not to say, he girded himself against them with such firmness that he would not even tell his name, or the nation or city to which he belonged, or whether he was bond or free, but answered in the Roman tongue to all their questions, 'I am a Christian.' He confessed this instead of name and city and race and everything besides, and the people heard from him no other word.'. . .

After these things, finally, their martyrdoms were divided into every form. For plaiting a crown of various colours and of all kinds of flowers, they presented it to the Father. It was proper therefore that the noble athletes, having endured a manifold strife, and conquered grandly, should receive the crown, great and incorruptible.

Maturus, therefore, and Sanctus and Blandina, and Attalus were led to the amphitheatre to be exposed to the wild beasts, and to give the heathen public a spectacle of cruelty, a day for fighting with wild beasts being specially appointed on account of our people. Both Maturus and Sanctus passed again through every torment in the amphitheatre, as if they had suffered nothing before, or rather, as if, having already conquered their antagonist in many contests, they were now striving for the crown itself. They endured again the customary running of the gauntlet and the violence of the wild beasts, and everything which the furious people called for or desired, and at last, the iron chair in which their bodies being roasted, tormented them with the fumes. And not with this did the persecutors cease, but were yet more mad against them, determined to overcome their patience. But even thus they did not hear a word from Sanctus except the confession which he had uttered from the beginning. These, then, after their life had continued for a long time

αὐτῶν τῆς ψυχῆς, τοὔσχατον ἐτύθησαν, διὰ τῆς ἡμέρας ἐκείνης, ἀντὶ πάσης τῆς ἐν τοῖς μονομαχίοις ποικιλίας, αὐτοὶ θέαμα γενόμενοι τῷ κόσμῳ.

Ἡ δὲ Βλανδῖνα ἐπὶ ξύλου κρεμασθεῖσα προὔκειτο βορὰ
5 τῶν εἰσβαλλομένων θηρίων· ἢ καὶ διὰ τοῦ βλέπεσθαι σταυροῦ σχήματι κρεμαμένη, διὰ τῆς εὐτόνου προσευχῆς, πολλὴν προθυμίαν τοῖς ἀγωνιζομένοις ἐνεποίει, βλεπόντων αὐτῶν ἐν τῷ ἀγῶνι καὶ τοῖς ἔξωθεν ὀφθαλμοῖς διὰ τῆς ἀδελφῆς τὸν ὑπὲρ αὐτῶν Ἐσταυρωμένον, ἵνα πείσῃ τοὺς
10 πιστεύοντας εἰς αὐτόν, ὅτι πᾶς ὁ ὑπὲρ τῆς Χριστοῦ δόξης παθὼν τὴν κοινωνίαν ἀεὶ ἔχει μετὰ τοῦ ζῶντος Θεοῦ. καὶ μηδενὸς ἀψαμένου τότε τῶν θηρίων αὐτῆς, καθαιρεθεῖσα ἀπὸ τοῦ ξύλου, ἀνελήφθη πάλιν εἰς τὴν εἱρκτήν, εἰς ἄλλον ἀγῶνα τηρουμένη, ἵνα διὰ πλειόνων γυμνασμά-
15 των νικήσασα τῷ μὲν σκολιῷ ὄφει ἀπαραίτητον ποιήσῃ τὴν καταδίκην, προτρέψηται δὲ τοὺς ἀδελφοὺς ἡ μικρὰ καὶ ἀσθενὴς καὶ εὐκαταφρόνητος, μέγαν καὶ ἀκαταγώνιστον ἀθλητὴν Χριστὸν ἐνδεδυμένη, διὰ πολλῶν κλήρων ἐκβιάσασα τὸν ἀντικείμενον, καὶ δι' ἀγῶνος τὸν τῆς
20 ἀφθαρσίας στεψαμένη στέφανον. . . . . . .

Ἐπὶ πᾶσι δὲ τούτοις τῇ ἐσχάτῃ λοιπὸν ἡμέρᾳ τῶν μονομαχιῶν, ἡ Βλανδῖνα πάλιν εἰσεκομίζετο μετὰ καὶ Ποντικοῦ παιδαρίου ὡς πεντεκαίδεκα ἐτῶν, οἳ καὶ καθημέραν εἰσήγοντο πρὸς τὸ βλέπειν τὴν τῶν λοιπῶν κόλασιν, καὶ
25 ἠναγκάζοντο ὀμνύναι κατὰ τῶν εἰδώλων αὐτῶν. καὶ διὰ τὸ ἐμμένειν εὐσταθῶς καὶ ἐξουθενεῖν αὐτούς, ἠγριώθη πρὸς αὐτοὺς τὸ πλῆθος, ὡς μήτε τὴν ἡλικίαν τοῦ παιδὸς οἰκτεῖραι, μήτε τὸ γύναιον αἰδεσθῆναι. πρὸς πάντα δὲ τὰ δεινὰ παρέβαλλον αὐτούς, καὶ διὰ πάσης ἐν κύκλῳ
30 διῆγον κολάσεως, ἐπαλλήλως ἀναγκάζοντες ὀμόσαι, ἀλλὰ μὴ δυνάμενοι τοῦτο πρᾶξαι· ὁ μὲν γὰρ Ποντικὸς ὑπὸ τῆς ἀδελφῆς παρωρμημένος, ὡς καὶ τὰ ἔθνη βλέπειν ὅτι ἐκείνη ἦν προτρεπομένη καὶ στηρίζουσα αὐτόν, πᾶσαν

through the great conflict, were at last sacrificed, having been made throughout that day a spectacle to the world, in place of the usual variety of combats.

But Blandina was suspended on a stake, and exposed to be devoured by the wild beasts who should attack her. And because she appeared as if hanging on a cross, and because of her earnest prayers, she inspired the combatants with great zeal. For they looked on her in her conflict, and beheld with their outward eyes, in the form of their sister, Him who was crucified for them, that He might persuade those who believe on Him, that every one who suffers for the glory of Christ has fellowship always with the living God. As none of the wild beasts at that time touched her, she was taken down from the stake, and cast again into prison. She was preserved thus for another contest, that, being victorious in more conflicts, she might make the punishment of the crooked serpent irrevocable; and, though small and weak and despised, yet clothed with Christ the mighty and conquering Athlete, she might arouse the zeal of the brethren, and, having overcome the adversary many times might receive, through her conflict, the crown incorruptible.

After all these, on the last day of the contests, Blandina was again brought in, with Ponticus, a boy about fifteen years old. They had been brought every day to witness the sufferings of the others, and had been pressed to swear by the idols. But because they remained steadfast and despised them, the multitude became furious, so that they had no compassion for the youth of the boy nor respect for the sex of the woman. Therefore they exposed them to all the terrible sufferings and took them through the entire round of torture, repeatedly urging them to swear, but being unable to effect this; for Ponticus, encouraged by his sister so that even the heathen could see that she was confirming and strengthening him, having

κόλασιν γενναίως ὑπομείνας, ἀπέδωκε τὸ πνεῦμα. ἡ δὲ μακαρία Βλανδίνα πάντων ἐσχάτη, καθάπερ μήτηρ εὐγενὴς παρορμήσασα τὰ τέκνα καὶ νικηφόρους προπέμψασα πρὸς τὸν Βασιλέα, ἀναμετρουμένη καὶ αὐτὴ
5 πάντα τὰ τῶν παίδων ἀγωνίσματα, ἔσπευδε πρὸς αὐτοὺς χαίρουσα καὶ ἀγαλλιωμένη ἐπὶ τῇ ἐξόδῳ, ὡς εἰς νυμφικὸν δεῖπνον κεκλημένη, ἀλλὰ μὴ πρὸς θηρία βεβλημένη. καὶ μετὰ τὰς μάστιγας, μετὰ τὰ θηρία, μετὰ τὸ τήγανον, τοὔσχατον εἰς γύργαθον βληθεῖσα, ταύρῳ παρεβλήθη·
10 καὶ ἱκανῶς ἀναβληθεῖσα πρὸς τοῦ ζώου, μηδὲ αἴσθησιν ἔτι τῶν συμβαινόντων ἔχουσα διὰ τὴν ἐλπίδα καὶ ἐποχὴν τῶν πεπιστευμένων καὶ ὁμίλιαν πρὸς Χριστόν, ἐτύθη καὶ αὐτή, καὶ αὐτῶν ὁμολογούντων τῶν ἐθνῶν ὅτι μηδὲ πώποτε παρ' αὐτοῖς γυνὴ τοιαῦτα καὶ τοσαῦτα ἔπαθεν.

15 Ἀλλ' οὐδ' οὕτως κόρον ἐλάμβανεν αὐτῶν ἡ μανία καὶ ἡ πρὸς τοὺς ἁγίους ὠμότης. ὑπὸ γὰρ ἀγρίου θηρὸς ἄγρια καὶ βάρβαρα φῦλα παραχθέντα δυσπαύστως εἶχε, καὶ ἄλλην ἰδίαν ἀρχὴν ἐπὶ τοῖς σώμασιν ἐλάμβανεν ἡ ὕβρις αὐτῶν. τὸ γὰρ νενικῆσθαι αὐτοὺς οὐκ ἐδυσώπει, διὰ τὸ
20 μὴ ἔχειν ἀνθρώπινον ἐπιλογισμόν, μᾶλλον δὲ καὶ ἐξέκαεν αὐτῶν τὴν ὀργὴν καθάπερ θηρίου, καὶ τοῦ ἡγεμόνος καὶ τοῦ δήμου τὸ ὅμοιον εἰς ἡμᾶς ἀδίκως ἐπιδεικνυμένων μῖσος· ἵνα ἡ γραφὴ πληρωθῇ, "Ὁ ἄνομος ἀνομησάτω ἔτι, καὶ ὁ δίκαιος δικαιωθήτω ἔτι." καὶ γὰρ τοὺς ἐν-
25 αποπνιγέντας ἐν τῇ εἱρκτῇ παρέβαλλον κυσίν, ἐπιμελῶς παραφυλάσσοντες νύκτωρ καὶ μεθημέραν, μὴ κηδευθῇ τις ὑφ' ἡμῶν. καὶ τότε δὴ προθέντες τά τε τῶν θηρίων, τά τε τοῦ πυρὸς λείψανα, πῇ μὲν ἐσπαραγμένα, πῇ δὲ ἠνθρακευμένα, καὶ τῶν λοιπῶν τὰς κεφαλὰς σὺν τοῖς
30 ἀποτμήμασιν αὐτῶν ὡσαύτως ἀτάφους παρεφύλαττον μετὰ στρατιωτικῆς ἐπιμελείας ἡμέραις συχναῖς. καὶ οἱ μὲν ἐνεβριμῶντο καὶ ἔβρυχον τοὺς ὀδόντας ἐπ' αὐτοῖς, ζητοῦντές τινα περισσοτέραν ἐκδίκησιν παρ' αὐτῶν λαβεῖν·

nobly endured every torture, gave up the ghost. But the blessed Blandina, last of all, having, as a noble mother, encouraged her children and sent them before her victorious to the King, endured herself all their conflicts and hastened after them, glad and rejoicing in her departure as if called to a marriage-supper, rather than cast to wild beasts. And, after the scourging, after the wild beasts, after the roasting-seat, she was finally enclosed in a net, and thrown before a bull. And having been tossed about by the animal, but feeling none of the things which were happening to her, on account of her hope and firm hold upon what had been entrusted to her, and her communion with Christ, she also was sacrificed. And the heathen themselves confessed that never among them had a woman endured so many and such terrible tortures.

But not even thus was their madness and cruelty toward the saints satisfied. For, incited by the Wild Beast, wild and barbarous tribes were not easily appeased, and their violence found another peculiar opportunity in the dead bodies. For, through their lack of manly reason, the fact that they had been conquered did not put them to shame, but rather the more enkindled their wrath as that of a wild beast, and aroused alike the hatred of governor and people to treat us unjustly; that the Scripture might be fulfilled: 'He that is lawless, let him be lawless still, and he that is righteous, let him be righteous still.' For they cast to the dogs those who had died of suffocation in the prison, carefully guarding them by night and day, lest any one should be buried by us. And they exposed the remains left by the wild beasts and by fire, mangled and charred, and placed the heads of the others by their bodies, and guarded them in like manner from burial by a watch of soldiers for many days. And some raged and gnashed their teeth against them, desiring to execute more severe vengeance upon them; but others laughed and

οἱ δὲ ἐνεγέλων καὶ ἐπετώθαζον, μεγαλύοντες ἅμα τὰ
εἴδωλα αὐτῶν, καὶ ἐκείνοις προσάπτοντες τὴν τούτων
τιμωρίαν. οἱ δὲ ἐπιεικέστεροι, καὶ κατὰ ποσὸν συμ-
παθεῖν δοκοῦντες, ὠνείδιζον πολὺ λέγοντες, "Ποῦ ὁ Θεὸς
αὐτῶν, καὶ τί αὐτοὺς ὤνησεν ἡ θρησκεία, ἣν καὶ πρὸ τῆς
ἑαυτῶν εἵλοντο ψυχῆς;" καὶ τὰ μὲν ἀπ' ἐκείνων τοιαύ-
την εἶχε τὴν ποικιλίαν, τὰ δὲ καθ' ἡμᾶς ἐν μεγάλῳ
καθειστήκει πένθει, διὰ τὸ μὴ δύνασθαι τὰ σώματα
κρύψαι τῇ γῇ. οὔτε γὰρ νὺξ συνεβάλλετο ἡμῖν πρὸς
τοῦτο, οὔτε ἀργύρια ἔπειθεν, οὔτε λιτανεία ἐδυσώπει,
παντὶ δὲ τρόπῳ παρετήρουν, ὡς μέγα τι κερδανοῦντες εἰ
μὴ τύχοιεν ταφῆς.

EUSEBIUS, *Hist. Eccl.* v. 1.

XXI A.

Passio Sanctorum Scilitanorum.

Praesente bis et Claudiano consulibus, XVI Kalendas
Augustas, Kartagine in secretario inpositis Sperato,
Nartzalo et Cittino, Donata, Secunda, Vestia; Saturninus
proconsul dixit: Potestis indulgentiam domini nostri
imperatoris promereri, si ad bonam mentem redeatis.

Speratus dixit: Numquam malefecimus, iniquitati
nullam operam praebuimus; numquam malediximus,
sed male accepti gratias egimus; propter quod imperatorem nostrum obseruamus.

Saturninus proconsul dixit: Et nos religiosi sumus, et
simplex est religio nostra, et iuramus per genium domini
nostri imperatoris, et pro salute eius supplicamus, quod et
uos quoque facere debetis.

Speratus dixit: Si tranquillas praebueris aures tuas,
dico mysterium simplicitatis.

Saturninus dixit: Initianti tibi mala de sacris nostris

mocked at them, magnifying their own idols, and imputed to them the punishment of the Christians. Even the more reasonable, and those who had seemed to sympathize somewhat, reproached them often, saying, 'Where is their God, and what has their religion, which they have chosen rather than life, profited them?' So various was their conduct toward us; but we were in deep affliction because we could not bury the bodies. For neither did night avail us for this purpose, nor did money persuade, nor entreaty move to compassion; but they kept watch in every way, as if the prevention of the burial would be of some great advantage to them.

A. N. L.

Acts of the Scillitan Martyrs.

When Praesens, for the second time, and Claudianus were the consuls, on the seventeenth day of July, at Carthage, there were set in the judgment-hall Speratus, Nartzalus, Cittinus, Donata, Secunda and Vestia.

Saturninus the proconsul said: Ye can win the indulgence of our lord the Emperor, if ye return to a sound mind.

Speratus said: We have never done ill, we have not lent ourselves to wrong, we have never spoken ill, but when ill-treated we have given thanks; because we pay heed to OUR EMPEROR.

Saturninus the proconsul said: We too are religious, and our religion is simple, and we swear by the genius of our lord the Emperor, and pray for his welfare, as ye also ought to do.

Speratus said: If thou wilt peaceably lend me thine ears, I can tell thee the mystery of simplicity.

Saturninus said: I will not lend mine ears to thee, when

aures non praebebo; sed potius iura per genium domini nostri imperatoris.

Speratus dixit: Ego imperium huius seculi non cognosco; sed magis illi Deo seruio, quem nemo hominum uidit nec uidere his oculis potest. furtum non feci; sed siquid emero teloneum reddo: quia cognosco dominum meum, regem regum et imperatorem omnium gentium.

Saturninus proconsul dixit ceteris: Desinite huius esse persuasionis.

Speratus dixit: Mala est persuasio homicidium facere, falsum testimonium dicere.

Saturninus proconsul dixit: Nolite huius dementiae esse participes.

Cittinus dixit: Nos non habemus alium quem timeamus, nisi dominum Deum nostrum qui est in caelis.

Donata dixit: Honorem Caesari quasi Caesari; timorem autem Deo.

Vestia dixit: Christiana sum.

Secunda dixit: Quod sum, ipsud uolo esse.

Saturninus proconsul Sperato dixit: Perseueras Christianus?

Speratus dixit: Christianus sum: et cum eo omnes consenserunt.

Saturninus proconsul dixit: Numquid ad deliberandum spatium uultis?

Speratus dixit: In re tam iusta nulla est deliberatio.

Saturninus proconsul dixit: Quae sunt res in capsa uestra?

Speratus dixit: Libri et epistulae Pauli uiri iusti.

Saturninus proconsul dixit: Moram XXX dierum habete et recordemini.

thou beginnest to speak evil things of our sacred rites; but rather swear thou by the genius of our lord the Emperor.

Speratus said: The empire of this world I know not; but rather I serve that God, *whom no man hath seen, nor with these eyes can see*[1]. I have committed no theft; but if I have bought anything I pay the tax; because I know my Lord, the King of kings and Emperor of all nations.

Saturninus the proconsul said to the rest: Cease to be of this persuasion.

Speratus said: It is an ill persuasion to do murder, to speak false witness.

Saturninus the proconsul said: Be not partakers of this folly.

Cittinus said: We have none other to fear, save only our Lord God, who is in heaven.

Donata said: Honour to Caesar as Caesar: but fear to God[2].

Vestia said: I am a Christian.

Secunda said: What I am, that I wish to be.

Saturninus the proconsul said to Speratus: Dost thou persist in being a Christian?

Speratus said: I am a Christian. And with him they all agreed.

Saturninus the proconsul said: Will ye have a space to consider?

Speratus said: In a matter so straightforward there is no considering.

Saturninus the proconsul said: What are the things in your chest?

Speratus said: Books and epistles of Paul, a just man.

Saturninus the proconsul said: Have a delay of thirty days and bethink yourselves.

[1] 1 Tim. vi. 16. [2] Cf. Rom. xiii. 7.

Speratus iterum dixit: Christianus sum: et cum eo omnes consenserunt.

Saturninus proconsul decretum ex tabella recitauit: Speratum, Nartzalum, Cittinum, Donatam, Vestiam, Secundam et ceteros ritu Christiano se uiuere confessos, quoniam oblâta sibi facultate ad Romanorum morem redeundi obstinanter perseuerauerunt, gladio animaduerti placet.

Speratus dixit: Deo gratias agimus.

Nartzalus dixit: Hodie martyres in caelis sumus: Deo gratias.

Saturninus proconsul per praeconem dici iussit: Speratum, Nartzalum, Cittinum, Veturium, Felicem, Aquilinum, Laetantium, Ianuariam, Generosam, Vestiam, Donatam, Secundam duci iussi.

Vniuersi dixerunt: Deo gratias.

Et ita omnes simul martyrio coronati sunt, et regnant cum Patre et Filio et Spiritu Sancto per omnia secula seculorum. amen.

ROBINSON, *Texts and Studies*, i. 112-116.

XXII.

Fragmentum Muratorianum.

quibus tamen interfuit et ita posuit
tertio euangelii librum secundo lucan
lucas iste medicus post ascensum X̃Pi
cum eo paulus quasi ut iuris studiosum
secundum adsumsisset numeni suo
ex opinione conscribset dn̄m tamen nec ipse
uidit in carne et idē prout asequi potuit
ita et ad natiuitate iohannis incipet dicere

Speratus said a second time: I am a Christian. And with him they all agreed.

Saturninus the proconsul read out the decree from the tablet: Speratus, Nartzalus, Cittinus, Donata, Vestia, Secunda and the rest having confessed that they live according to the Christian rite, since after opportunity offered them of returning to the custom of the Romans they have obstinately persisted, it is determined that they be put to the sword.

Speratus said: We give thanks to God.

Nartzalus said: To-day we are martyrs in heaven; thanks be to God.

Saturninus the proconsul ordered it to be declared by the herald: Speratus, Nartzalus, Cittinus, Veturius, Felix, Aquilinus, Laetantius, Januaria, Generosa, Vestia, Donata and Secunda, I have ordered to be executed.

They all said: Thanks be to God.

And so they all together were crowned with martyrdom; and they reign with the Father and the Son and the Holy Ghost, for ever and ever. Amen.

R.

Fragment of Muratori on the Canon.

.... but at some he was present, and so he set them down.

The third book of the Gospel, that according to Luke, was compiled in his own name in order by Luke the physician, when after Christ's ascension Paul had taken him to be with him like a student of law. Yet neither did *he* see the Lord in the flesh; and he too, as he was able to ascertain [events, so set them down][1]. So he began his story from the birth of John.

---

[1] l. 8 *ita + posuit ita* e coni. Lightfoot.

quarti euangeliorum iohannis ex decipolis
cohortantibus condescipulis et ẽps suis
dixit conieiunate mihi odie triduo et quid
cuique fuerit reuelatum alterutrum
nobis ennarremus eadem nocte reue
latum andreae ex apostolis ut recognis
centibus cuntis iohannis suo nomine
cuncta discriberet et ideo licit uaria sin
culis euangeliorum libris principia
doceantur nihil tamen differt creden
tium fidei cum uno ac principali sp̃u de
clarata sint in omnibus omnia de natiui
tate de passione de resurrectione
de conuersatione cum decipulis suis
ac de gemino eius aduentu
primo in humilitate dispectus quod fo
it secundum potestate regali . . . pre
clarum quod foturum est quid ergo
mirum si iohannes tam constanter
sincula etiã in epistulis suis proferam
dicens in semeipsu quae uidimus oculis
nostris et auribus audiuimus et manus
nostrae palpauerunt haec scripsimus uobis
sic enim non solum uisurem sed et auditorem
sed et scriptorẽ omnium mirabiliũ dñi per ordi
nem profetetur acta autẽ omniũ apostolorum
sub uno libro scribta sunt lucas obtime theofi
le comprindit quia sub praesentia eius sincula
gerebantur sicuti et semote passionẽ petri
euidenter declarat sed et profectionẽ pauli ab ur
be ad spaniã proficiscentis epistulae autem
pauli quae a quo loco uel qua ex causa directe
sint uolentibus intellegere ipse declarant
primũ omnium corintheis scysmae heresis in
terdicens deinceps b callaetis circumcisione

The fourth of the Gospels [was written by] John, one
of the disciples. When exhorted by his fellow-disciples
and bishops, he said, 'Fast with me this day for three
days; and what may be revealed to any of us, let us
relate it to one another.' The same night it was revealed
to Andrew, one of the apostles, that John was to write all
things in his own name, and they were all to certify.

And therefore, though various elements are taught in
the several books of the Gospels, yet it makes no difference
to the faith of believers, since by one guiding Spirit all
things are declared in all of them concerning the Nativity,
the Passion, the Resurrection, the conversation with his
disciples and his two comings, the first in lowliness and
contempt, which has come to pass, the second glorious
with royal power, which is to come.

What marvel therefore if John so firmly sets forth each
statement in his Epistle too, saying of himself, 'What we
have seen with our eyes and heard with our ears and our
hands have handled, these things we have written to you'?
For so he declares himself not an eyewitness and a hearer
only, but a writer of all the marvels of the Lord in order.

The Acts however of all the Apostles are written in
one book. Luke puts it shortly to the most excellent
Theophilus, that the several things were done in his own
presence, as he also plainly shows by leaving out the
passion of Peter, and also the departure of Paul from
town on his journey to Spain.

The Epistles however of Paul themselves make plain
to those who wish to understand it, what epistles were
sent by him, and from what place and for what cause.
He wrote at some length first of all to the Corinthians,
forbidding schisms and heresies; next to the Galatians,

romanis autē ordine scripturarum sed et
principium earum . . . esse X̄Pm intimans
prolexius scripsit de quibus sincolis neces
se est ad nobis desputari cum ipse beatus
apostolus paulus sequens prodecessoris sui
iohannis ordinē non nisi nomenatĩ semptē
ecclesiis scribat ordine tali a corenthios
prima ad efesius seconda ad philippinses ter
tia ad colosensis quarta ad calatas quin
ta ad tensaolenecinsis sexta ad romanos
septima uerum corintheis et thesaolecen
sibus licet pro correbtione iteretur una
tamen per omnem orbem terrae ecclesia
deffusa esse denoscitur et iohannis enĩ in a
pocalebsy licet septē eccleseis scribat
tamen omnibus dicit uerū ad filemonem una
et at titū una et ad tymotheū duas pro affec
to et dilectione in honore tamen eclesiae ca
tholice in ordinatione eclesiastice
discepline s̄cificate sunt fertur etiam ad
laudecenses alia ad alexandrinos pauli no
mine fincte ad heresem marcionis et alia plu
ra quae in catholicam eclesiam recepi non
potest fel enim cum melle misceri non con
cruit epistola sane iude et superscrictio
iohannis duas in catholica habentur et sapi
entia ab amicis salomonis in honorē ipsius
scripta apocalapse etiam iohanis et pe
tri tantum recipimus quam quidam ex nos
tris legi in eclesia nolunt pastorem uero
nuperrim e temporibus nostris in urbe
roma herma conscripsit sedente cathe
tra urbis romae aecclesiae pio ep̄s fratre

forbidding circumcision; then to the Romans, impressing on them the plan of the Scriptures, and also that Christ is the first principle of them, concerning which severally it is [not] necessary for us to discuss, since the blessed Apostle Paul himself, following the order of his predecessor John, writes only by name to seven churches in the following order—to the Corinthians a first, to the Ephesians a second, to the Philippians a third, to the Colossians a fourth, to the Galatians a fifth, to the Thessalonians a sixth, to the Romans a seventh; whereas, although for the sake of admonition there is a second to the Corinthians and to the Thessalonians, yet *one* Church is recognized as being spread over the entire world. For John too in the Apocalypse, though he writes to seven churches, yet speaks to all. Howbeit to Philemon one, to Titus one, and to Timothy two were put in writing from personal inclination and attachment, to be in honour however with the Catholic Church for the ordering of the ecclesiastical mode of life. There is current also one to the Laodicenes, another to the Alexandrians, [both] forged in Paul's name to suit the heresy of Marcion, and several others, which cannot be received into the Catholic Church; for it is not fitting that gall be mixed with honey.

The Epistle of Jude no doubt, and the couple bearing the name of John, are accepted in the Catholic [Church]; and the Wisdom written by the friends of Solomon in his honour. The Apocalypse also of John, and of Peter [one Epistle, which] only we receive; [there is also a second][1] which some of our friends will not have read in the Church. But the Shepherd was written quite lately in our times by Hermas, while his brother Pius, the bishop, was sitting in the chair of the church of the city of Rome;

---

[1] l. 72 as restored in Greek by Zahn: Πέτρου [ἐπιστολὴ μία, ἣν] μόνην ἀποδεχόμεθα· [ἔστι δὲ καὶ ἑτέρα] ἥν τινες κ.τ.λ.

eius et ideo legi eum quidē oportet se pu
plicare vero in eclesia populo neque inter
profetas completum numero neque inter
apostolos in finē temporum potest 80
5 arsinoi autem seu ualentini uel mitiadis [?]
nihil in totum recipemus qui etiam nouū
psalmorum librum marcioni conscripse
runt una cum basilide assianom catafry
cum constitutorem.

XXIII.

10 Ὁ μὲν δὴ Ματθαῖος ἐν τοῖς Ἑβραίοις τῇ ἰδίᾳ αὐτῶν
διαλέκτῳ καὶ γραφὴν ἐξήνεγκεν Εὐαγγελίου, τοῦ Πέτρου
καὶ τοῦ Παύλου ἐν Ῥώμῃ εὐαγγελιζομένων καὶ θεμε-
λιούντων τὴν ἐκκλησίαν. μετὰ δὲ τὴν τούτων ἔξοδον,
Μάρκος ὁ μαθητὴς καὶ ἑρμηνευτὴς Πέτρου καὶ αὐτὸς τὰ
15 ὑπὸ Πέτρου κηρυσσόμενα ἐγγράφως ἡμῖν παραδέδωκε·
καὶ Λουκᾶς δὲ ὁ ἀκόλουθος Παύλου τὸ ὑπ᾽ ἐκείνου κη-
ρυσσόμενον Εὐαγγέλιον ἐν βιβλίῳ κατέθετο. ἔπειτα
Ἰωάννης ὁ μαθητὴς τοῦ Κυρίου, ὁ καὶ ἐπὶ τὸ στῆθος
αὐτοῦ ἀναπεσών, καὶ αὐτὸς ἐξέδωκε τὸ Εὐαγγέλιον, ἐν
20 Ἐφέσῳ τῆς Ἀσίας διατρίβων.

Ταῦτα μὲν οὖν ἐν τρίτῳ τῆς εἰρημένης ὑποθέσεως τῷ
προδηλωθέντι [Εἰρηναίῳ] εἴρηται. ἐν δὲ τῷ πέμπτῳ
περὶ τῆς Ἰωάννου Ἀποκαλύψεως, καὶ τῆς ψήφου τῆς
περὶ τοῦ Ἀντιχρίστου προσηγορίας οὕτω διαλαμβάνει·
25 Τούτων δὲ οὕτως ἐχόντων, καὶ ἐν πᾶσι δὲ τοῖς σπου-
δαίοις καὶ ἀρχαίοις ἀντιγράφοις τοῦ ἀριθμοῦ τούτου
κειμένου, καὶ μαρτυρούντων αὐτῶν ἐκείνων τῶν κατ᾽ ὄψιν
τὸν Ἰωάννην ἑωρακότων, καὶ τοῦ λόγου διδάσκοντος ἡμᾶς
ὅτι ὁ ἀριθμὸς τοῦ ὀνόματος τοῦ θηρίου κατὰ τὴν τῶν
30 Ἑλλήνων ψῆφον διὰ τῶν ἐν αὐτῷ γραμμάτων ἐμφαίνεται.

Καὶ ὑποκαταβὰς περὶ τοῦ αὐτοῦ φάσκει·
Ἡμεῖς οὖν οὐκ ἀποκινδυνεύομεν περὶ τοῦ ὀνόματος τοῦ

and therefore it ought indeed to be read, but it cannot to the end of time be publicly read in the Church to the people, either among the prophets, who are complete in number, or among the Apostles.

But of Valentinus the Arsinoite and his friends[1] we receive nothing at all; who have also composed a long[2] new book of Psalms; together with Basilides and the Asiatic founder of the Montanists.

Origin of the Gospels.

MATTHEW published a written Gospel among the Hebrews in their own language, while Peter and Paul were preaching and founding the church in Rome. After their decease Mark, the disciple and interpreter of Peter— he also transmitted to us in writing those things which Peter had preached; and Luke, the attendant of Paul, recorded in a book the Gospel which Paul had declared. Afterwards John, the disciple of the Lord, who also reclined on his bosom—he too published the Gospel, while staying at Ephesus in Asia.

[Irenaeus] states these things in the third book of his above-mentioned work. In the fifth book he speaks as follows of the Apocalypse of John, and the number of the name of Antichrist:—

'As these things are so, and this number is found in all the approved and ancient copies, and those who saw John face to face confirm it, and reason teaches us that the number of the name of the beast, according to the mode of calculation among the Greeks, appears in its letters' ...

And farther on he says concerning the same:—

'We are not bold enough to speak confidently of the

---

[1] l. 81 = τοῦ δὲ Ἀρσινοΐτου Οὐαλεντίνου καὶ τῶν μετ' αὐτοῦ Zahn
[2] l. 83 marcioni = μακρύν Zahn.

Ἀντιχρίστου ἀποφαινόμενοι βεβαιωτικῶς. εἰ γὰρ ἔδει ἀναφανδὸν τῷ νῦν καιρῷ κηρύττεσθαι τοὔνομα αὐτοῦ, δι' ἐκείνου ἂν ἐρρέθη τοῦ καὶ τὴν ἀποκάλυψιν ἑωρακότος· οὐδὲ γὰρ πρὸ πολλοῦ χρόνου ἑωράθη, ἀλλὰ σχεδὸν ἐπὶ 5 τῆς ἡμετέρας γενεᾶς, πρὸς τῷ τέλει τῆς Δομετιανοῦ ἀρχῆς.

Ταῦτα καὶ περὶ τῆς Ἀποκαλύψεως ἱστόρηται τῷ δεδηλωμένῳ. μέμνηται δὲ καὶ τῆς Ἰωάννου πρώτης Ἐπιστολῆς, μαρτύρια ἐξ αὐτῆς πλεῖστα εἰσφέρων, ὁμοίως δὲ 10 καὶ τῆς Πέτρου προτέρας. οὐ μόνον δὲ οἶδεν, ἀλλὰ καὶ ἀποδέχεται, τὴν τοῦ Ποιμένος γραφήν, λέγων·

Καλῶς οὖν εἶπεν ἡ γραφὴ ἡ λέγουσα, 'Πρῶτον πάντων πίστευσον ὅτι εἷς ἐστὶν ὁ Θεός, ὁ τὰ πάντα κτίσας καὶ τὰ ἑξῆς.'

15 Καὶ ῥητοῖς δέ τισιν ἐκ τῆς Σολομῶνος Σοφίας κέχρηται μονονουχὶ φάσκων· 'ὅρασις δὲ Θεοῦ περιποιητικὴ ἀφθαρσίας, ἀφθαρσία δὲ ἐγγὺς εἶναι ποιεῖ Θεοῦ.' καὶ ἀπομνημονευμάτων δὲ ἀποστολικοῦ τινὸς πρεσβυτέρου, οὗ τοὔνομα σιωπῇ παρέδωκε, μνημονεύει, ἐξηγήσεις τε αὐτοῦ 20 θείων γραφῶν παρατίθεται. ἔτι καὶ Ἰουστίνου τοῦ μάρτυρος καὶ Ἰγνατίου μνήμην πεποίηται, μαρτυρίαις αὖθις καὶ ἀπὸ τῶν τούτοις γραφέντων κεχρημένος. ἐπήγγελται δὲ ὁ αὐτὸς ἐκ τῶν Μαρκίωνος συγγραμμάτων ἀντιλέξειν αὐτῷ ἐν ἰδίῳ σπουδάσματι.

EUSEBIUS, *Hist. Eccles.* v. 8.

XXIV.

25 Ἕτεροι δὲ καὶ αὐτοὶ αἱρετικώτεροι τὴν φύσιν, Φρύγες τὸ γένος, προληφθέντες ὑπὸ γυναίων ἠπάτηνται, Πρισκίλλης τινὸς καὶ Μαξιμίλλης καλουμένων, ἃς προφήτιδας νομίζουσιν, ἐν ταύταις τὸ παράκλητον πνεῦμα κεχωρηκέναι λέγοντες, καί τινα πρὸ αὐτῶν Μοντανὸν ὁμοίως δοξάζουσιν 30 ὡς προφήτην, ὧν βίβλους ἀπείρους ἔχοντες πλανῶνται,

name of Antichrist. For if it were necessary that his name should be declared clearly at the present time, it would have been announced by him who saw the revelation. For it was seen, not long ago, but almost in our generation, toward the end of the reign of Domitian.'

These things concerning the Apocalypse are stated by the writer referred to. He also mentions the first Epistle of John, taking many proofs from it, and likewise the first Epistle of Peter. And he not only knows, but also receives, the Shepherd, writing as follows:—

'Well did the Scripture speak, saying, "First of all believe that God is one, who has created and completed all things,"' &c.

And he uses almost the precise words of the Wisdom of Solomon, saying, 'the vision of God produces immortality, but immortality renders us near to God.' He mentions also the memoirs of a certain apostolic presbyter, whose name he passes by in silence, and gives his expositions of the sacred Scriptures. And he refers to Justin the Martyr, and to Ignatius, using quotations also from their writings. Moreover, he promises to refute Marcion from his own writings, in a special work.

Montanism.

BUT there are others who are themselves in nature more heretical [than the Quartodecimans]. These are Phrygians by birth, and have been deceived through having been overcome by womenkind, called a certain Priscilla and Maximilla, whom they hold for prophetesses, saying that the Comforter Spirit dwelt in them; and they likewise glorify one Montanus before them as a prophet. So having endless books of these people they go astray,

μήτε τὰ ὑπ' αὐτῶν λελαλημένα λόγῳ κρίναντες, μήτε
τοῖς κρῖναι δυναμένοις προσέχοντες, ἀλλ' ἀκρίτως τῇ πρὸς
αὐτοὺς πίστει προσφέρονται, πλεῖόν τι δι' αὐτῶν φάσκοντες
[ὡς] μεμαθηκέναι ἢ ἐκ νόμου καὶ προφητῶν καὶ τῶν
5 εὐαγγελίων. ὑπὲρ δὲ ἀποστόλους καὶ πᾶν χάρισμα
ταῦτα τὰ γύναια δοξάζουσιν, ὡς τολμᾶν πλεῖόν τι Χριστοῦ ἐν τούτοις λέγειν τινὰς αὐτῶν γεγονέναι. οὗτοι
τὸν μὲν πατέρα τῶν ὅλων Θεὸν καὶ πάντων κτίστην ὁμοίως
τῇ ἐκκλησίᾳ ὁμολογοῦσι καὶ ὅσα τὸ εὐαγγέλιον περὶ τοῦ
10 Χριστοῦ μαρτυρεῖ, καινίζουσι δὲ νηστείας καὶ ἑορτὰς καὶ
ξηροφαγίας καὶ ῥαφανοφαγίας φάσκοντες ὑπὸ τῶν γυναίων
δεδιδάχθαι. τινὲς δὲ αὐτῶν τῇ τῶν Νοητιανῶν αἱρέσει
συντιθέμενοι τὸν Πατέρα αὐτὸν εἶναι τὸν Υἱὸν λέγουσι, καὶ
τοῦτον ὑπὸ γένεσιν καὶ πάθος καὶ θάνατον ἐληλυθέναι.

HIPPOLYTUS, *Ref. Omn. Haer.* viii. 19.

XXV.

15 Ταῦτα τὰ δόγματα, Φλωρῖνε, ἵνα πεφεισμένως εἴπω,
οὐκ ἔστιν ὑγιοῦς γνώμης· ταῦτα τὰ δόγματα ἀσύμφωνά
ἐστι τῇ ἐκκλησίᾳ, εἰς τὴν μεγίστην ἀσέβειαν περιβάλλοντα τοὺς πειθομένους αὐτοῖς· ταῦτα τὰ δόγματα οὐδὲ
οἱ ἔξω τῆς ἐκκλησίας αἱρετικοὶ ἐτόλμησαν ἀποφήνασθαί
20 ποτε· ταῦτα τὰ δόγματα οἱ πρὸ ἡμῶν πρεσβύτεροι, οἱ
καὶ τοῖς ἀποστόλοις συμφοιτήσαντες, οὐ παρέδωκάν σοι.
εἶδον γάρ σε παῖς ἔτι ὢν ἐν τῇ κάτω Ἀσίᾳ παρὰ Πολυκάρπῳ, λαμπρῶς πράττοντα ἐν τῇ βασιλικῇ αὐλῇ, καὶ
πειρώμενον εὐδοκιμεῖν παρ' αὐτῷ. μᾶλλον γὰρ τὰ τότε
25 διαμνημονεύω τῶν ἔναγχος γινομένων. αἱ γὰρ ἐκ παίδων
μαθήσεις συναύξουσαι τῇ ψυχῇ ἑνοῦνται αὐτῇ, ὥστε με
δύνασθαι εἰπεῖν καὶ τὸν τόπον ἐν ᾧ καθεζόμενος διελέγετο
ὁ μακάριος Πολύκαρπος, καὶ τὰς προόδους αὐτοῦ καὶ τὰς
εἰσόδους, καὶ τὸν χαρακτῆρα τοῦ βίου, καὶ τὴν τοῦ

neither judging their statements by reason, nor heeding those that are able to judge, but behave without judgement in the faith they give them, saying that through them they have learned something more than from the Law and the Prophets and the Gospels. But they glorify these womenkind above Apostles and every gift, so that some of them presume to say that there was something more in them than in Christ. These confess God the Father of the universe and creator of all things like the Church, and all that the Gospel witnesses concerning Christ, but invent new fasts and feasts and meals of dry food and meals of radishes, saying that they were taught them by the womenkind. And some of them agree with the heresy of the Noëtians in saying that the Father is the same with the Son, and that this One became subject to birth and suffering and death.

Letter of Irenaeus to Florinus.

THESE opinions, Florinus, that I may speak without harshness, are not of sound judgement; these opinions are not in harmony with the Church, but involve those adopting them in the greatest impiety; these opinions even the heretics outside the pale of the Church have never ventured to broach; these opinions the elders before us, who also were disciples of the Apostles, did not hand down to thee. For I saw thee, when I was still a boy, in Lower Asia in company with Polycarp, while thou wast faring prosperously in the royal court, and endeavouring to stand well with him. For I distinctly remember the incidents of that time better than events of recent occurrence; for the lessons received in childhood, growing with the growth of the soul, become identified with it; so that I can describe the very place in which the blessed Polycarp used to sit when he discoursed, and his goings out and his comings in, and his manner of life, and his personal appearance, and the

σώματος ἰδέαν, καὶ τὰς διαλέξεις ἃς ἐποιεῖτο πρὸς τὸ
πλῆθος, καὶ τὴν κατὰ Ἰωάννου συναναστροφὴν ὡς
ἀπήγγελλε, καὶ τὴν μετὰ τῶν λοιπῶν τῶν ἑωρακότων
τὸν Κύριον· καὶ ὡς ἀπεμνημόνευε τοὺς λόγους αὐτῶν, καὶ
5 περὶ τοῦ Κυρίου τίνα ἦν ἃ παρ' ἐκείνων ἀκηκόει, καὶ περὶ
τῶν δυνάμεων αὐτοῦ, καὶ περὶ τῆς διδασκαλίας, ὡς παρὰ
τῶν αὐτοπτῶν 'τῆς ζωῆς τοῦ Λόγου' παρειληφὼς ὁ
Πολύκαρπος ἀπήγγελλε πάντα σύμφωνα ταῖς γραφαῖς.
ταῦτα καὶ τότε διὰ τὸ ἔλεος τοῦ Θεοῦ τὸ ἐπ' ἐμοὶ γεγονὸς
10 σπουδαίως ἤκουον, ὑπομνηματιζόμενος αὐτὰ οὐκ ἐν χάρτῃ,
ἀλλ' ἐν τῇ ἐμῇ καρδίᾳ· καὶ ἀεὶ διὰ τὴν χάριν τοῦ Θεοῦ
γνησίως αὐτὰ ἀναμαρυκῶμαι· καὶ δύναμαι διαμαρτύ-
ρασθαι ἔμπροσθεν τοῦ Θεοῦ, ὅτι εἴ τι τοιοῦτον ἀκηκόει
ἐκεῖνος ὁ μακάριος καὶ ἀποστολικὸς πρεσβύτερος, ἀνα-
15 κράξας ἂν καὶ ἐμφράξας τὰ ὦτα αὐτοῦ, καὶ τὸ σύνηθες
αὐτῷ εἰπών, 'Ὦ καλὲ Θεέ, εἰς οἵους με καιροὺς τετήρηκας,
ἵνα τούτων ἀνέχωμαι,' πεφεύγει ἂν καὶ τὸν τόπον ἐν ᾧ
καθεζόμενος ἢ ἑστὼς τῶν τοιούτων ἀκηκόει λόγων. καὶ
ἐκ τῶν ἐπιστολῶν δὲ αὐτοῦ ὧν ἐπέστειλεν ἤτοι ταῖς
20 γειτνιώσαις ἐκκλησίαις, ἐπιστηρίζων αὐτάς, ἢ τῶν ἀδελφῶν τισι, νουθετῶν αὐτοὺς καὶ προτρεπόμενος, δύναται
φανερωθῆναι.

EUSEBIUS, *Hist. Eccles.* v. 20.

XXVI.

Ἡμεῖς οὖν ἀραδιούργητον ἄγομεν τὴν ἡμέραν, μήτε
προστιθέντες, μήτε ἀφαιρούμενοι. καὶ γὰρ κατὰ τὴν
25 Ἀσίαν μεγάλα στοιχεῖα κεκοίμηται, ἅ τινα ἀναστήσεται
τῇ ἡμέρᾳ τῆς παρουσίας τοῦ Κυρίου, ἐν ᾗ ἔρχεται μετὰ
δόξης ἐξ οὐρανῶν, καὶ ἀναστήσει πάντας τοὺς ἁγίους,
Φίλιππον τῶν δώδεκα ἀποστόλων, ὃς κεκοίμηται ἐν Ἱερα-
πόλει, καὶ δύο θυγατέρες αὐτοῦ γεγηρακυῖαι παρθένοι·
30 καὶ ἡ ἑτέρα αὐτοῦ θυγάτηρ ἐν Ἁγίῳ Πνεύματι πολι-

discourses which he held before the people, and how he
would describe his intercourse with John and with the rest
who had seen the Lord, and how he would relate their
words. And whatsoever things he had heard from them
about the Lord, and about his miracles, and about his 5
teaching, Polycarp, as having received them from eye-
witnesses of the life of the Word, would relate altogether
in accordance with the Scriptures. To these discourses
I used to listen at the time with attention by God's mercy
which was bestowed upon me, noting them down, not 10
on paper, but in my heart; and by the grace of God I
constantly ruminate upon them faithfully. And I can
testify in the sight of God, that if the blessed and Apostolic
elder had heard anything of this kind, he would have
cried out, and stopped his ears, and said after his wont, 15
'O good God, for what times hast Thou kept me, that
I should endure such things?' and would even have fled
from the place where he was sitting or standing when
he heard such words. And indeed, this can be shown
from his letters which he wrote either to the neighbouring 20
Churches for their confirmation, or to certain of the
brethren for their warning and exhortation. L.

Letter of Polycrates to Victor.

WE observe the exact day; neither adding, nor taking
away. For in Asia also great lights have fallen asleep,
which shall rise again on the day of the Lord's coming, 25
when he shall come with glory from heaven, and shall raise
up all the saints. Among these are Philip, one of the twelve
Apostles, who fell asleep in Hierapolis; and his two daughters who grew old in virginity, and his other daughter who

τευσαμένη ἐν Ἐφέσῳ ἀναπαύεται· ἔτι δὲ καὶ Ἰωάννης ὁ ἐπὶ τὸ στῆθος τοῦ Κυρίου ἀναπεσών, ὃς ἐγενήθη ἱερεὺς τὸ πέταλον πεφορεκώς, καὶ μάρτυς καὶ διδάσκαλος· οὗτος ἐν Ἐφέσῳ κεκοίμηται. ἔτι δὲ καὶ Πολύκαρπος ἐν
5 Σμύρνῃ καὶ ἐπίσκοπος καὶ μάρτυς· καὶ Θρασέας καὶ ἐπίσκοπος καὶ μάρτυς ἀπὸ Εὐμενίας, ὃς ἐν Σμύρνῃ κεκοίμηται. τί δὲ δεῖ λέγειν Σάγαριν ἐπίσκοπον καὶ μάρτυρα, ὃς ἐν Λαοδικείᾳ κεκοίμηται; ἔτι δὲ καὶ Παπείριον τὸν μακάριον, καὶ Μελίτωνα τὸν εὐνοῦχον, τὸν ἐν Ἁγίῳ
10 Πνεύματι πάντα πολιτευσάμενον· ὃς κεῖται ἐν Σάρδεσι περιμένων τὴν ἀπὸ τῶν οὐρανῶν ἐπισκοπήν, ἐν ᾗ ἐκ νεκρῶν ἀναστήσεται. οὗτοι πάντες ἐτήρησαν τὴν ἡμέραν τῆς τεσσαρεσκαιδεκάτης τοῦ Πάσχα κατὰ τὸ εὐαγγέλιον, μηδὲν παρεκβαίνοντες, ἀλλὰ κατὰ τὸν κανόνα τῆς
15 πίστεως ἀκολουθοῦντες. ἔτι δὲ κἀγὼ ὁ μικρότερος πάντων ὑμῶν Πολυκράτης, κατὰ παράδοσιν τῶν συγγενῶν μου, οἷς καὶ παρηκολούθησά τισιν αὐτῶν· ἑπτὰ μὲν ἦσαν συγγενεῖς μου ἐπίσκοποι, ἐγὼ δὲ ὄγδοος· καὶ πάντοτε τὴν ἡμέραν ἤγαγον οἱ συγγενεῖς μου, ὅταν ὁ λαὸς ἤρνυε τὴν
20 ζύμην· ἐγὼ οὖν, ἀδελφοί, ἑξήκοντα πέντε ἔτη ἔχων ἐν Κυρίῳ, καὶ συμβεβληκὼς τοῖς ἀπὸ τῆς οἰκουμένης ἀδελφοῖς, καὶ πᾶσαν ἁγίαν γραφὴν διεληλυθώς, οὐ πτύρομαι ἐπὶ τοῖς καταπλησσομένοις. οἱ γὰρ ἐμοῦ μείζονες εἰρήκασι, 'πειθαρχεῖν δεῖ Θεῷ μᾶλλον ἢ ἀνθρώποις.'

Ibid. v. 24.

XXVII.

25 Κέρδων δέ τις ἀπὸ τῶν περὶ τὸν Σίμωνα τὰς ἀφορμὰς λαβὼν καὶ ἐπιδημήσας ἐν τῇ Ῥώμῃ ἐπὶ Ὑγίνου, ἔννατον κλῆρον τῆς ἐπισκοπικῆς διαδοχῆς ἀπὸ τῶν ἀποστόλων ἔχοντος, ἐδίδαξε τὸν ὑπὸ τοῦ νόμου καὶ προφητῶν κεκηρυγμένον Θεόν, μὴ εἶναι πατέρα τοῦ Κυρίου ἡμῶν Ἰησοῦ

lived in the Holy Spirit and rests at Ephesus; and, moreover, John, who was both a martyr and a teacher, who leaned upon the bosom of the Lord, and became a priest wearing the sacerdotal plate. He fell asleep at Ephesus. And Polycarp too in Smyrna, who was a bishop and martyr; and Thraseas, bishop and martyr from Eumenia, who fell asleep in Smyrna. Why need I mention the bishop and martyr Sagaris who fell asleep in Laodicea, or the blessed Papirius, or Melito the eunuch, who lived altogether in the Holy Spirit, and who lies in Sardis, awaiting the visitation from heaven, when he shall rise from the dead? All these observed the fourteenth day for the passover according to the Gospel, deviating in no respect, but following the rule of faith. And I also, Polycrates, the least of you all, do according to the tradition of my relatives, some of whom I have closely followed. For seven of my relatives were bishops, and I am the eighth. And my relatives always observed the day when the people put away the leaven. I, therefore, brethren, who have lived sixty-five years in the Lord, and have met with the brethren throughout the world, and have gone through every holy scripture, am not affrighted by terrifying words. For those greater than I have said 'We ought to obey God rather than men.'

Marcion.

ONE Cerdon, who had taken his principles from the school of Simon, and stayed in Rome in the time of Hyginus, who held the ninth place of the episcopal succession from the Apostles—he taught that the God preached by the law and prophets is not the Father of our Lord

Χριστοῦ, τὸν μὲν γὰρ γνωρίζεσθαι, τὸν δὲ ἀγνῶτα εἶναι· καὶ τὸν μὲν δίκαιον, τὸν δὲ ἀγαθὸν ὑπάρχειν.

Διαδεξάμενος δὲ αὐτὸν Μαρκίων ὁ Ποντικός, ηὔξησε τὸ διδασκαλεῖον, ἀπηρυθριασμένως βλασφημῶν eum qui a
5 lege et prophetis annuntiatus est Deus; malorum factorem et bellorum concupiscentem et inconstantem quoque sententia et contrarium sibi ipsum dicens. Iesum autem ab eo Patre, qui est super mundi fabricatorem Deum, venientem in Iudaeam temporibus Pontii Pilati praesidis,
10 qui fuit procurator Tiberii Caesaris, in hominis forma manifestatum his, qui in Iudaea erant, dissolventem prophetas et legem et omnia opera eius Dei, qui mundum fecit, quem et Cosmocratorem dicit. Et super haec id quod est secundum Lucam evangelium circumcidens et
15 omnia, quae sunt de generatione Domini conscripta, auferens, et de doctrina sermonum Domini multa auferens, in quibus manifestissime conditorem huius universitatis suum Patrem confitens Dominus conscriptus est; semet ipsum esse veraciorem, quam sunt hi, qui evangelium
20 tradiderunt, apostoli, suasit discipulis suis, non evangelium, sed particulam evangelii tradens eis. Similiter autem et apostoli Pauli epistolas abscidit, auferens quaecunque manifeste dicta sunt ab apostolo de eo Deo, qui mundum fecit, quoniam hic Pater Domini nostri Iesu Christi, et
25 quaecunque ex propheticis memorans apostolus docuit, praenuntiantibus adventum Domini.

IRENAEUS, *Adv. Haer.* i. 27.

XXVIII.

TRADITIONEM itaque apostolorum in toto mundo manifestatam, in omni ecclesia adest respicere omnibus qui vera velint videre; et habemus annumerare eos, qui ab
30 apostolis instituti sunt episcopi in ecclesiis, et succes-

Jesus Christ; for the former is known, but the latter unknown, and the former is by nature righteous, but the other good. And Marcion of Pontus succeeding him developed the school, blaspheming shamelessly him who is proclaimed as God by the law and the prophets; calling him a maker of evils and a lover of wars, unsettled of purpose also, and inconsistent with himself. [He said] however that Jesus coming from the Father, who is above the God who made the world, into Judaea in the times of the governor Pontius Pilate, procurator of Tiberius Caesar, was manifested in the form of a man to those that were in Judaea, destroying the prophets and the law, and all the works of the God who made the world, whom he also calls Cosmocrator[1]. Besides this, by mutilating the Gospel which is according to Luke, and removing all that refers to the generation of the Lord, and removing many passages of the teaching of the Lord's discourses, in which the Lord is recorded as very plainly confessing the framer of this universe to be his own Father, Marcion has persuaded his disciples that he is himself truer than those Apostles who delivered the Gospel; so he delivers to them not the Gospel, but a part of the Gospel. But likewise he has cut down also the Epistles of the Apostle Paul, removing all that is plainly said by the Apostle concerning the God that made the world, that *he* is the Father of our Lord Jesus Christ; and all that the Apostle taught by quotation from the prophetical writings which foretold the coming of the Lord.

The Argument of Irenaeus from Tradition.

THE tradition therefore of the Apostles, manifested in the entire world, is a thing which all who wish to see facts can clearly perceive in every Church; and we are able to count up those who were by the Apostles appointed

[1] Eph. vi. 12.

sores eorum usque ad nos, qui nihil tale docuerunt neque cognoverunt, quale ab his deliratur. Etenim si recondita mysteria scissent apostoli, quae seorsim et latenter ab reliquis perfectos docebant, his vel maxime traderent ea
5 quibus etiam ipsas ecclesias committebant. Valde enim perfectos et irreprehensibiles in omnibus eos volebant esse, quos et successores relinquebant, suum ipsorum locum magisterii tradentes; quibus emendate agentibus fieret magna utilitas, lapsis autem summa calamitas.
10 Sed quoniam valde longum est in hoc tali volumine omnium ecclesiarum enumerare successiones; maximae et antiquissimae, et omnibus cognitae, a gloriosissimis duobus apostolis Petro et Paulo Romae fundatae et constitutae ecclesiae, eam, quam habet ab apostolis tradi-
15 tionem, et annuntiatam hominibus fidem, per successiones episcoporum pervenientem usque ad nos indicantes, confundimus omnes eos, qui quoquo modo, vel per sibiplacentiam, vel vanam gloriam, vel per caecitatem et malam sententiam, praeterquam oportet colligunt. Ad hanc enim
20 ecclesiam propter potentiorem principalitatem necesse est omnem convenire ecclesiam, hoc est, eos qui sunt undique fideles, in qua semper ab his, qui sunt undique, conservata est ea quae est ab apostolis traditio.

Θεμελιώσαντες οὖν καὶ οἰκοδομήσαντες οἱ μακάριοι
25 ἀπόστολοι τὴν ἐκκλησίαν, Λίνῳ τὴν τῆς ἐπισκοπῆς λειτουργίαν ἐνεχείρισαν. τούτου τοῦ Λίνου Παῦλος ἐν ταῖς πρὸς Τιμόθεον ἐπιστολαῖς μέμνηται. διαδέχεται δὲ αὐτὸν Ἀνέγκλητος. μετὰ τοῦτον δὲ τρίτῳ τόπῳ ἀπὸ τῶν ἀποστόλων τὴν ἐπισκοπὴν κληροῦται Κλήμης, ὁ καὶ
30 ἑωρακὼς τοὺς μακαρίους ἀποστόλους καὶ συμβεβληκὼς αὐτοῖς, καὶ ἔτι ἔναυλον τὸ κήρυγμα τῶν ἀποστόλων καὶ τὴν παράδοσιν πρὸ ὀφθαλμῶν ἔχων, οὐ μόνος· ἔτι γὰρ

bishops in the Churches, and the series of their successors to our own time, who neither taught nor knew anything resembling these men's dotage. For if the Apostles had known hidden mysteries which they used to teach the perfect apart from and without the knowledge of the rest, they would deliver them to those especially to whom they were also committing the Churches themselves. For they desired them to be very perfect and blameless in all things, whom they were also leaving as their successors, delivering over to them their own proper seat of government; for if these should act rightly, great advantage would result, but if they fell away, the most disastrous calamity. But since it would be very long in such a volume as this to count up the series of bishops in all the Churches, we confound all those who in any way, whether through self-pleasing or vain glory, or through blindness and evil opinion meet for worship otherwise than they ought—by pointing out the tradition (which it has from the Apostles) of the most great and ancient and universally-known Church, founded and established at Rome by the two most glorious Apostles Peter and Paul; and also the faith declared to men, which comes down to our own time through the successions of bishops. For unto this Church, on account of its more powerful lead, every Church, meaning the faithful who are from everywhere, must needs resort; since in it that tradition which is from the Apostles has always been preserved by those who are from everywhere.

The blessed Apostles having founded and established the Church, entrusted the office of the episcopate to Linus. Paul speaks of this Linus in his Epistles to Timothy. Anencletus succeeded him, and after Anencletus, in the third place from the Apostles, Clement received the episcopate. He had seen and conversed with the blessed Apostles, and their preaching was still sounding in his ears, and their tradition was still before his eyes. Nor

πολλοὶ ὑπελείποντο τότε ἀπὸ τῶν ἀποστόλων δεδιδαγμένοι. ἐπὶ τούτου οὖν τοῦ Κλήμεντος στάσεως οὐκ ὀλίγης τοῖς ἐν Κορίνθῳ γενομένης ἀδελφοῖς, ἐπέστειλεν ἡ ἐν Ῥώμῃ ἐκκλησία ἱκανωτάτην γραφὴν τοῖς Κορινθίοις, εἰς εἰρήνην
5 συμβιβάζουσα αὐτούς, καὶ ἀνανεοῦσα τὴν πίστιν αὐτῶν, καὶ ἣν νεωστὶ ἀπὸ τῶν ἀποστόλων παράδοσιν εἰλήφει.

Τὸν δὲ Κλήμεντα τοῦτον διαδέχεται Εὐάρεστος· καὶ τὸν Εὐάρεστον Ἀλέξανδρος· εἶθ᾽ οὕτως ἕκτος ἀπὸ τῶν ἀποστόλων καθίσταται Ξύστος. μετὰ δὲ τοῦτον Τελεσ-
10 φόρος, ὃς καὶ ἐνδόξως ἐμαρτύρησεν· ἔπειτα Ὑγῖνος, εἶτα Πῖος· μεθ᾽ ὃν Ἀνίκητος. διαδεξαμένου τὸν Ἀνίκητον Σωτῆρος, νῦν δωδεκάτῳ τόπῳ τὸν τῆς ἐπισκοπῆς ἀπὸ τῶν ἀποστόλων κατέχει κλῆρον Ἐλεύθερος. τῇ αὐτῇ τάξει, καὶ τῇ αὐτῇ διδαχῇ [διαδοχῇ], ἥ τε ἀπὸ τῶν ἀπο-
15 στόλων ἐν τῇ ἐκκλησίᾳ παράδοσις καὶ τὸ τῆς ἀληθείας κήρυγμα κατήντηκεν εἰς ἡμᾶς.

Καὶ Πολύκαρπος δὲ οὐ μόνον ὑπὸ ἀποστόλων μαθητευθείς, καὶ συναναστραφεὶς πολλοῖς τοῖς τὸν Χριστὸν ἑωρακόσιν, ἀλλὰ καὶ ὑπὸ ἀποστόλων κατασταθεὶς εἰς τὴν
20 Ἀσίαν, ἐν τῇ ἐν Σμύρνῃ ἐκκλησίᾳ, ἐπίσκοπος, ὃν καὶ ἡμεῖς ἑωράκαμεν ἐν τῇ πρώτῃ ἡμῶν ἡλικίᾳ· (ἐπιπολὺ γὰρ παρέμεινε, καὶ πάνυ γηραλέος, ἐνδόξως καὶ ἐπιφανέστατα μαρτυρήσας, ἐξῆλθε τοῦ βίου) ταῦτα διδάξας ἀεί, ἃ καὶ παρὰ τῶν ἀποστόλων ἔμαθεν, ἃ καὶ ἡ ἐκκλησία
25 παραδίδωσιν, ἃ καὶ μόνα ἐστὶν ἀληθῆ. μαρτυροῦσι τούτοις αἱ κατὰ τὴν Ἀσίαν ἐκκλησίαι πᾶσαι, καὶ οἱ μέχρι νῦν διαδεδεγμένοι τὸν Πολύκαρπον, πολλῷ ἀξιοπιστότερον καὶ βεβαιότερον ἀληθείας μάρτυρα ὄντα Οὐαλεντίνου καὶ Μαρκίωνος, καὶ τῶν λοιπῶν κακογνω-
30 μόνων. ὃς καὶ ἐπὶ Ἀνικήτου ἐπιδημήσας τῇ Ῥώμῃ, πολλοὺς ἀπὸ τῶν προειρημένων αἱρετικῶν ἐπέστρεψεν εἰς τὴν ἐκκλησίαν τοῦ Θεοῦ, μίαν καὶ μόνην ταύτην ἀλήθειαν κηρύξας ὑπὸ τῶν ἀποστόλων παρειληφέναι, τὴν ὑπὸ τῆς

was he alone in this, for many who had been taught by the Apostles yet survived. In the times of Clement, a serious dissension having arisen among the brethren in Corinth, the Church of Rome sent a most powerful letter to the Corinthians, reconciling them in peace, renewing their faith, and proclaiming the doctrine lately received from the Apostles.

Evarestus succeeded Clement, and Alexander Evarestus. Then Xystus, the sixth from the Apostles, was appointed. After him Telesphorus, who suffered martyrdom gloriously; then Hyginus; then Pius; and after him Anicetus; Soter succeeded Anicetus; and now, in the twelfth place from the Apostles, Eleutherus holds the office of bishop. In the same order and succession the tradition in the Church and the preaching of the truth has descended from the Apostles unto us.

But Polycarp also was not only instructed by Apostles, and familiar with many that had seen Christ, but was also appointed by Apostles in Asia bishop of the Church of Smyrna. We too saw him in our early youth; for he lived a long time, and died, when a very old man, a glorious and most illustrious martyr's death, having always taught the things which he had learned from the Apostles, which the Church also hands down, and which alone are true. To these things all the Asiatic Churches testify, as do also those who, down to the present time, have succeeded Polycarp, who was a much more trustworthy and certain witness of the truth than Valentinus and Marcion and the rest of the evil-minded. He was also in Rome in the time of Anicetus and caused many to turn away from the above-mentioned heretics to the Church of God, proclaiming that he had received from the Apostles this one and only system of truth which has been trans-

ἐκκλησίας παραδεδομένην. καὶ εἰσὶν οἱ ἀκηκοότες αὐτοῦ, ὅτι Ἰωάννης, ὁ τοῦ Κυρίου μαθητής, ἐν τῇ Ἐφέσῳ πορευθεὶς λούσασθαι, καὶ ἰδὼν ἔσω Κήρινθον, ἐξήλατο τοῦ βαλανείου μὴ λουσάμενος, ἀλλ᾽ ἐπειπών· Φύγωμεν, μὴ καὶ τὸ βαλανεῖον συμπέσῃ, ἔνδον ὄντος Κηρίνθου, τοῦ τῆς ἀληθείας ἐχθροῦ. καὶ αὐτὸς δὲ ὁ Πολύκαρπος Μαρκίωνι ποτὲ εἰς ὄψιν αὐτῷ ἐλθόντι καὶ φήσαντι· Ἐπιγινώσκεις ἡμᾶς; ἀπεκρίθη· Ἐπιγινώσκω τὸν πρωτότοκον τοῦ Σατανᾶ. τοσαύτην οἱ ἀπόστολοι καὶ οἱ μαθηταὶ αὐτῶν ἔσχον εὐλάβειαν, πρὸς τὸ μηδὲ μέχρι λόγου κοινωνεῖν τινι τῶν παραχαρασσόντων τὴν ἀλήθειαν, ὡς καὶ Παῦλος ἔφησεν· Αἱρετικὸν ἄνθρωπον μετὰ μίαν καὶ δευτέραν νουθεσίαν παραιτοῦ, εἰδὼς ὅτι ἐξέστραπται ὁ τοιοῦτος, καὶ ἁμαρτάνει, ὢν αὐτοκατάκριτος. ἔστι δὲ ἐπιστολὴ Πολυκάρπου πρὸς Φιλιππησίους γεγραμμένη ἱκανωτάτη, ἐξ ἧς καὶ τὸν χαρακτῆρα τῆς πίστεως αὐτοῦ καὶ τὸ κήρυγμα τῆς ἀληθείας οἱ βουλόμενοι καὶ φροντίζοντες τῆς ἑαυτῶν σωτηρίας δύνανται μαθεῖν.

Ibid. iii. 3.

XXIX.

Ὡς οἱ πρεσβύτεροι λέγουσι, τότε καὶ οἱ μὲν καταξιωθέντες τῆς ἐν οὐρανῷ διατριβῆς, ἐκεῖσε χωρήσουσιν, οἱ δὲ τῆς τοῦ παραδείσου τρυφῆς ἀπολαύσουσιν, οἱ δὲ τὴν λαμπρότητα τῆς πόλεως καθέξουσιν· πανταχοῦ γὰρ ὁ Σωτὴρ ὁραθήσεται, [καὶ] καθὼς ἄξιοι ἔσονται οἱ ὁρῶντες αὐτόν. εἶναι δὲ τὴν διαστολὴν ταύτην τῆς οἰκήσεως τῶν τὰ ἑκατὸν καρποφορούντων καὶ τῶν τὰ ἑξήκοντα καὶ τῶν τὰ τριάκοντα· ὧν οἱ μὲν εἰς τοὺς οὐρανοὺς ἀναληφθή-

mitted by the Church. And there are those that heard from him that John, the disciple of the Lord, going to bathe in Ephesus and seeing Cerinthus within, ran out of the bath-house without bathing, crying, 'Let us flee, lest even the bath-house fall, because Cerinthus, the enemy of the truth, is within.' And Polycarp himself, when Marcion once met him and said, 'Knowest thou us?' replied, 'I know the first-born of Satan.' Such caution did the Apostles and their disciples exercise that they might not even converse with any of those who perverted the truth; as Paul also said, 'A man that is a heretic, after the first and second admonition, reject; knowing that he that is such is subverted, and sinneth, being condemned of himself.' There is also a very powerful epistle of Polycarp written to the Philippians, from which those that wish to do so, and that are concerned for their own salvation, may learn the character of his faith and the preaching of the truth.

A. N. L.

A Tradition of the Elders.

As the Elders say, then also shall they which have been deemed worthy of the abode in heaven go thither, while others shall enjoy the delight of paradise, and others again shall possess the brightness of the city; for in every place the Saviour shall be seen, according as they shall be worthy who see Him. They say moreover that this is the distinction between the habitation of them that bring forth a hundred-fold, and them that bring forth sixty-fold, and them that bring forth thirty-fold; of whom the first

σονται, οἱ δὲ ἐν τῷ παραδείσῳ διατρίψουσιν, οἱ δὲ τὴν
πόλιν κατοικήσουσιν· καὶ διὰ τοῦτο εἰρηκέναι τὸν Κύριον,
ἐν τοῖς τοῦ πατρός μου μονὰς εἶναι πολλάς. τὰ πάντα
γὰρ τοῦ Θεοῦ, ὃς τοῖς πᾶσι τὴν ἁρμόζουσαν οἴκησιν
5 παρέχει.   *Ibid.* v. 36.

XXX.

Ἦν μὲν οὖν πρὸ τῆς τοῦ Κυρίου παρουσίας εἰς
δικαιοσύνην Ἕλλησιν ἀναγκαία φιλοσοφία, νυνὶ δὲ χρη-
σίμη πρὸς θεοσέβειαν γίνεται, προπαιδεία τις οὖσα τοῖς
τὴν πίστιν δι᾽ ἀποδείξεως καρπουμένοις, ὅτι ʽὁ πούς
10 σου᾽ φησὶν ʽοὐ μὴ προσκόψῃ,᾽ ἐπὶ τὴν πρόνοιαν τὰ
καλὰ ἀναφέροντος, ἐάν τε Ἑλληνικὰ ᾖ ἐάν τε ἡμέτερα.
πάντων μὲν γὰρ αἴτιος τῶν καλῶν ὁ Θεός, ἀλλὰ τῶν μὲν
κατὰ προηγούμενον ὡς τῆς τε διαθήκης τῆς παλαιᾶς καὶ
τῆς νέας, τῶν δὲ κατ᾽ ἐπακολούθημα ὡς τῆς φιλοσοφίας.
15 τάχα δὲ καὶ προηγουμένως τοῖς Ἕλλησιν ἐδόθη τότε πρὶν
ἢ τὸν Κύριον καλέσαι καὶ τοὺς Ἕλληνας· ἐπαιδαγώγει
γὰρ καὶ αὐτὴ τὸ Ἑλληνικὸν ὡς ὁ νόμος τοὺς Ἑβραίους
εἰς Χριστόν. προπαρασκευάζει τοίνυν ἡ φιλοσοφία προοδο-
ποιοῦσα τὸν ὑπὸ Χριστοῦ τελειούμενον.... μία μὲν οὖν
20 ἡ τῆς ἀληθείας ὁδός, ἀλλ᾽ εἰς αὐτὴν καθάπερ εἰς ἀέναον
ποταμὸν ἐκρέουσι τὰ ῥεῖθρα ἄλλα ἄλλοθεν.

CLEMENS ALEXANDRINUS, *Strom.* i. 5, p. 331.

XXXI.

Ὁ τοίνυν μετριοπαθήσας τὰ πρῶτα καὶ εἰς ἀπάθειαν
μελετήσας αὐξήσας τε εἰς εὐποιίαν γνωστικῆς τελειότητος
ἰσάγγελος μὲν ἐνταῦθα, φωτεινὸς δὲ ἤδη καὶ ὡς ὁ ἥλιος
25 λάμπων κατὰ τὴν εὐεργεσίαν σπεύδει τῇ γνώσει τῇ δικαίᾳ
δι᾽ ἀγάπης Θεοῦ ἐπὶ τὴν ἁγίαν μονήν.

Ibid. vi. 13, p. 792.

shall be taken up into the heavens, and the second shall dwell in paradise, and the third shall inhabit the city; and that therefore our Lord has said, In my Father's abode are many mansions; for all things are of God, Who giveth to all their appropriate dwelling.

Philosophy a preparation for the Gospel.

PHILOSOPHY then before the coming of the Lord was necessary to the Greeks for righteousness, but now it is profitable for piety, seeing that it is a sort of training for those who by means of demonstration have the enjoyment of faith, for 'thy foot shall not stumble,' says he, if thou refer good things to providence, whether they be Greek or Christian. For God is the cause of all good things, but of some primarily, as of the old and new covenants, and of others indirectly, as of philosophy. Peradventure also it was given primarily to the Greeks in times before the Lord called also the Greeks; for this was a schoolmaster to the Greek world as the law was to the Hebrews to bring them unto Christ. Philosophy therefore is a preparation, making ready the way for him who is being perfected by Christ.... The way then of truth is one; but into it as into a never-failing river flow the streams from all sides.

The true Gnostic.

HE then who has first moderated his passions and trained himself for impassibility, and developed to the beneficence of gnostic perfection, is here equal to the angels. Luminous already, and like the sun shining in the exercise of beneficence, he speeds by righteous knowledge through the love of God to the holy mansion.

XXXII.

Ἡ μὲν οὖν πίστις σύντομός ἐστιν, ὡς εἰπεῖν, τῶν κατεπειγόντων γνῶσις, ἡ γνῶσις δὲ ἀπόδειξις τῶν διὰ πίστεως παρειλημμένων ἰσχυρὰ καὶ βέβαιος διὰ τῆς κυριακῆς διδασκαλίας ἐποικοδομουμένη τῇ πίστει εἰς τὸ ἀμετάπτωτον
5 καὶ μετ᾽ ἐπιστήμης καταληπτικὸν παραπέμπουσα. καί μοι δοκεῖ πρώτη τις εἶναι μεταβολὴ σωτήριος ἡ ἐξ ἐθνῶν εἰς πίστιν, ὡς προεῖπον, δευτέρα δὲ ἡ ἐκ πίστεως εἰς γνῶσιν· ἡ δὲ εἰς ἀγάπην περαιουμένη ἐνθένδε ἤδη φίλον φίλῳ τὸ γινῶσκον τῷ γινωσκομένῳ παρίστησιν. καὶ
10 τάχα ὁ τοιοῦτος ἐνθένδε ἤδη προλαβὼν ἔχει τὸ ἰσάγγελος εἶναι. μετὰ γοῦν τὴν ἐν σαρκὶ τελευταίαν ὑπεροχὴν ἀεὶ κατὰ τὸ προσῆκον ἐπὶ τὸ κρεῖττον μεταβάλλων εἰς τὴν πατρῴαν αὐλὴν ἐπὶ τὴν κυριακὴν ὄντως διὰ τῆς ἁγίας ἑβδομάδος ἐπείγεται μονήν, ἐσόμενος, ὡς εἰπεῖν, φῶς ἑστὸς
15 καὶ μένον ἀϊδίως, πάντη πάντως ἄτρεπτον.

Ibid. vii. 10, p. 865.

XXXIII.

Κἂν τολμήσωσι προφητικαῖς χρήσασθαι γραφαῖς καὶ οἱ τὰς αἱρέσεις μετιόντες πρῶτον μὲν οὐ πάσαις, ἔπειτα οὐ τελείαις οὐδὲ ὡς τὸ σῶμα καὶ τὸ ὕφος τῆς προφητείας ὑπαγορεύει, ἀλλ᾽ ἐκλεγόμενοι τὰ ἀμφιβόλως εἰρημένα εἰς
20 τὰς ἰδίας μετάγουσι δόξας, ὀλίγας σποράδην ἀπανθιζόμενοι φωνάς, οὐ τὸ σημαινόμενον ἀπ᾽ αὐτῶν σκοποῦντες, ἀλλ᾽ αὐτῇ ψιλῇ ἀποχρώμενοι τῇ λέξει. σχεδὸν γὰρ ἐν πᾶσιν οἷς προσφέρονται ῥητοῖς εὕροις ἂν αὐτοὺς ὡς τοῖς ὀνόμασι μόνοις προσανέχουσι τὰ σημαινόμενα ὑπαλλάτ-
25 τοντες, οὔθ᾽ ὡς λέγονται γινώσκοντες οὔθ᾽ ὡς ἔχειν πεφύκασι χρώμενοι, αἷς καὶ δὴ κομίζουσιν ἐκλογαῖς.

Ibid. vii. 16, p. 891.

Faith and Knowledge.

FAITH is then, so to speak, a compendious knowledge of the essentials; and knowledge is the strong and sure demonstration of what is received by faith, built upon faith by the Lord's teaching, conveying [the soul] on to unchangeableness, and scientific comprehension. And, in my view, the first saving change is that from heathenism to faith, as I said before; and the second, that from faith to knowledge. And the latter terminating in love, here in this life introduces as friend to friend, that which knows to that which is known. And, perchance, such an one has already attained the condition of 'being equal to the angels.' At any rate, after the highest excellence in the flesh, changing always duly to the better, he hastens to the ancestral hall, through the holy Hebdomad to the Lord's own mansion; to be, so to say, a light, steady, and continuing eternally, entirely and in every part immutable.

Misuse of Scripture by Heretics.

AND if those also who follow heresies venture to avail themselves of the prophetic Scriptures; in the first place they will not make use of all the Scriptures, and then they will not quote them entire, nor as the body and texture of the prophecy prescribe. But, selecting ambiguous expressions, they wrest them to their own opinions, gathering a few expressions here and there; not looking to the sense, but making use of the mere diction. For in almost all the quotations they make, you will find that they attend to the words alone, while they alter the meanings; neither knowing how they are spoken, nor using the quotations they do bring according to their natural meaning.

XXXIV.

Ut de origine aliquid retractemus eiusmodi legum, vetus erat decretum, ne qui deus ab imperatore consecraretur, nisi a senatu probatus. Scit M. Aemilius de deo suo Alburno. Facit et hoc ad caussam nostram, quod apud
5 vos de humano arbitratu divinitas pensitatur. Nisi homini deus placuerit, deus non erit; homo iam deo propitius esse debebit. Tiberius ergo, cuius tempore nomen Christianum in saeculum introivit, annuntiatum sibi ex Syria Palaestina, quod illic veritatem illius divinitatis revelaverat,
10 detulit ad senatum cum praerogativa suffragii sui. Senatus, quia non ipse probaverat, respuit; Caesar in sententia mansit, comminatus periculum accusatoribus Christianorum. Consulite commentarios vestros; illic reperietis primum Neronem in hanc sectam cum maxime Romae
15 orientem Caesariano gladio ferocisse. Sed tali dedicatore damnationis nostrae etiam gloriamur. Qui enim scit illum, intelligere potest, non nisi grande aliquod bonum a Nerone damnatum. Tentaverat et Domitianus, portio Neronis de crudelitate; sed qua et homo, facile coeptum repressit,
20 restitutis etiam quos relegaverat. Tales semper nobis insecutores, iniusti, impii, turpes, quos et ipsi damnare consuestis, et a quibus damnatos restituere soliti estis. Ceterum de tot exinde principibus, usque ad hodiernum divinum humanumque sapientibus, edite aliquem debella-
25 torem Christianorum. At nos e contrario edimus protectorem, si litterae M. Aurelii gravissimi imperatoris

Bad Emperors the only Persecutors.

To say something of the origin of laws of that sort. There was an old decree, that no god should be consecrated by any general without the approval of the Senate. M. Aemilius found it out with his god Alburnus. This too helps our case, that with you divinity depends on human judgement. Unless a god pleases men, he shall not be a god at all—man will positively have to be propitious to his god. Tiberius then, in whose time the Christian name came into the world, referred to the Senate the news which had reached himself from Palestine of the events which had revealed the truth of Christ's divinity, with the recommendation of his own vote in favour of it. The Senate refused, because it had not itself approved. Caesar held to his opinion, and threatened punishment to the accusers of Christians. Consult your own records. There you will find that Nero was the first who raged with the imperial sword against our sect, just when it was coming into notice at Rome. But we are proud indeed of having such a man to inaugurate our condemnation; for any one who knows him can understand that what Nero condemned cannot but have been something very good indeed. Domitian tried it too, another Nero for cruelty; but as having some humanity too, he soon stopped his effort, and even restored those whom he had exiled. Our persecutors are always men of this sort, unrighteous, impious and shameful; men whose memory even you are used to brand with infamy, whose judicial victims it is your custom to restore. However, out of all the emperors from that time to the present who have tasted of divine and human wisdom, name a single one as an antagonist of Christians! Nay, we, on the contrary, name one as a protector, if you will call for the letter of the grave and reverend emperor M. Aurelius, in which he bears witness

requirantur, quibus illam Germanicam sitim Christianorum
forte militum precationibus impetrato imbri discussam contestatur. Qui sicut non palam ab eiusmodi hominibus
poenam dimovit, ita alio modo palam dispersit, adiecta
etiam accusatoribus damnatione, et quidem tetriore. Quales
ergo leges istae, quas adversus nos soli exsequuntur
impii, iniusti, turpes, truces, vani, dementes? quas Traia-
nus ex parte frustratus est vetando inquiri Christianorum;
quas nullus Hadrianus, quamquam curiositatum omnium
explorator, nullus Vespasianus, quamquam Iudaeorum
debellator, nullus Pius, nullus Verus impressit.

TERTULLIAN, *Apol.* 5

XXXV.

VULTIS ex operibus ipsius tot ac talibus, quibus con-
tinemur, quibus sustinemur, quibus oblectamur, etiam
quibus exterremur, vultis ex animae ipsius testimonio
comprobemus? Quae licet carcere corporis pressa, licet
institutionibus pravis circumscripta, licet libidinibus ac
concupiscentiis evigorata, licet falsis diis exancillata, cum
tamen resipiscit, ut ex crapula, ut ex somno, ut ex aliqua
valetudine, et sanitatem suam patitur, deum nominat, hoc
solo nomine, quia proprio dei veri: deus magnus, deus
bonus, et quod deus dederit, omnium vox est. Iudicem
quoque contestatur illum, deus videt, et deo commendo,
et deus mihi reddet. O testimonium animae naturaliter
Christianae! Denique pronuntians haec, non ad Capito-
lium, sed ad coelum respicit. Novit enim sedem dei vivi;
ab illo, et inde descendit. *Ibid.* 17.

that the great drought in Germany was removed by a shower of rain obtained by the prayers of Christians who chanced to be serving in the army. As on one side he did not openly free such men from the penalties of law, so on the other he openly made these of none effect, imposing also a sentence, and that a severer one, on their accusers. What sort of laws then are these, which are put in force against us only by the impious, the unrighteous, the shameful, the savage, the senseless, the demented—laws which Trajan partly defeated by forbidding Christians to be sought out, which neither a Hadrian, though so curious a student of every novelty, nor a Vespasian, conqueror of the Jews as he was, nor a Pius, nor a Verus ever enforced?

Testimony of the Soul.

WILL you have our proof from his works in all their magnitude and number, which contain or sustain us, which delight us or again dismay us; or will you have it from the witness of the soul itself? Though it be shut up in the prison of the body, though it be limited by evil customs, though it be enervated by lusts and longings, though it be a slave to false gods, yet when it comes to itself as after a debauch or after sleep or after a sickness, and feels its proper health, it makes mention of God, and by that name only, for it is peculiar to the true God. 'God is great,' 'God is good,' 'which may God grant,' are all men's words. It appeals also to Him as judge—'God sees,' 'I commend to Him,' and 'God will repay me.' O testimony of the soul by nature Christian! Finally, in using these words, it looks up not to the Capitol but to heaven, for it recognizes the throne of the living God. From Him it is, and thence came down.

XXXVI.

Est et alia maior necessitas nobis orandi pro imperatoribus, etiam pro omni statu imperii rebusque Romanis
qui vim maximam universo orbi imminentem, ipsamque
clausulam seculi acerbitates horrendas comminantem Ro-
5 mani imperii commeatu scimus retardari. Ita quae nolumus
experiri, ea dum precamur differri, Romanae diuturnitati
favemus. Sed et iuramus, sicut non per genios Caesarum
ita per salutem eorum, quae est augustior omnibus geniis.
Nescitis genios daemonas dici, et inde diminutiva voce
10 daemonia? Nos iudicium dei suspicimus in imperatoribus
qui gentibus illos praefecit.

Ibid. 32.

XXXVII.

Hesterni sumus et vestra omnia implevimus, urbes,
insulas, castella, municipia, conciliabula, castra ipsa, tribus,
decurias, palatium, senatum, forum; sola vobis reliquimus
15 templa. Cui bello non idonei, non prompti fuissemus,
etiam impares copiis, qui tam libenter trucidamur, si non
apud istam disciplinam magis occidi liceret, quam occidere?
Potuimus et inermes, nec rebelles, sed tantummodo dis-
cordes, solius divortii invidia adversus vos dimicasse. Si
20 enim tanta vis hominum in aliquem orbis remoti sinum
abrupissemus a vobis, suffudisset pudore utique domi-
nationem vestram tot qualiumcunque amissio civium, imo
etiam et ipsa destitutione punisset.

Ibid. 37.

Christians not disloyal.

WE are under another and a greater need of praying for the emperors, and further for the good estate of the Empire and the interests of Rome, knowing as we do that a mighty shock impending over the entire world and the end of the age itself with the fearful calamities it threatens are delayed by the respite which the Roman Empire gives. Thus when we pray for those things to be put off which we do not wish ourselves to experience, we are in favour of the long endurance of Rome. Furthermore, even as we do not swear by the genii of the Caesars, so we do swear by their health, which is more august than all the genii. Do you not know that the genii are called *daemones*, and thence by the diminutive word *daemonia*? We in the emperors look up to the judgement of God, who has set them over the nations.

Numbers of the Christians.

WE are men of yesterday; yet we have filled all your places of resort—cities, lodging-houses, villages, towns, markets, even the camp, tribes, town-councils, palace, senate, forum; we have left you nothing but your temples. For what war should not we have been fit and ready, though with unequal forces, who are so willing to be slaughtered, if according to our teaching it were not better to be killed than to kill? We could have fought against you even without arms, yet without rebellion, simply by the civil discord of an unfriendly separation. For if such a force of men as we had broken off from you to some far corner of the world, your empire would undoubtedly have been put to shame by the loss of so many citizens of whatever sort, or rather actual bankruptcy would have been your punishment.

XXXVIII.

Corpus sumus de conscientia religionis et disciplinae unitate et spei foedere. Coimus in coetum et congregationem, ut ad deum, quasi manu facta, precationibus ambiamus. Haec vis deo grata est. Oramus etiam pro imperatoribus, pro ministeriis eorum ac potestatibus, pro statu saeculi, pro rerum quiete, pro mora finis. Cogimur ad litterarum divinarum commemorationem, si quid praesentium temporum qualitas aut praemonere cogit aut recognoscere. Certe fidem sanctis vocibus pascimus, spem erigimus, fiduciam figimus, disciplinam praeceptorum nihilominus inculcationibus densamus; ibidem etiam exhortationes, castigationes et censura divina. Nam et iudicatur magno cum pondere, ut apud certos de dei conspectu, summumque futuri iudicii praeiudicium est, si quis ita deliquerit, ut a communicatione orationis et conventus et omnis sancti commercii relegetur. Praesident probati quique seniores, honorem istum non pretio sed testimonio adepti; neque enim pretio ulla res dei constat. Etiam si quod arcae genus est, non de honoraria summa, quasi redemptae religionis congregatur; modicam unusquisque stipem menstrua die, vel quum velit, et si modo velit et si modo possit, apponit: nam nemo compellitur, sed sponte confert. Haec quasi deposita pietatis sunt. Nam inde non epulis nec potaculis, nec ingratis voratrinis dispensatur, sed egenis alendis humandisque, et pueris ac puellis re ac parentibus destitutis, iamque domesticis senibus, item naufragis, et si qui in metallis, et si qui in insulis, vel in custodiis, dumtaxat ex causa dei sectae, alumni confessionis suae fiunt.

Ibid. 39.

Christian Worship.

WE are made a body by common religious feeling, unity of discipline, and the bond of hope. We come together in a meeting and assembly, that we may as it were form a troop, and so in prayer to God beset Him with our supplications. This violence is well-pleasing to God. We pray also for emperors, for their ministers and for them that are in power, for the welfare of the world, for peace therein, for the delay of the end. We meet together for the reading of the divine writings, if the character of the times compels us in any way to forewarning or reminder. However that may be, with the holy words we nourish our faith, lift up our hope, confirm our confidence, and no less make strong our discipline by impressing the precepts. At these meetings we have also exhortations, rebukes, and a Divine censorship. For judgement also is executed with much gravity, as before men who are sure that they are in the sight of God; and it is a notable foretaste of judgement to come if a man has so sinned as to be banished from the communion of our prayer and meeting and all holy intercourse. Our presidents are the approved elders, obtaining that honour not for a price, but by attested character; for indeed the things of God are not sold for a price. Even if there is a sort of common fund, it is not made up of money paid in fees, as for a worship by contract. Each of us puts in a trifle on the monthly day, or when he pleases; but only if he pleases, and only if he is able, for no man is obliged, but contributes of his own free will. These are as it were deposits of piety; for it is not paid out thence for feasts and drinkings and thankless eating-houses, but for feeding and burying the needy, for boys and girls deprived of means and parents, for old folk now confined to the house: also for them that are shipwrecked, for any who are in the mines, and for any who in the islands or in the prisons, if only it be for the cause of God's people, become the nurslings of their own confession.

XXXVIII A.

DENIQUE ut a baptismate ingrediar, aquam adituri, ibidem, sed et aliquanto prius in ecclesia sub antistitis manu contestamur, nos renuntiare diabolo et pompae et angelis eius. Dehinc ter mergitamur amplius aliquid
5 respondentes quam dominus in evangelio determinavit. Inde suscepti, lactis et mellis concordiam praegustamus[1], exque ea die lavacro quotidiano per totam hebdomadem abstinemus. Eucharistiae sacramentum, et in tempore victus et omnibus mandatum a domino, etiam antelucanis
10 coetibus, nec de aliorum manu quam praesidentium sumimus. Oblationes pro defunctis, pro natalitiis, annua die facimus. Die dominico ieiunium nefas ducimus vel geniculis adorare. Eadem immunitate a die Paschae in Pentecosten usque gaudemus. Calicis aut panis etiam
15 nostri aliquid decuti in terram anxie patimur.

Ad omnem progressum atque promotum, ad omnem aditum et exitum, ad vestitum et calceatum, ad lavacra, ad mensas, ad lumina, ad cubilia, ad sedilia, quaecunque nos conversatio exercet, frontem crucis signaculo terimus.

20 Harum et aliarum ejusmodi disciplinarum si legem expostules scripturarum, nullam invenies; traditio tibi praetendetur auctrix, consuetudo confirmatrix, et fides observatrix.

ID. *De Corona Mil.* 3, 4.

XXXIX.

IPSAE denique haereses a philosophia subornantur. Inde
25 aeones et formae, nescio quae, et trinitas hominis apud Valentinum: Platonicus fuerat. Inde Marcionis deus melior de tranquillitate: a Stoicis venerat. Et uti anima interire dicatur, ab Epicureis observatur; et ut carnis restitutio negetur, de una omnium philosophorum schola

---

[1] *Apol.* 9. Non prius discumbitur, quam oratio ad deum praegustetur.

Non-scriptural Customs.

[For customs not prescribed in Scripture, but sanctioned by usage,] I will begin with baptism. Before we enter the water we make our protest, both on the spot and a little before in the church and under the bishop's hand, that we renounce the devil, his pomp and his angels. Thereupon we are thrice immersed, making a somewhat longer answer than the Lord prescribed in the Gospel. Thence we are received (by sponsors), and taste first of all a mixture of milk and honey; and from that day we abstain from our daily bath for a whole week. The sacrament also of Thanksgiving, which the Lord delivered at a meal time and to all of us, we receive in meetings before daybreak, but from the hand of none but our presidents. On the proper day of the year we make our offerings for the dead and for the 'birthdays' (of martyrs). On the Lord's day we count it unlawful to fast or to worship on our knees; and in the same privilege we rejoice from Easter Day till Pentecost. Of this cup, aye, and of this bread of ours, we are careful that none be cast on the ground. At every step and advance, in all our going out and coming in, when we dress and put on our shoes, at the bath and at the table, when we light our lamps, or go to bed, or take a seat, in every action of our lives, we sign our forehead with the cross. For these and the like observances, if you ask for the Scripture rule, there is none for you to read. You will be told, Tradition has originated, Custom has sanctioned, Loyalty observes them.

R.

Philosophy the Mother of Heresy.

FINALLY the heresies themselves are equipped by philosophy. Thence came the aeons, the—I know not what—infinite forms, and the trinity of man taught by Valentinus: he had been a Platonist. Thence came Marcion's better god, the better for his tranquillity: *he* had come from the Stoics. The statement that the soul dies is a note taken from the Epicureans, and the denial of the restoration of the flesh is assumed from the entire school of all the philosophers.

sumitur; et ubi materia cum deo aequatur, Zenonis disciplina est; et ubi aliquid de igneo deo allegatur, Heraclitus intervenit. Eaedem materiae apud haereticos et philosophos volutantur; iidem retractatus implicantur: unde malum, et quare? et unde homo, et quomodo? et quod proxime Valentinus proposuit: unde deus? scilicet de enthymesi et ectromate. ID. *de Praescr.* 7.

XL.

(APOSTOLUS prohibet) haereticum post unam correptionem convenire, non post disputationem. Adeo interdixit disputationem ... quoniam nihil proficiat congressio scripturarum, nisi plane aut stomachi quis ineat eversionem aut cerebri ...

Ergo non ad scripturas provocandum est. ... Nunc solum disputandum est, quibus competat fides ipsa cujus sint scripturae, a quo, per quos et quando, et quibus sit tradita disciplina, qua fiunt Christiani. ...

Christus Jesus ... undecim ... jussit ire et docere nationes ... statim igitur apostoli ... ecclesias apud unamquamque civitatem condiderunt, a quibus traducem fidei et semina doctrinae ceterae exinde ecclesiae mutuatae sunt et quotidie mutuantur, ut ecclesiae fiant. Ac per hoc et ipsae apostolicae deputabuntur ut soboles apostolicarum ecclesiarum. Omne genus ad originem suam censeatur necesse est. Itaque tot ac tantae ecclesiae una est illa ab apostolis prima, ex qua omnes. Sic omnes primae et omnes apostolicae, dum una omnes probant unitate communicatio pacis et appellatio fraternitatis et contesseratio hospitalitatis, quae iura non alia ratio regit, quam eiusdem sacramenti una traditio.

Where matter is made equal to God, it is the teaching of Zeno; and where anything is stated about a god of fire, it is Heraclitus who comes in. We have the same subjects repeatedly discussed by heretics and philosophers with the same complicated reconsiderations. Whence is evil, and why? Whence is man, and how? and—the very latest problem of Valentinus—whence is God? From *enthymesis* and *ectroma,* no doubt.

The Argument of Tertullian from Tradition.

IT is after a single rebuke, not after a discussion, that the Apostle forbids us to converse with a heretic. Discussion then he has forbidden . . . for (amongst other reasons) a debate over Scripture plainly does no good, unless it be to disturb either temper or brains. . . . Therefore we must not appeal to Scripture. . . . The only question we just now have to discuss is, With whom is that very faith to which Scripture belongs? From whom, through whom, when and to whom was the rule delivered by which men become Christians?

Christ Jesus . . . commanded the Eleven to go and teach the nations . . . straightway therefore the Apostles . . . founded in the several cities Churches from which the rest have thenceforth borrowed and daily borrow the shoot of faith and seeds of teaching, in order that they may become Churches; and it is from this fact that they too will be counted Apostolic, as the offspring of Apostolic Churches. Every kind of thing must be estimated by reference back to its origin. Therefore the Churches, whatever their size or number, form but the single primitive Church which comes from the Apostles, and its offspring are they all. Thus they are all primitive and all Apostolic, since they are all approved together by their union in the communion of peace, the title of brotherhood, and the interchange of hospitality—rights which are governed by no other rule than the single tradition of the same mystery in all. Here then we enter

Hinc igitur dirigimus praescriptionem, si dominus Iesus
Christus apostolos misit ad praedicandum, alios non esse
recipiendos praedicatores, quam quos Christus instituit.
... Si haec ita sunt, constat proinde omnem doctrinam,
quae cum illis ecclesiis apostolicis, matricibus et origina-
libus fidei, conspiret, veritati deputandam, id sine dubio
tenentem, quod ecclesiae ab apostolis, apostoli a Christo,
Christus a deo accepit; reliquam vero omnem doctrinam
de mendacio praeiudicandam, quae sapiat contra veritatem
ecclesiarum et apostolorum et Christi et dei.

Ibid. 16-21.

XLI.

Non omittam ipsius etiam conversationis haereticae
descriptionem, quam futilis, quam terrena, quam humana
sit, sine gravitate, sine auctoritate, sine disciplina, ut fidei
suae congruens. Inprimis quis catechumenus, quis fidelis,
incertum est; pariter adeunt, pariter audiunt, pariter orant,
etiam ethnici, si supervenerint; sanctum canibus et porcis
margaritas, licet non veras, iactabunt. Simplicitatem volunt
esse prostrationem disciplinae, cuius penes nos curam
lenocinium vocant. Pacem quoque passim cum omnibus
miscent. Nihil enim interest illis, licet diversa tractantibus,
dum ad unius veritatis expugnationem conspirent. Omnes
scientiam pollicentur. Ante sunt perfecti catechumeni,
quam edocti. Ipsae mulieres haereticae, quam procaces!
quae audeant docere, contendere, exorcismos agere, cura-
tiones repromittere, forsitan et tingere. Ordinationes
eorum temerariae, leves, inconstantes. Nunc neophytos
collocant, nunc saeculo obstrictos, nunc apostatas nostros,

our demurrer, that if the Lord Christ Jesus sent Apostles to preach, other than those whom Christ appointed ought not to be received as preachers. . . . If these things be so, it is in the same way plain that all teaching which agrees with those Apostolic Churches which are the wombs and origins of the faith must be ascribed to the truth, such teaching doubtless containing that which the Churches received from the Apostles, the Apostles from Christ, and Christ from God, whereas all other teaching must be summarily set down as false, since its tenor is opposed to the truth of the Churches and Apostles, and Christ and God.

Disorderly Worship of Heretics.

I WILL not leave out a description of the conduct also of the heretics—how empty it is, how earthly, how merely human, without sobriety, without impressiveness, without discipline—as suits their faith. In the first place, who is catechumen and who faithful, is doubtful. They all come up alike, all hear, all pray alike—heathens too, if they come in. That which is holy they will cast to the dogs, and their pearls (though they are but shams) to the swine. They will have it that simplicity means the destruction of discipline, and the care of it with us they call pandering. Peace, too, they mix up at random with all comers; for with all their differences of thinking they care for nothing so long as they are agreed on assailing the one single Truth. They all promise knowledge. The catechumens are perfect before they are fully taught. The very women of the heretics—how pert they are! For they have the impudence to teach to wrangle, to perform exorcisms, to undertake healings, possibly even to baptize. Their ordinations are random, capricious, unsettled. Sometimes they appoint novices, sometimes secular officials, sometimes renegades of ours, in order to bind them by vain-

ut gloria eos obligent, quia veritate non possunt. Nusquam facilius proficitur, quam in castris rebellium, ubi ipsum esse illic, promereri est. Itaque alius hodie episcopus, cras alius; hodie diaconus, qui cras lector; hodie presbyter, qui cras laicus; nam et laicis sacerdotalia munera iniungunt.

Ibid. 41.

XLII.

AUDIO etiam edictum esse propositum, et quidem peremptorium. Pontifex scilicet Maximus, episcopus episcoporum edicit: Ego et moechiae et fornicationis delicta poenitentia functis dimitto. O edictum, cui adscribi non poterit: Bonum factum! Et ubi proponetur liberalitas ista? Ibidem, opinor, in ipsis libidinum ianuis, sub ipsis libidinum titulis. Illic eiusmodi poenitentia promulganda est, ubi delinquentia ipsa versabitur. Illic legenda est venia, quo cum spe eius intrabitur. Sed hoc in ecclesia legitur, et in ecclesia pronuntiatur, et virgo est.

ID. *De Pudicit.* 1.

XLIII.

RECENSEAMUS nunc cetera pericula et vulnera, ut dixi, fidei ab apostolo provisa non carnis tantum verum etiam ipsius spiritus molestissima. ... Domino certe non potest pro disciplina satisfacere, habens in latere diaboli servum, procuratorem domini sui ad impedienda fidelium studia et officia: ut si statio facienda est, maritus de die condicat ad balneas; si ieiunia observanda sunt, maritus eadem die convivium exerceat; si procedendum erit, nunquam magis

glory, for by truth they cannot. Nowhere is promotion easier than in the camp of rebels, where the mere fact of being there is a merit. Thus one man is bishop to-day, another to-morrow: he is deacon to-day who to-morrow is reader, and he is presbyter to-day who to-morrow is layman; for even on laymen they impose priestly functions.

The Roman Bishop's Edict.

I HEAR also that an edict has been issued, and that a decisive one. The sovereign Pontiff forsooth, the bishop of bishops puts forth his edict. 'I,' says he, 'to them that have done penitence remit the sins of both adultery and fornication.' What an edict it is, to which we cannot add Well done! And where shall that gracious message be posted up? On the very spot, I suppose—on the very door-posts of lust, beneath the advertisements themselves of lust. *There* ought penitence of that sort to be published, where the offence itself shall dwell. *There* ought the pardon to be read, where men enter in the hope of it. But this—in the Church it is read, and in the Church pronounced, and—she is a virgin!

Inconveniences of a mixed Marriage.

LET us now recount the other dangers and wounds, as I said, of faith foreseen by the Apostle as not to the flesh only, but likewise even to the spirit very grievous. . . . Without doubt she cannot satisfy the Lord according to discipline, when she has at her side a servant of the devil, an agent of *his* lord to hinder the works and duties of believers; so that if there is a meeting to attend, her husband the first thing in the morning makes her an appointment for the baths; if there are fasts to be observed, her husband that same day gives a dinner; if she has to go out [on charitable errands], never is household

familiae occupatio obveniat. Quis enim sinat coniugem
suam visitandorum fratrum gratia vicatim aliena et quidem
pauperiora quaeque tuguria circuire? quis nocturnis con-
vocationibus, si ita oportuerit, a latere suo adimi libenter
feret? quis denique sollemnibus Paschae abnoctantem
securus sustinebit? quis ad convivium dominicum illud
quod infamant sine sua suspicione dimittet? quis in car-
cerem ad osculanda vincula martyris reptare patietur?
Iam vero alicui fratrum ad osculum convenire? aquam
sanctorum pedibus offerre? de cibo, de poculo invadere,
desiderare, in mente habere? si et peregre frater adveniat,
quod in aliena domo hospitium? si cui largiendum erit,
horreum, proma praeclusa sunt.... Moratur dei ancilla
cum laboribus alienis, et inter illos omnibus honoribus
daemonum, omnibus sollemnibus regum, incipiente anno,
incipiente mense, nidore thuris agitabitur. Et procedet
de ianua laureata et lucernata, ut de novo consistorio
libidinum publicarum; discumbet cum marito in sodalitiis,
saepe in popinis; et ministrabit nonnunquam iniquis, solita
quondam sanctis ministrare; et non hinc praeiudicium
damnationis suae agnoscet, eos observans, quos erat
iudicatura[1]?

Id. *Ad Uxorem*, ii. 3-6.

XLIV.

Nam iste primus ex Asia hoc genus perversitatis intulit
Romae, homo et alias inquietus, insuper de iactatione
martyrii inflatus ob solum et simplex et breve carceris
taedium, quando, etsi corpus suum tradidisset exurendum,

[1] 1 Cor. vi. 2.

business more in the way. For who would let his wife go
round from street to street to other men's houses, and
indeed to all the poorer cottages, for the sake of visiting
the brethren ? Who will willingly allow her to be taken
from his side for nocturnal meetings, if her duty be so ?
Who in short will bear without anxiety her absence all
night for the ceremonial of Easter ? Who will let her go
without suspicion of his own to that Lord's Supper which
they defame ? Who will suffer her to creep into a prison
to kiss a martyr's bonds ? or indeed to meet one of the
brethren for the kiss ? to offer water for the feet of the
saints ? to seize [for them] from her food or from her cup,
to long for them, to keep them in mind ? If a brother on
a journey come, what welcome is there for him in an alien
house ? If there is a case for liberality, the granary and
the larder are shut up.... The handmaid of God dwells
with alien labours, and amongst them she will be persecuted with the odour of incense at all the festivals of
demons, all the ceremonials of kings, the beginning of the
year, the beginning of the month. She will come forth
too from a laurelled gateway hung with lanterns as from
some new abode of public lusts. She will dine with her
husband in clubs, often in taverns, and sometimes she will
minister to the unjust, who was used to minister to saints ;
and will she not recognize in this a sentence that carries
her damnation, as she attends on those whom she was to
judge hereafter ?

The Misdeeds of Praxeas.

FOR Praxeas it was who first imported from Asia to
Rome this kind of perversity—a man in other ways unquiet,
and moreover puffed up with pride of confessorship merely
on the strength of a short annoyance of imprisonment
without further hardship; whereas even though he had
given his body to be burned, he would have gained

nihil profecisset, dilectionem dei non habens, cuius charismata quoque expugnavit. Nam idem tunc episcopum Romanum agnoscentem iam prophetias Montani, Priscae, Maximillae, et ex ea agnitione pacem ecclesiis Asiae et
Phrygiae inferentem, falsa de ipsis prophetis et ecclesiis eorum adseverando et praecessorum eius auctoritates defendendo coegit et literas pacis revocare iam emissas et a proposito recipiendorum charismatum concessare. Ita duo negotia diaboli Praxeas Romae procuravit, prophetiam expulit et haeresim intulit, paracletum fugavit et patrem crucifixit.

ID. *Adv. Prax.* 1.

XLV.

ITAQUE pro cuiusque personae conditione ac dispositione, etiam aetate, cunctatio baptismi utilior est, praecipue tamen circa parvulos. Quid enim necesse est, sponsores etiam periculo ingeri, qui et ipsi per mortalitatem destituere promissiones suas possunt et proventu malae indolis falli? Ait quidem dominus: Nolite illos prohibere ad me venire. Veniant ergo, dum adolescunt; veniant, dum discunt, dum quo veniant docentur; fiant Christiani, quum Christum nosse potuerint. Quid festinat innocens aetas ad remissionem peccatorum? Cautius agetur in secularibus, ut cui substantia terrena non creditur, divina credatur.

ID. *De Baptismo*, 18.

XLVI.

Τοιαῦτα ὁ γόης τολμήσας συνεστήσατο διδασκαλεῖον κατὰ τῆς ἐκκλησίας οὕτως διδάξας, καὶ πρῶτος τὰ πρὸς

nothing by it, not having the love of God, whose gifts too he has fought against. For he it was again, who when the then bishop of Rome was ready to recognize the prophecies of Montanus, Prisca and Maximilla, and in consequence of that recognition to give his peace to the Churches of Asia and Phrygia—he by making false statements about the prophets themselves and their Churches, and by urging the authority of the bishop's predecessors, obliged him to recall the letters of peace he had already sent out, and to give up his purpose of acknowledging the gifts. Thus Praxeas managed two of the devil's businesses in Rome: he drove out prophecy and brought in heresy; he put to flight the Comforter and crucified the Father.

Infant Baptism.

THEREFORE according to the circumstances and temper and even age of each is the delay of baptism more profitable, yet especially in the case of little children. For where is the need of involving sponsors also in danger? They too through mortality may fail to perform their promises, or may be deceived by the growth of an evil disposition. The Lord says, indeed, Forbid them not to come unto me. Let them come then when they are grown up; let them come when they have learned, when they are taught where they are coming; let them become Christians when they are able to know Christ. Why does an age which is innocent hasten to the remission of sins? There will be more caution used in worldly matters, so that one who is not trusted with earthly substance is trusted with divine.

Misdeeds of Callistus.

THE impostor had the impudence to adopt opinions of this kind, setting up a school against the Church, and

τὰς ἡδονὰς τοῖς ἀνθρώποις συγχωρεῖν ἐπενόησε, λέγων πᾶσιν ὑπ' αὐτοῦ ἀφίεσθαι ἀμαρτίας. ... οὗτος ἐδογμάτισεν ὅπως εἰ ἐπίσκοπος ἁμάρτοι τι, εἰ καὶ πρὸς θάνατον, μὴ δεῖν κατατίθεσθαι. ἐπὶ τούτου ἤρξαντο ἐπίσκοποι καὶ πρεσβύτεροι καὶ διάκονοι δίγαμοι καὶ τρίγαμοι καθίστασθαι εἰς κλήρους· εἰ δὲ καί τις ἐν κλήρῳ ὢν γαμοίη, μένειν τὸν τοιοῦτον ἐν τῷ κλήρῳ ὡς μὴ ἡμαρτηκότα. ... καὶ γὰρ καὶ γυναιξὶν ἐπέτρεψεν, †εἰ ἄνανδροι εἶεν καὶ ἡλικίᾳ γε ἐκκαίοιντο ἀναξίᾳ, ἢ ἑαυτῶν ἀξίαν μὴ βούλοιντο καθαιρεῖν διὰ τὸ νομίμως γαμηθῆναι†, ἔχειν ἕνα ὃν ἂν αἱρήσωνται σύγκοιτον, εἴτε οἰκέτην, εἴτε ἐλεύθερον, καὶ τοῦτον κρίνειν ἀντὶ ἀνδρὸς μὴ νόμῳ γεγαμημένην. ... καὶ ἐπὶ τούτοις τοῖς τολμήμασιν ἑαυτοὺς οἱ ἀπηρυθριασμένοι καθολικὴν ἐκκλησίαν ἀποκαλεῖν ἐπιχειροῦσι, καί τινες νομίζοντες εὖ πράττειν συντρέχουσιν αὐτοῖς. ἐπὶ τούτου πρώτως τετόλμηται δεύτερον αὐτοῖς βάπτισμα.

HIPPOLYTUS, *Ref. Omn. Haer.* ix. 12.[1]

XLVII.

Ἐν τούτῳ καὶ Ἀμβρόσιος τὰ τῆς Οὐαλεντίνου φρονῶν αἱρέσεως, πρὸς τῆς ὑπὸ Ὠριγένους πρεσβευομένης ἀληθείας ἐλεγχθείς, καὶ ὡς ἂν ὑπὸ φωτὸς καταυγασθεὶς τὴν διάνοιαν, τῷ τῆς ἐκκλησιαστικῆς ὀρθοδοξίας προστίθεται λόγῳ· καὶ ἄλλοι δὲ πλείους τῶν ἀπὸ παιδείας, τῆς περὶ τὸν Ὠριγένην φήμης πανταχόσε βοωμένης, ἦσαν ὡς αὐτόν, πεῖραν τῆς ἐν τοῖς ἱεροῖς λόγοις ἱκανότητος τἀνδρὸς ληψόμενοι· μυρίοι δὲ τῶν αἱρετικῶν, φιλοσόφων τε τῶν μάλιστα ἐπιφανῶν οὐκ ὀλίγοι, διὰ σπουδῆς αὐτῷ προσεῖχον, πρὸς τοῖς θείοις καὶ τὰ τῆς ἔξωθεν φιλοσοφίας πρὸς αὐτοῦ παιδευόμενοι. εἰσῆγέ τε γὰρ ὅσους εὐφυῶς ἔχοντας ἑώρα καὶ ἐπὶ τὰ φιλόσοφα μαθήματα, γεωμετρίαν καὶ ἀριθμητικὴν καὶ τὰ ἄλλα προπαιδεύματα παρα-

[1] *Liberian Catalogue.* Eo tempora Pontianus episcopus et Yppolitus presbyter exoles sunt deportati in Sardinia, in insula nociva, Severo et Quintiano cons. In eadem insula discinctus est iiii Kl. Octobr, et loco eius ordinatus est Antheros xi Kl. Dec. cons. ss.

teaching accordingly; and he was the first who found out
the device of yielding to men in their sensual pleasures by
saying that all men had their sins forgiven by him. . . . He
it was who laid it down, that if a bishop committed a sin,
though it were a sin unto death, he ought not to be 5
deposed. In his time began twice married and thrice
married men to be appointed to clerical office as bishops,
elders and deacons; and if one married who was in the
clergy, such a one remained in the clergy as if he had not
sinned [quoting Rom. xiv. 4, Matt. xiii. 29, and the clean 10
and unclean in the ark]. For he even allowed women, if
they were unmarried and inflamed with love unworthy of
their age, or did not wish to forfeit their rank for the
sake of a legal marriage, to have one whomsoever they
chose for a companion, whether he were slave or free, and 15
though not legally married to him to count him for a
husband. . . . And on the strength of these audacious
doings the shameless fellows endeavour to call themselves
a Catholic Church; and some thinking they are faring well
agree with them. In his time a second baptism was first 20
impudently attempted by them.

Origen's conception of education.

ABOUT this time Ambrose, who held the heresy of
Valentinus, was convinced by Origen's presentation of the
truth, and, as if his mind were illumined by light, he
accepted the orthodox doctrine of the Church. Many other 25
lovers of learning also, drawn by the fame of Origen,
which resounded everywhere, came to him to make trial
of his skill in sacred literature. And a great many heretics
and not a few of the most distinguished philosophers
studied under him diligently, receiving instruction from 30
him not only in divine things, but also in secular philosophy. For when he perceived that any persons had
superior intelligence he instructed them also in philosophic studies—in geometry, arithmetic and other pre-

διδούς, εἴς τε τὰς αἱρέσεις τὰς παρὰ τοῖς φιλοσόφοις προάγων, καὶ τὰ παρὰ τούτοις συγγράμματα διηγούμενος, ὑπομνηματιζόμενός τε καὶ θεωρῶν εἰς ἕκαστα, ὥστε μέγαν καὶ παρ' αὐτοῖς Ἕλλησι φιλόσοφον τὸν ἄνδρα κηρύτ-
5 τεσθαι. πολλοὺς δὲ καὶ τῶν ἰδιωτικωτέρων ἐνῆγεν ἐπὶ τὰ ἐγκύκλια γράμματα, οὐ μικρὰν αὐτοῖς ἔσεσθαι φάσκων ἐξ ἐκείνων ἐπιτηδειότητα εἰς τὴν τῶν θείων γραφῶν θεωρίαν τε καὶ παρασκευήν. ὅθεν μάλιστα καὶ ἑαυτῷ ἀναγκαίαν ἡγήσατο τὴν περὶ τὰ κοσμικὰ καὶ φιλόσοφα
10 μαθήματα ἄσκησιν.

EUSEBIUS, *Hist. Eccles.* vi. 18.

XLVIII.

Ἐπεὶ οὖν συνέστηκεν ἡ γραφὴ καὶ αὐτὴ οἱονεὶ ἐκ σώματος μὲν τοῦ βλεπομένου, ψυχῆς δὲ τῆς ἐν αὐτῷ νοουμένης καὶ καταλαμβανομένης, καὶ πνεύματος τοῦ κατὰ τὰ ὑποδείγματα καὶ σκιὰν τῶν ἐπουρανίων· φέρε, ἐπι-
15 καλεσάμενοι τὸν ποιήσαντα τῇ γραφῇ σῶμα καὶ ψυχὴν καὶ πνεῦμα, σῶμα μὲν τοῖς πρὸ ἡμῶν, ψυχὴν δὲ ἡμῖν, πνεῦμα δὲ τοῖς ἐν τῷ μέλλοντι αἰῶνι κληρονομήσουσι ζωὴν αἰώνιον καὶ μέλλουσιν ἥκειν ἐπὶ τὰ ἐπουράνια καὶ ἀληθινὰ τοῦ νόμου, ἐρευνήσωμεν οὐ τὸ γράμμα ἀλλὰ τὴν
20 ψυχὴν ἐπὶ τοῦ παρόντος· εἰ δὲ οἷοί τέ ἐσμεν, ἀναβησόμεθα καὶ ἐπὶ τὸ πνεῦμα, κατὰ τὸν λόγον τὸν περὶ τῶν ἀναγνωσθεισῶν θυσιῶν.

ORIGEN, *In Lev. Hom.* v (*Philocalia*, 1, *ad fin.*).

XLIX.

Ἑξῆς δὲ τούτοις ὁ Κέλσος ὑπιδόμενος τὰ ἐπιδειχθησόμενα ὑπὸ τοῦ Ἰησοῦ γεγενημένα μεγάλα, περὶ ὧν ὀλίγα
25 ἀπὸ πολλῶν εἰρήκαμεν· προσποιεῖται συγχωρεῖν ἀληθῆ εἶναι, ὅσα περὶ θεραπειῶν, ἢ ἀναστάσεως, ἢ περὶ ἄρτων

paratory studies—and then advanced to the systems of
the philosophers and explained their writings. And he
made observations and comments upon each of them, so that
he became celebrated as a great philosopher even among
the Greeks themselves. And he instructed many of the
less learned in the common school studies, saying that
these would be no small help to them in the study and
understanding of the Divine Scriptures. On this account
he considered it especially necessary for himself to be
skilled in secular and philosophic learning.

N. L.

The Letter and the Spirit.

SINCE then Scripture itself also consists as it were of
a visible body, and of the soul in it that is perceived and
understood, and of the spirit which is according to the
patterns and shadow of the heavenly things—come, let us
call on Him who made for Scripture body and soul and
spirit, a body for them that came before us, a soul for us,
and a spirit for them that in the age to come shall inherit
life eternal, and shall attain to the heavenly and true things
of the law; and so let us for the present search not the
letter but the soul. And if we are able, we shall ascend
also to the spirit, in our account of the sacrifices whereof
we have just read.

The Argument from our Lord's Miracles.

IN the next place Celsus, suspecting that we shall put
forward the mighty works of Jesus, of which we have
already spoken very slightly, professes to grant that they
may be true—all that is recorded of healings, or of a

ὀλίγων θρεψάντων πολλοὺς ἀναγέγραπται, ἀφ' ὧν λείψανα
πολλὰ καταλέλειπται, ἢ ὅσα ἄλλα οἴεται τερατευσαμένους
τοὺς μαθητὰς ἱστορηκέναι, καὶ ἐπιφέρει αὐτοῖς· ' Φέρε
πιστεύσωμεν εἶναί σοι ταῦτ' εἰργασμένα.' καὶ εὐθέως
5 κοινοποιεῖ αὐτὰ πρὸς τὰ ἔργα τῶν γοήτων, ὡς ὑπισχνουμένων θαυμασιώτερα, καὶ πρὸς τὰ ὑπὸ τῶν μαθόντων ἀπὸ
Αἰγυπτίων ἐπιτελούμενα, ἐν μέσαις ἀγοραῖς ὀλίγων
ὀβολῶν ἀποδομένων τὰ σεμνὰ μαθήματα, καὶ δαίμονας
ἀπὸ ἀνθρώπων ἐξελαυνόντων, καὶ νόσους ἀποφυσώντων,
10 καὶ ψυχὰς ἡρώων ἀνακαλούντων, δεῖπνά τε πολυτελῆ, καὶ
τραπέζας, καὶ πέμματα, καὶ ὄψα τὰ οὐκ ὄντα δεικνύντων,
καὶ ὡς ζῷα κινούντων οὐκ ἀληθῶς ὄντα ζῷα, ἀλλὰ μέχρι
φαντασίας φαινόμενα τοιαῦτα. καί φησιν· 'Ἆρ' ἐπεὶ
ταῦτα ποιοῦσιν ἐκεῖνοι, δεήσει ἡμᾶς αὐτοὺς ἡγεῖσθαι
15 υἱοὺς εἶναι θεοῦ; ἢ λεκτέον αὐτὰ ἐπιτηδεύματα εἶναι
ἀνθρώπων πονηρῶν καὶ κακοδαιμόνων;' ID. c. Cels. i. 68.

L.

Τίς τοῦτο εἶδε; γυνὴ πάροιστρος, ὥς φατε, καὶ εἴ τις
ἄλλος τῶν ἐκ τῆς αὐτῆς γοητείας, ἤτοι κατά τινα διάθεσιν
ὀνειρώξας, ἢ κατὰ τὴν αὐτοῦ βούλησιν δόξῃ πεπλανημένῃ
10 φαντασιωθείς, ὅπερ δὴ μυρίοις συμβέβηκεν· ἤ, ὅπερ
μᾶλλον, ἐκπλῆξαι τοὺς λοιποὺς τῇ τερατείᾳ ταύτῃ θελήσας,
καὶ διὰ τοῦ τοιούτου ψεύσματος ἀφορμὴν ἄλλοις ἀγύρταις
παρασχεῖν. *Ibid.* ii. 55.

LI.

Ψεῦδος δὲ καὶ τὸ ' μόνους ἠλιθίους καὶ ἀγεννεῖς καὶ
25 ἀναισθήτους καὶ ἀνδράποδα καὶ γύναια καὶ παιδάρια
πείθειν ἐθέλειν τοὺς διδάσκοντας τὸν θεῖον λόγον.' καὶ
τούτους μὲν γὰρ καλεῖ ὁ λόγος, ἵνα αὐτοὺς βελτιώσῃ·

resurrection, or of the many who fed on a few loaves and left of them many fragments, and all the rest of the stories in telling which he thinks the disciples were romancing—and adds, 'Well, suppose we believe that you really did them.' Then straightway he puts them on a level with the works of the jugglers, on the ground that their professions are still more marvellous, and with the performances of those who have learned from the Egyptians, who sell their venerated arts for a few pence in the open market-place, and cast out demons from men, and puff away diseases, and call up souls of heroes, and exhibit costly dinners with tables and cakes and dainties non-existent, and set in motion as living animals lifeless things which have only the appearance of animals. Then he says, 'Since the jugglers do these things, must we needs think them sons of God, or shall we say that these are practices of wicked wretches?'

Celsus on the Lord's Resurrection.

WHO saw this? A frantic woman, as you say, and possibly some other in the same imposture, either dreaming it through some personal peculiarity, or by a wandering imagination shaping it according to his own will, which is just what has happened in so many cases; or, what is more likely, desiring to scare the rest with this quackery, and by a falsehood of this sort to give an opening to other impostors.

The Gospel not specially addressed to Fools.

THAT again is false, that it is 'only simpletons and low people, and stupid, and slaves, and womenkind, and children,' whom the teachers of the Divine word desire to persuade. For though the word does call these, that

καλεῖ δὲ καὶ τοὺς πολλῷ τούτων διαφέροντας· ἐπεὶ σωτήρ
ἐστι πάντων ἀνθρώπων ὁ Χριστός, καὶ μάλιστα πιστῶν,
εἴτε συνετῶν εἴτε καὶ ἁπλουστέρων.
Ibid. iii. 49.

LI A.

Ἀποδεικνύντες δὲ ὡς ἐν ἐπιτομῇ περὶ τῆς θεότητος
5 Ἰησοῦ, καὶ χρώμενοι τοῖς περὶ αὐτοῦ λόγοις προφητικοῖς,
συναποδείκνυμεν θεοπνεύστους εἶναι τὰς προφητευούσας
περὶ αὐτοῦ γραφάς· καὶ τὰ καταγγέλλοντα τὴν ἐπι-
δημίαν αὐτοῦ γράμματα καὶ διδασκαλίαν μετὰ πάσης
δυνάμεως καὶ ἐξουσίας εἰρημένα, καὶ διὰ τοῦτο τῆς
10 ἀπὸ τῶν ἐθνῶν ἐκλογῆς κεκρατηκότα. Λεκτέον δὲ
ὅτι τὸ τῶν προφητικῶν λόγων ἔνθεον, καὶ τὸ πνευ-
ματικὸν τοῦ Μωσέως νόμου, ἔλαμψεν ἐπιδημήσαντος
Ἰησοῦ. ἐναργῆ γὰρ παραδείγματα περὶ τοῦ θεοπνεύστους εἶναι τὰς παλαιὰς γραφὰς πρὸ τῆς ἐπιδημίας
15 τοῦ Χριστοῦ παραστῆσαι οὐ πάνυ δυνατὸν ἦν· ἀλλ᾿ ἡ
Ἰησοῦ ἐπιδημία δυναμένους ὑποπτεύεσθαι τὸν νόμον καὶ
τοὺς προφήτας ὡς οὐ θεῖα εἰς τοὐμφανὲς ἤγαγεν ὡς
οὐρανίῳ χάριτι ἀναγεγραμμένα. ὁ δὲ μετ᾿ ἐπιμελείας καὶ
προσοχῆς ἐντυγχάνων τοῖς προφητικοῖς λόγοις, παθὼν ἐξ
20 αὐτοῦ τοῦ ἀναγινώσκειν ἴχνος ἐνθουσιασμοῦ, δι᾿ ὧν πάσχει
πεισθήσεται οὐκ ἀνθρώπων εἶναι συγγράμματα τοὺς πεπι-
στευμένους ἡμῖν εἶναι θεοῦ λόγους. καὶ τὸ ἐνυπάρχον δὲ
φῶς τῷ Μωσέως νόμῳ, καλύμματι ἐναποκεκρυμμένον,
συνέλαμψε τῇ Ἰησοῦ ἐπιδημίᾳ, περιαιρεθέντος τοῦ καλύμ-
25 ματος, καὶ τῶν ἀγαθῶν κατὰ βραχὺ εἰς γνῶσιν ἐρχομένων,
ὧν σκιὰν εἶχε τὸ γράμμα.

ORIGEN, *De Principiis*, iv. 6 = *Philoc.* p. 12.

LI B.

Τίς γοῦν νοῦν ἔχων οἰήσεται πρώτην καὶ δευτέραν καὶ
τρίτην ἡμέραν, ἑσπέραν τε καὶ πρωΐαν, χωρὶς ἡλίου γε-

it may make them better, yet it also calls those who are much better than these, since the Christ is the Saviour of all men, and specially of such as believe, whether prudent or simple.

The true ground of Old Testament Inspiration.

IN this our Demonstration in brief of the divinity of Jesus, and in our use of the words of the Prophets concerning Him, we are making simultaneous demonstration of the inspiration of those scriptures which prophesy about Him, and proving the literature which proclaims His coming to be an utterance of full power and authority, which for that reason has laid firm hold of the elect of the Gentiles. Indeed, we may say that the inspired character of the prophetic writings and the spirituality of the law of Moses shone out when Jesus came. Clear proofs of the inspiration of the Old Testament could not well be given before the Christ had come. Till then the law and the prophets were open to a suspicion of not being truly divine: it was the coming of Jesus that set them in a plain light as records made by the grace of heaven. He who with diligent attention reads the words of the prophets will from his very reading experience a trace and vestige of inspiration in himself, and this personal experience will convince him that those are no compilations of men, which we are firmly persuaded are the words of God. The light, too, that was always there in the Mosaic law, though covered with a vail, shone out simultaneously with the coming of Jesus, when the vail was taken away and the good things came little by little into view, those good things whose shadow was found in the letter.

R.

The Parabolic Element in Scripture Narratives.

WHAT intelligent person would fancy, for instance, that a first, second, and third day, evening and morning, took

γονέναι καὶ σελήνης καὶ ἀστέρων; τὴν δὲ οἱονεὶ πρώτην καὶ χωρὶς οὐρανοῦ; τίς δ᾽ οὕτως ἠλίθιος ὡς οἰηθῆναι τρόπον ἀνθρώπου γεωργοῦ τὸν θεὸν πεφυτευκέναι παράδεισον ἐν Ἐδὲμ κατὰ ἀνατολάς, καὶ ξύλον ζωῆς ἐν αὐτῷ
5 πεποιηκέναι ὁρατὸν καὶ αἰσθητόν, ὥστε διὰ τῶν σωματικῶν ὀδόντων γευσάμενον τοῦ καρποῦ τὸ ζῆν ἀναλαμβάνειν· καὶ πάλιν καλοῦ καὶ πονηροῦ μετέχειν τινὰ παρὰ τὸ μεμασῆσθαι τὸ ἀπὸ τοῦδε τοῦ ξύλου λαμβανόμενον; ἐὰν δὲ καὶ θεὸς τὸ δειλινὸν ἐν τῷ παραδείσῳ περιπατεῖν
10 λέγηται, καὶ ὁ Ἀδὰμ ὑπὸ τὸ ξύλον κρύπτεσθαι· οὐκ οἶμαι διστάξειν τινὰ περὶ τοῦ αὐτὰ τροπικῶς διὰ δοκούσης ἱστορίας καὶ οὐ σωματικῶς γεγενημένης, μηνύειν τινὰ μυστήρια. ἀλλὰ καὶ Κάιν ἐξερχόμενος ἀπὸ προσώπου τοῦ θεοῦ σαφῶς τοῖς ἐπιστήσασι φαίνεται κινεῖν τὸν
15 ἐντυγχάνοντα ζητεῖν πρόσωπον θεοῦ καὶ ἐξέρχεσθαί τινα ἀπ᾽ αὐτοῦ. καὶ τί δεῖ πλείω λέγειν, τῶν μὴ πάνυ ἀμβλέων μυρία ὅσα τοιαῦτα δυναμένων συναγαγεῖν, ἀναγεγραμμένα μὲν ὡς γεγονότα, οὐ γεγενημένα δὲ κατὰ τὴν λέξιν; ἀλλὰ καὶ τὰ εὐαγγέλια δὲ τοῦ αὐτοῦ εἴδους τῶν
20 λόγων πεπλήρωται· εἰς ὑψηλὸν ὄρος τὸν Ἰησοῦν ἀναβιβάζοντος τοῦ διαβόλου, ἵν᾽ ἐκεῖθεν αὐτῷ δείξῃ τοῦ παντὸς κόσμου τὰς βασιλείας καὶ τὴν δόξαν αὐτῶν. τίς γὰρ οὐκ ἂν τῶν μὴ παρέργως ἀναγινωσκόντων τὰ τοιαῦτα καταγινώσκοι τῶν οἰομένων τῷ τῆς σαρκὸς ὀφθαλμῷ,
25 δεηθέντι ὕψους ὑπὲρ τοῦ κατανοηθῆναι δύνασθαι τὰ κατωτέρω καὶ ὑποκείμενα, ἑωρᾶσθαι τὴν Περσῶν καὶ Σκυθῶν καὶ Ἰνδῶν καὶ Παρθυαίων βασιλείαν, καὶ ὡς δοξάζονται παρὰ ἀνθρώποις οἱ βασιλεύοντες; παραπλησίως δὲ τούτοις καὶ ἄλλα μυρία ἀπὸ τῶν εὐαγγελίων ἔνεστι τὸν
30 ἀκριβοῦντα τηρῆσαι, ὑπὲρ τοῦ συγκαταθέσθαι συνυφαίνεσθαι ταῖς κατὰ τὸ ῥητὸν γεγενημέναις ἱστορίαις ἕτερα μὴ συμβεβηκότα.

ID. *De Principiis*, iv. 16 = *Philoc.* p. 24

place without sun, moon, and stars; and the first, as we call it, without even a heaven? Who would be so childish as to suppose that God after the manner of a human gardener planted a garden in Eden towards the east, and made therein a tree, visible and sensible, so that one could get the power of living by the bodily eating of its fruit with the teeth; or again, could partake of good and evil by feeding on what came from that other tree? If God is said to walk at eventide in the garden, and Adam to hide himself under the tree, I fancy that no one will question that these statements are figurative, declaring mysterious truths by the means of a seeming history, not one that took place in a bodily form. And Cain's going forth from the presence of God, as is plain and clear to attentive minds, stirs the reader to look for the meaning of the presence of God, and of any one's going forth from it. What need of more, when all but the dullest eyes can gather innumerable instances, in which things are recorded as having happened which did not take place in the literal sense? Nay, even the Gospels are full of sayings of the same class: as when the devil takes Jesus up into a high mountain, to show him from thence the kingdoms of the whole world and the glory of them. Who but a careless reader of such words would fail to condemn those who think that by the eye of flesh, which needed a height to bring into view what lay far down beneath, the kingdoms of Persians, and Scythians, and Indians, and Parthians, were seen, and the glory men give to their rulers? Countless cases such as this the accurate reader is able to observe, to make him agree that with the histories which literally took place other things are interwoven which did not actually happen.

LII.

Οὐκοῦν ἐγκαταλείπεται θείᾳ κρίσει ὁ ἐγκαταλειπόμενος, καὶ μακροθυμεῖ ἐπί τινας τῶν ἁμαρτανόντων ὁ Θεὸς οὐκ ἀλόγως, ἀλλ' ὡς αὐτοῖς συνοίσοντος ὡς πρὸς τὴν ἀθανασίαν τῆς ψυχῆς καὶ τὸν ἄπειρον αἰῶνα τοῦ μὴ ταχὺ
5 συνεργηθῆναι εἰς σωτηρίαν, ἀλλὰ βράδιον ἐπὶ ταύτην ἀχθῆναι μετὰ τὸ πειραθῆναι πολλῶν κακῶν. ὥσπερ γάρ τινα καὶ ἰατροὶ δυνάμενοι τάχιον ἰάσασθαι, ὅταν ἐγκεκρυμμένον ἰὸν ὑπονοῶσιν ὑπάρχειν περὶ τὰ σώματα, τὸ ἐναντίον τῷ ἰάσασθαι ἐργάζονται, διὰ τὸ ἰᾶσθαι βούλεσθαι ἀσφαλέ-
10 στερον τοῦτο ποιοῦντες· ἡγούμενοι κρεῖττον εἶναι πολλῷ χρόνῳ παρακατασχεῖν τινα ἐν τῷ φλεγμαίνειν καὶ κάμνειν ὑπὲρ τοῦ βεβαιότερον αὐτὸν τὴν ὑγείαν ἀπολαβεῖν, ἤπερ τάχιον μὲν ῥῶσαι δοκεῖν ὕστερον δὲ ἀναδῦναι καὶ πρόσκαιρον γενέσθαι τὴν ταχυτέραν ἴασιν·· τὸν αὐτὸν τρόπον
15 καὶ ὁ Θεός, γινώσκων τὰ κρύφια τῆς καρδίας καὶ προγινώσκων τὰ μέλλοντα, διὰ τῆς μακροθυμίας ἐπιτρέπει τάχα καὶ διὰ τῶν ἔξωθεν συμβαινόντων ἐφελκόμενος τὸ ἐν κρυπτῷ κακόν, ὑπὲρ τοῦ καθᾶραι τὸν δι' ἀμέλειαν τὰ σπέρματα τῆς ἁμαρτίας κεχωρηκότα, ἵνα εἰς ἐπιπολὴν
20 ἐλθόντα αὐτά τις ἐμέσας, εἰ καὶ ἐπὶ πλεῖον ἐν κακοῖς γεγένηται, ὕστερον δυνηθῇ καθαρσίυ τυχὼν τοῦ μετὰ τὴν κακίαν ἀναστοιχειωθῆναι. Θεὸς γὰρ οἰκονομεῖ τὰς ψυχὰς οὐχ ὡς πρὸς τὴν φέρ' εἰπεῖν πεντηκονταετίαν τῆς ἐνθάδε ζωῆς, ἀλλ' ὡς πρὸς τὸν ἀπέραντον αἰῶνα·
25 ἄφθαρτον γὰρ φύσιν πεποίηκε τὴν νοερὰν καὶ αὐτῷ συγγενῆ, καὶ οὐκ ἀποκλείεται ὥσπερ ἐπὶ τῆς ἐνταῦθα ζωῆς ἡ λογικὴ ψυχὴ τῆς θεραπείας.

ID. *De Principiis*, iii. 13.

The Method of God's dealing with Sinners.

HE therefore that is left is left to the divine judgement; and God is long-suffering towards certain sinners, not unreasonably, but with intent to profit them, with a view to the immortality of the soul and the unending age, that they be not quickly brought into salvation, but led to it more slowly, after they have had trial of many evils. For even as physicians (though able to heal a man more quickly), when they suspect that there is hidden poison anywhere in the body, do the reverse of healing, and this they do because they wish to heal the more surely; counting it better to keep a man for a long time in inflammation and sickness that he may the more certainly recover his health, than that he should seem to gain strength more quickly and afterward fall back again, so that the quicker healing is but for a time; in the same way God also, knowing the secret things of the heart and foreknowing the things to come, through His long-suffering permits [sins], peradventure by means of outside events drawing together the evil that is in secret, for the sake of cleansing him who by reason of carelessness has received the seeds of sin, to the end that when they have come to the surface a man may spue them out, and even if he have been deep in wickednesses, may afterward be able to obtain cleansing after his wickedness and be renewed. For God disposes souls not as for say the fifty years of life on earth, but as for the unending age; for He has made the intelligent nature incorruptible and akin to Himself, and the rational soul is not shut out from cure as in this present life.

LIII.

Τῆς δὲ μοχθηρίας τῶν Ἰουδαϊκῶν γραφῶν οὐκ ἀπόστασιν, λύσιν δέ τινες εὑρεῖν προθυμηθέντες, ἐπ' ἐξηγήσεις ἐτράποντο ἀσυγκλώστους καὶ ἀναρμόστους τοῖς γεγραμμένοις, οὐκ ἀπολογίαν μᾶλλον ὑπὲρ τῶν ὀθνείων, παραδοχὴν δὲ καὶ ἔπαινον τοῖς οἰκείοις φερούσας. αἰνίγματα γὰρ τὰ φανερῶς παρὰ Μωϋσεῖ λεγόμενα εἶναι κομπάσαντες, καὶ ἐπιθειάσαντες ὡς θεσπίσματα πλήρη κρυφίων μυστηρίων, διά τε τοῦ τύφου τὸ κριτικὸν τῆς ψυχῆς καταγοητεύσαντες, ἐπάγουσιν ἐξηγήσεις.

EUSEBIUS, *Hist. Eccles.* vi. 19.

LIV.

Ἔτι πρὸς τούτοις περὶ τῆς πρὸς Ἑβραίους ἐπιστολῆς ἐν ταῖς εἰς αὐτὴν ὁμιλίαις ταῦτα διαλαμβάνει·

Ὅτι ὁ χαρακτὴρ τῆς λέξεως τῆς πρὸς Ἑβραίους ἐπιγεγραμμένης ἐπιστολῆς οὐκ ἔχει τὸ ἐν λόγῳ ἰδιωτικὸν τοῦ ἀποστόλου, ὁμολογήσαντος ἑαυτὸν 'ἰδιώτην εἶναι τῷ λόγῳ,' τουτέστι τῇ φράσει, ἀλλὰ ἐστὶν ἡ ἐπιστολὴ συνθέσει τῆς λέξεως Ἑλληνικωτέρα, πᾶς ὁ ἐπιστάμενος κρίνειν φράσεων διαφορὰς ὁμολογήσαι ἄν. πάλιν τε αὖ ὅτι τὰ νοήματα τῆς ἐπιστολῆς θαυμάσιά ἐστι, καὶ οὐ δεύτερα τῶν ἀποστολικῶν ὁμολογουμένων γραμμάτων, καὶ τοῦτο ἂν συμφήσαι εἶναι ἀληθὲς πᾶς ὁ προσέχων τῇ ἀναγνώσει τῇ ἀποστολικῇ.

Τούτοις μεθ' ἕτερα ἐπιφέρει λέγων·

Ἐγὼ δὲ ἀποφαινόμενος εἴποιμ' ἄν, ὅτι τὰ μὲν νοήματα τοῦ ἀποστόλου ἐστίν, ἡ δὲ φράσις καὶ ἡ σύνθεσις ἀπομνημονεύσαντός τινος τὰ ἀποστολικά, καὶ ὡσπερεὶ σχολιογραφήσαντός τινος τὰ εἰρημένα ὑπὸ τοῦ διδασκάλου. εἴ τις οὖν ἐκκλησία ἔχει ταύτην τὴν ἐπιστολὴν ὡς Παύλου, αὕτη εὐδοκιμείτω καὶ ἐπὶ τούτῳ. οὐ γὰρ εἰκῇ οἱ

Porphyry's Objections to Allegorical Interpretations.

SOME persons, desiring to find a solution of the baseness of the Jewish Scriptures rather than abandon them, have had recourse to interpretations inconsistent and incongruous with the words written, which explanations instead of supplying a defence of the foreigners, contain rather approval and praise of themselves. For they boast that the plain words of Moses are enigmas, and regard them as oracles full of hidden mysteries; and having bewildered the mental judgement by their folly, they foist interpretations on them.

N. L.

Origen on the Authorship of the Epistle to the Hebrews.

IN addition Origen makes the following statements in regard to the Epistle to the Hebrews in his Homilies upon it:

'That the verbal style of the epistle entitled "To the Hebrews," is not rude like the language of the Apostle, who acknowledged himself "rude in speech," that is, in expression; but that its diction is purer Greek, any one who has the power to discern differences of phraseology will acknowledge. Moreover, that the thoughts of the epistle are admirable, and not inferior to the acknowledged Apostolic writings, any one who carefully examines the Apostolic text will admit.'

Farther on he adds:

'If I gave my opinion, I should say that the thoughts are those of the Apostle, but the diction and phraseology are those of some one who remembered the Apostolic teachings, and wrote down at his leisure what had been said by his teacher. Therefore if any Church holds that this epistle is by Paul, let it be commended for this. For

ἀρχαῖοι ἄνδρες ὡς Παύλου αὐτὴν παραδεδώκασι. τίς δὲ ὁ γράψας τὴν ἐπιστολήν, τὸ μὲν ἀληθὲς Θεὸς οἶδεν. ἡ δὲ εἰς ἡμᾶς φθάσασα ἱστορία, ὑπό τινων μὲν λεγόντων, ὅτι Κλήμης ὁ γενόμενος ἐπίσκοπος Ῥωμαίων ἔγραψε τὴν ἐπιστολήν, ὑπό τινων δέ, ὅτι Λουκᾶς ὁ γράψας τὸ εὐαγγέλιον καὶ τὰς Πράξεις. *Ibid.* vi. 25.

LIV A.[1]

Τοῖς ἐπὶ τῶν θυσιῶν ᾑρη
μένοις κώ(μης) Ἀλεξ(άνδρου) Νήσου
παρὰ Αὐρηλ(ίου) Διογένου(ς) Σατα
βοῦτος ἀπὸ κώ(μης) Ἀλεξανδ(ρου)
Νήσου ὡς Lοβ οὐλ(ὴ)
ὀφρύι δεξ(ιᾷ) καὶ ἀεὶ
θύων τοῖς θεοῖς διετέ
λεσα καὶ νῦν ἐπὶ πα
ροῦσιν ὑμεῖν κατὰ
τὰ προστετα[γμέ]
να ἔθυσα καὶ ἔ[πιον] or ἔ[σπεισα]
[κά]ι τῶν ἱ[ε]ρείων [ἐγευ]
σάμην καὶ ἀξιῶ [ὑμᾶς]
ὑποσημιώσασθαι
Διευτυχεῖται
Αὐρήλ(ιος) [Δι]ογένης ἐπιδ[έδωκα]
Αὐρήλ(ιος) σ...ρ...
θύοντα Μυσ....
...νωνος σεσ[ημείωμαι?]
[Lά] Αὐτοκράτορο[ς] Καί[σαρος]
[Γα]ίου Μεσσίου Κ[ο]ίν[του]
[Τρ]αι[ανοῦ] Δε]κίου Εὐσ[εβοῦς]
[Ε]ὐτ[υχοῦς] Σε[β]α[σ]τοῦ
Ἐπ[ειφ]β...

[1] Brackets ( ) indicate contractions; clams [ ] supply defects in the MS.

not without reason have the ancients handed it down as Paul's. But who wrote the epistle, in truth God knows. The statement of some who have gone before us is that Clement, bishop of the Romans, wrote the epistle, and of others that Luke, the author of the Gospel and the Acts, wrote it.

N. L.

A Libellus of the Decian Persecution.

To the officers in charge of the sacrifices of the village of Alexander's Isle, from Aurelius Diogenes, the son of Satabus, of the village of Alexander's Isle, aged about 72, with a scar on his right eyebrow. I have always sacrificed to the gods; and now in your presence, according to the commands, I have sacrificed and made a libation and tasted of the victims; and I desire you to subscribe. Fare ye well.

I, Aurelius Diogenes, have delivered this . . .

I, Mys[. . . the son of . . .]non[1], [saw him] sacrificing, and have subscribed

In the first year of Imperator Caesar Caius Messius Quintus Trajanus Decius Pius Felix Augustus, on Epiphi 2 (=June 26, 250).

[1] The parts in clams will show the sort of matter which must have occupied the space.

LV.

Νοουατιανῷ μὲν γὰρ εὐλόγως ἀπεχθανόμεθα, διακό-
ψαντι τὴν ἐκκλησίαν, καί τινας τῶν ἀδελφῶν εἰς ἀσεβείας
καὶ βλασφημίας ἑλκύσαντι, καὶ περὶ τοῦ Θεοῦ διδασκαλίαν ἀνοσιωτάτην ἐπεισκυκλήσαντι, καὶ τὸν χρηστότατον
5 Κύριον ἡμῶν Ἰησοῦν Χριστὸν ὡς ἀνηλεῆ συκοφαντοῦντι,
ἐπὶ πᾶσι δὲ τούτοις τὸ λουτρὸν ἀθετοῦντι τὸ ἅγιον, καὶ
τήν τε πρὸ αὐτοῦ πίστιν καὶ ὁμολογίαν ἀνατρέποντι, τό
τε Πνεῦμα τὸ ἅγιον ἐξ αὐτῶν, εἰ καί τις ἦν ἐλπὶς τοῦ
παραμεῖναι ἢ καὶ ἐπανελθεῖν πρὸς αὐτούς, παντελῶς
10 φυγαδεύοντι. *Ibid.* vii. 8.

LVI.

QUAM unitatem tenere firmiter et vindicare debemus,
maxime episcopi qui in ecclesia praesidemus, ut episco-
patum quoque ipsum unum atque indivisum probemus.
Nemo fraternitatem mendacio fallat, nemo fidem veritatis
15 perfida prevaricatione corrumpat. Episcopatus unus est,
cuius a singulis in solidum pars tenetur. Ecclesia una est,
quae in multitudinem latius incremento fecunditatis ex-
tenditur, quomodo solis multi radii sed lumen unum, et
rami arboris multi sed robur unum tenaci radice fundatum,
20 et cum de fonte uno rivi plurimi defluunt, numerositas licet
diffusa videatur exundantis copiae largitate, unitas tamen
servatur in origine. . . . Qui reliquit ecclesiam Christi
alienus est, profanus est, hostis est. Habere non potest
Deum patrem qui ecclesiam non habet matrem. Si potuit
25 evadere quisquis extra arcam Noe fuit, et qui extra ecclesiam fuerit evadet. CYPRIAN, *De Cath. Eccles. Unitate,* 5.

Dionysius of Alexandria on Novatian.

FOR we hate Novatian with good reason, in that he divided the Church and led some of the brethren into impieties and blasphemies and introduced a most unholy doctrine concerning God, and slanders our most compassionate Lord Jesus Christ as merciless. In addition to all this he rejects the holy washing, and overthrows the faith and confession which go before it, and utterly banishes from them the Holy Spirit, if there were any hope at all that he would remain with them or return to them.

The Unity of the Church.

AND this unity we ought firmly to hold and assert, especially those of us that are bishops who preside in the Church, that we may also prove the episcopate itself to be one and undivided. Let no one deceive the brotherhood by a falsehood: let no one corrupt the faithfulness of the truth by perfidious prevarication. The episcopate is one, each part of which is held by each one for the whole. The Church also is one, which is spread abroad far and wide into a multitude by an increase of fruitfulness. As there are many rays of the sun, but one light; and many branches of a tree, but one strength based in its tenacious root; and since from one spring flow many streams, although the multiplicity seems diffused in the liberality of an overflowing abundance, yet the unity is still preserved in the source.... He who has left the Church of Christ is an alien, a profane person, an enemy. He cannot have God for his Father who has not the Church for his mother. If he could escape who was outside the ark of Noah, then he too will escape who was outside the Church.

A. N. L.

LVII.

Cyprianvs Presbyteris et Diaconibvs Romae Consistentibvs Fratribvs S.

Factis ad vos litteris, fratres carissimi, quibus actus noster expositus et disciplinae ac diligentiae quantulaecumque ratio declarata est, aliud accessit quod nec ipsum latere vos debuit. Nam frater noster Lucianus et ipse unus de confessoribus, fide quidem calidus et virtute robustus sed bene minus dominica lectione fundatus, quaedam conatus est inperite, iam pridem se auctorem constituens, ut manu eius scripti libelli gregatim multis nomine Pauli darentur, cum Mappalicus martyr cautus et verecundus, legis ac disciplinae memor, nullas contra evangelium litteras fecerit, sed tantum domestica pietate commotus matri et sorori suae quae lapsae fuerant mandaverit pacem dari, Saturninus quoque post tormenta adhuc in carcere constitutus nullas eiusmodi litteras emiserit. Lucianus vero non tantum Paulo adhuc in carcere posito nomine eius libellos manu sua scriptos passim dedit, sed et post eius excessum eadem facere sub eius nomine perseveravit, dicens hoc sibi ab illo esse mandatum et nesciens domino magis quam conservo obtemperandum. Aureli quoque adulescentis tormenta perpessi nomine libelli multi dati sunt eiusdem Luciani manu scripti, quod litteras ille non nosset. Cui rei ut aliquantum possit obsisti, litteras ad eos feci quas ad vos sub epistola priore transmisi, quibus petere et suadere non destiti ut dominicae legis et evangelii ratio teneretur.

On Church Discipline.

CYPRIAN to the presbyters and deacons abiding at Rome, his brethren, greeting. After the letters that I wrote to you, beloved brethren, in which what I had done was explained, and an account was given of my discipline and diligence, such as it is, there came another matter which, any more than the others, ought not to be concealed from you. For our brother Lucian, who himself also is one of the confessors, earnest indeed in faith, and robust in virtue, but little established in the reading of the Lord's word, has attempted certain things in a foolish way, having now for some time made himself the cause that certificates written by his hand were given indiscriminately to many persons in the name of Paulus; whereas Mappalicus the martyr, cautious and modest, mindful of the law and discipline, wrote no letters contrary to the Gospel, but only, moved with domestic affection for his mother and sister, who had fallen, commanded peace to be given to them. Saturninus, moreover, after his torture, still remaining in prison, sent out no letters of this kind. But Lucian, not only while Paulus was still in prison, gave everywhere in his name certificates written with his own hand, but even after his decease persisted in doing the same things under his name, saying that this had been commanded him by Paulus, ignorant that he must obey the Lord rather than his fellow-servant. In the name also of Aurelius, a young man who had undergone the torture, many certificates were given, written by the hand of the same Lucian, because Aurelius did not know how to write himself.

In order, in some measure, to put a stop to this practice, I wrote letters to them, which I have sent to you under the enclosure of the former letter, in which I did not cease to ask and persuade them that consideration might be had for the law of the Lord and the Gospel. But after I sent

Post quas litteras quasi moderatius aliquid et temperantius fieret, universorum confessorum nomine Lucianus epistolam scripsit, qua paene omne vinculum fidei et timor dei et mandatum domini et evangelii sanctitas et firmitas
5 solveretur. Scripsit enim omnium nomine universos eos pacem dedisse et hanc formam per me aliis episcopis innotescere velle, cuius epistolae exemplum ad vos transmisi.

ID. *Ep.* 27.

LVIII.

PROPTER quod [Num. xvi. 26] plebs obsequens prae-
10 ceptis dominicis et Deum metuens a peccatore praeposito separare se debet, nec se ad sacrilegi sacerdotis sacrificia miscere, quando ipsa maxime habeat potestatem vel eligendi dignos sacerdotes vel indignos recusandi. Quod et ipsum videmus et divina auctoritate descendere, ut sacer-
15 dos plebe praesente sub omnium oculis deligatur et dignus atque idoneus publico iudicio ac testimonio conprobetur, sicut in Numeris Dominus Moysi praecipit dicens [Num. xx. 25, 26]. Coram omni synagoga iubet Deus constitui sacerdotem, id est instruit et ostendit ordinationes sacer-
20 dotales non nisi sub populi adsistentis conscientia fieri oportere, ut plebe praesente vel detegantur malorum crimina vel bonorum merita praedicentur et sit ordinatio iusta et legitima quae omnium suffragio et iudicio fuerit examinata.... Propter quod diligenter de traditione
25 divina et apostolica observatione servandum est et tenendum quod apud nos quoque et fere per provincias

my letters to them, as if something were being done more
moderate and temperate; the same Lucian wrote a letter
in the name of all the confessors, in which well nigh every
bond of faith, and fear of God, and the Lord's command,
and the sacredness and fixity of the Gospel were dissolved. 5
For he wrote in the name ot all, that they had all given
peace, and that he wished that this decree should be
communicated through me to the other bishops, of which
letter I have transmitted a copy to you.

A. N. L.

Appointment of Bishops.

ON which account [Num. xvi. 26] a people obedient to 10
the Lord's precepts, and fearing God, ought to separate
themselves from a sinful prelate, and not to associate
themselves with the sacrifices of a sacrilegious priest[1],
especially since they themselves have the power either of
choosing worthy priests, or of rejecting unworthy ones. 15
Which very thing, too, we observe to come from divine
authority, that the priest should be chosen in the presence
of the people under the eyes of all, and should be approved
worthy and suitable by public judgement and testimony;
as in the book of Numbers the Lord commanded Moses, 20
saying [Num. xx. 25, 26]. God commands a priest to be
appointed in the presence of all the assembly; that is, He
instructs and shows that the ordination of priests ought
not to be solemnized except with the knowledge of the
people standing near, that in the presence of the people 25
either the crimes of the wicked may be disclosed, or the
merits of the good may be declared, and the ordination,
which shall have been examined by the suffrage and
judgement of all, may be just and legitimate. . . . For
which reason you must diligently observe and keep the 30
practice delivered from divine tradition and Apostolic
observance, which is also maintained among us, and
almost throughout all the provinces; that for the proper

[1] i.e. bishop: as always in Cyprian.

universas tenetur, ut ad ordinationes rite celebrandas ad
eam plebem cui praepositus ordinatur episcopi eiusdem
provinciae proximi quique conveniant et episcopus deligatur plebe praesente, quae singulorum vitam plenissime
novit et uniuscuiusque actum de eius conversatione per-
spexit.   ID. *Ep.* 67.

LIX.

QUOD si aliquis illud opponit ut dicat eandem Nova-
tianum legem tenere quam catholica ecclesia teneat, eodem
symbolo quo et nos baptizare, eundem nosse deum
patrem, eundem filium Christum, eundem spiritum sanctum, ac propter hoc usurpare eum potestatem baptizandi
posse quod videatur interrogatione baptismi a nobis non
discrepare: sciat quisque hoc opponendum putat primum
non esse unam nobis et schismaticis symboli legem neque
eandem interrogationem. Nam cum dicunt, Credis in
remissionem peccatorum et vitam aeternam per sanctam
ecclesiam, mentiuntur interrogatione, quando non habeant
ecclesiam. Tunc deinde voce sua ipsi confitentur remissionem peccatorum non dari nisi per sanctam ecclesiam
posse, quam non habentes ostendunt remitti illic peccata
non posse.   ID. *Ep.* 69.

LX.

NESCIO qua etenim praesumptione ducuntur quidam de
collegis nostris ut putent eos qui apud haereticos tincti
sunt, quando ad nos venerint, baptizari non oportere, eo
quod dicant unum baptisma esse: quod unum scilicet in
ecclesia catholica est, quia ecclesia una est et esse
baptisma praeter ecclesiam non potest. Nam cum duo
baptismata esse non possint, si haeretici vere baptizant,

celebration of ordinations all the neighbouring bishops of
the same province should assemble with that people for
which a prelate is ordained; and the bishop should be
chosen in the presence of the people, who have most fully
known the life of each one, and have looked into the doings
of each one as respects his habitual conduct.

A. N. L.

Schismatical Baptism worthless.

BUT if any one says by way of objection that Novatian
holds the same law as the Catholic Church holds, baptizes
with the same creed as ourselves, and recognizes the same
God as Father, the same Christ as Son, and the same
Holy Spirit; and that for this reason he can take to himself the power of baptizing, because he seems not to differ
from ourselves in his baptismal questioning—whoso
thinks this a good objection, let him know first that we
and the schismatics have neither one law of the creed nor
the same questioning, for when they say, 'Dost thou
believe in the forgiveness of sins and life eternal through
the Holy Church?' they lie in their questioning, because
they have no Church. Then, again, with their own voice
they themselves confess that forgiveness of sins is not
given except through the Holy Church; and, as they
have not this, they show that with them sins cannot be
forgiven.

Heretical Baptism invalid.

FOR I know not by what argument some of our colleagues
are led to think that when those come to us who have been
dipped by heretics, they ought not to be baptized, on the
ground as they say that there is one baptism; which one
of course is in the Catholic Church, for the Church is one,
and baptism there is none outside the Church. For since
there cannot be two baptisms, then if heretics in truth

ipsi habent baptisma ... nos autem dicimus eos qui inde veniunt non rebaptizari apud nos sed baptizari. Neque enim accipiunt illic aliquid ubi nihil est, sed veniunt ad nos ut hic accipiant ubi et gratia et veritas omnis est, quia
5 et gratia et veritas una est.

ID. *Ep.* 71.

LXI.

Eos autem qui Romae sunt non ea in omnibus observare quae sint ab origine tradita et frustra apostolorum auctoritatem praetendere scire quis etiam inde potest, quod circa celebrandos dies Paschae et circa multa alia
10 divinae rei sacramenta videat esse apud illos aliquas diversitates nec observari illic omnia aequaliter quae Hierosolymis observantur, secundum quod in ceteris quoque plurimis provinciis multa pro locorum et hominum diversitate variantur, nec tamen propter hoc ab ecclesiae
15 catholicae pace atque unitate aliquando discessum est. Quod nunc Stephanus ausus est facere rumpens adversus vos pacem, quam semper antecessores eius vobiscum amore et honore mutuo custodierunt, adhuc etiam infamans Petrum et Paulum beatos apostolos, quasi hoc
20 ipsi tradiderint, qui in epistolis suis haereticos execrati sunt et ut eos evitemus monuerunt. Unde apparet traditionem hanc humanam esse quae haereticos asserit et baptisma quod non nisi solius ecclesiae est eos habere defendit.

ID. *Ep.* 75.

LXII.

CYPRIANVS SVCCESSO FRATRI S. ...

25 .. Quae autem sunt in vero ita se habent, rescripsisse Valerianum ad senatum ut episcopi et presbyteri et

baptize, it is they who have the baptism. . . . We however
say that those who come thence are not rebaptized with us
but baptized, for indeed they receive not anything there
where nothing is, but come to us that they may here
receive where there is all grace and truth, since there
is but one grace and truth.

Firmilian's Letter to Cyprian.

BUT that they who are at Rome do not observe those
things in all cases which are handed down from the beginning, and vainly allege the authority of Apostles; any
one may know even from the fact, that concerning the
celebration of Easter, and concerning many other sacra-
ments of divine matters, he may see that there are some
diversities among them, and that all things are not observed
among them alike, which are observed at Jerusalem, just
as in very many other provinces also many things are
varied because of the difference of the places and peoples.
And yet on this account there is no departure at all from
the peace and unity of the Catholic Church, such as
Stephen has now dared to make; breaking the peace
against you, which his predecessors have always kept with
you in mutual love and honour, even herein defaming
Peter and Paul the blessed Apostles, as if the very men
delivered this who in their epistles execrated heretics,
and warned us to avoid them. Whence it appears
that this tradition is of men which maintains heretics,
and asserts that they have baptism, which belongs to the
Church alone. A. N. L.

The Edict of Valerian.

CYPRIAN to his brother Successus, greeting. . . . But the
truth concerning them is as follows, that Valerian had
sent a rescript to the Senate, to the effect that bishops and

diaconi in continenti animadvertantur, senatores vero et
egregii viri et equites Romani dignitate amissa etiam
bonis spolientur et si ademptis facultatibus Christiani
[esse] perseveraverint, capite quoque multentur, matronae
ademptis bonis in exilium relegentur, Caesariani autem
quicumque vel prius confessi fuerant vel nunc confessi
fuerint confiscentur et vincti in Caesarianas possessiones
descripti mittantur.

ID. *Ep.* 80.

LXIII.

Καὶ ἀπὸ τῶν νοημάτων δέ, καὶ ἀπὸ τῶν ῥημάτων καὶ
τῆς συντάξεως αὐτῶν, εἰκότως ἕτερος οὗτος παρ' ἐκείνον
ὑπονοηθήσεται. συνᾴδουσι μὲν γὰρ ἀλλήλοις τὸ εὐαγγέλιον καὶ ἡ ἐπιστολή, ὁμοίως τε ἄρχονται. τὸ μὲν
φησίν, ''Ἐν ἀρχῇ ἦν ὁ λόγος·' ἡ δέ, ''Ὁ ἦν ἀπ' ἀρχῆς.'
τὸ μὲν φησί, 'Καὶ ὁ λόγος σὰρξ ἐγένετο, καὶ ἐσκή-
νωσεν ἐν ἡμῖν, καὶ ἐθεασάμεθα τὴν δόξαν αὐτοῦ, δόξαν
ὡς μονογενοῦς παρὰ πατρός·' ἡ δὲ τὰ αὐτὰ σμικρῷ
παρηλλαγμένα· ''Ὃ ἀκηκόαμεν, ὃ ἑωράκαμεν τοῖς ὀφθαλμοῖς ἡμῶν, ὃ ἐθεασάμεθα, καὶ αἱ χεῖρες ἡμῶν ἐψηλάφησαν,
περὶ τοῦ λόγου τῆς ζωῆς· καὶ ἡ ζωὴ ἐφανερώθη.' ταῦτα
γὰρ προανακρούεται διατεινόμενος, ὡς ἐν τοῖς ἑξῆς ἐδή-
λωσε πρὸς τοὺς 'οὐκ ἐν σαρκὶ' φάσκοντας 'ἐληλυθέναι'
τὸν Κύριον· διὸ καὶ συνῆψεν ἐπιμελῶς, 'Καὶ ὃ ἑωράκαμεν μαρτυροῦμεν, καὶ ἀπαγγέλλομεν ὑμῖν τὴν ζωὴν
τὴν αἰώνιον, ἥ τις ἦν πρὸς τὸν πατέρα, καὶ ἐφανερώθη
ἡμῖν· ὃ ἑωράκαμεν καὶ ἀκηκόαμεν, ἀπαγγέλλομεν ὑμῖν.'
ἔχεται αὐτοῦ, καὶ τῶν προθέσεων οὐκ ἀφίσταται, διὰ δὲ
τῶν αὐτῶν κεφαλαίων καὶ ὀνομάτων πάντα διεξέρχεται·
ὧν τινὰ μὲν ἡμεῖς συντόμως ὑπομνήσομεν. ὁ δὲ προσ-

presbyters and deacons should immediately be punished;
but that senators, and men of importance, and Roman
knights, should lose their dignity, and moreover be deprived of their property; and if, when their means were
taken away, they should persist in being Christians, then
they should also lose their heads; that matrons should be
deprived of their property, and sent into banishment;
but that people of Caesar's household, whoever of them
had either confessed before, or should now confess, should
have their property confiscated, and should be sent in
chains by assignment to Caesar's estates.

Dionysius of Alexandria on the authorship of the Apocalypse.

AND from the thoughts too, and from the words and
their arrangement, this writer may reasonably be supposed
different from the other. For the Gospel and the Epistle
agree together, and begin in like manner. The one says,
'In the beginning was the Word'; the other, 'That which
was from the beginning.' The one says, 'And the Word
became flesh, and dwelt among us, and we beheld His
glory, glory as of an only-begotten from the Father'; the
other the same a little varied, 'That which we have heard,
which we have seen with our eyes, which we beheld, and
our hands handled, of the Word of life, and the life was
manifested.' For this he makes his prelude and steadfastly maintains, as he makes plain in what follows, against
those who say 'That the Lord has not come in flesh':
wherefore also he carefully adds, 'And that which we have
seen we testify, and we declare unto you the eternal life
which was with the Father and was manifested to us: that
which we have seen and heard declare we unto you.' He
is consistent with himself, and does not depart from his
purposes, but goes through all things under the same
heads and names, of which we will shortly mention some.

ἐχῶς ἐντυγχάνων εὑρήσει ἐν ἑκατέρῳ πολλὴν 'τὴν ζωήν,' πολὺ 'τὸ φῶς, ἀποτροπὴν τοῦ σκότους,' συνεχῆ 'τὴν ἀλήθειαν, τὴν χάριν, τὴν χαράν, τὴν σάρκα καὶ τὸ αἷμα τοῦ Κυρίου, τὴν κρίσιν, τὴν ἄφεσιν τῶν ἁμαρτιῶν,
5 τὴν πρὸς ἡμᾶς ἀγάπην τοῦ Θεοῦ, τὴν πρὸς ἀλλήλους ἡμᾶς ἀγάπης ἐντολήν, ὡς πάσας δεῖ φυλάσσειν τὰς ἐντολάς· ὁ ἔλεγχος τοῦ κόσμου, τοῦ διαβόλου, τοῦ ἀντιχρίστου, ἡ ἐπαγγελία τοῦ ἁγίου Πνεύματος, ἡ υἱοθεσία τοῦ Θεοῦ,' ἡ δι' ὅλου 'πίστις' ἡμῶν ἀπαιτουμένη, 'ὁ
10 Πατὴρ καὶ ὁ Υἱὸς' πανταχοῦ· καὶ ὅλως διὰ πάντων χαρακτηρίζοντας, ἕνα καὶ τὸν αὐτὸν συνορᾶν τοῦ τε εὐαγγελίου καὶ τῆς ἐπιστολῆς χρῶτα πρόκειται. ἀλλοιοτάτη δὲ καὶ ξένη παρὰ ταῦτα ἡ ἀποκάλυψις, μήτε ἐφαπτομένη, μήτε γειτνιῶσα τούτων μηδενὶ σχεδόν, ὡς
15 εἰπεῖν, μηδὲ συλλαβὴν πρὸς αὐτὰ κοινὴν ἔχουσα· ἀλλ' οὐδὲ μνήμην τινα οὐδὲ ἔννοιαν οὔτε ἡ ἐπιστολὴ τῆς ἀποκαλύψεως ἔχει· (ἐῶ γὰρ τὸ εὐαγγέλιον·) οὔτε τῆς ἐπιστολῆς ἡ ἀποκάλυψις· Παύλου διὰ τῶν ἐπιστολῶν ὑποφήναντός τι καὶ περὶ τῶν ἀποκαλύψεων αὐτοῦ, ἃς οὐκ
20 ἐνέγραψε καθ' αὑτάς. ἔτι δὲ καὶ διὰ τῆς φράσεως τὴν διαφορὰν ἔστι τεκμήρασθαι τοῦ εὐαγγελίου καὶ τῆς ἐπιστολῆς πρὸς τὴν ἀποκάλυψιν. τὰ μὲν γὰρ οὐ μόνον ἀπταίστως κατὰ τὴν Ἑλλήνων φωνήν, ἀλλὰ καὶ λογιώτατα ταῖς λέξεσι, τοῖς συλλογισμοῖς, ταῖς συντάξεσι
25 τῆς ἑρμηνείας γέγραπται. πολλοῦ γε δεῖ βάρβαρόν τινα φθόγγον, ἢ σολοικισμόν, ἢ ὅλως ἰδιωτισμὸν ἐν αὐτοῖς εὑρεθῆναι. ἑκάτερον γὰρ εἶχεν, ὡς ἔοικε, τὸν λόγον, ἀμφοτέρους αὐτῷ χαρισαμένου τοῦ Κυρίου, τόν τε τῆς γνώσεως, τόν τε τῆς φράσεως. τούτῳ δὲ ἀποκάλυψιν μὲν ἑωρακέναι,

He that reads carefully will find in either much mention of
the life, the light, the turning away of darkness ; and continually the truth, the grace, the joy, the flesh and the blood
of the Lord, the judgement, the forgiveness of sins, the love
of God for us, the command to us to love one another, the
need of keeping all the commandments, the conviction of
the world, of the devil and of Antichrist, the promise of the
Holy Spirit, the adoption of God, the faith which is
throughout required of us, everywhere the Father and the
Son. In short, if we mark them by all their characters, it
is plain to see that the complexion of the Gospel and of
the Epistle is one and the same. But the Apocalypse is
entirely different from these and foreign to them, neither
touching nor bordering on any of them ; scarcely, so to
say, having even a syllable in common with them. Nay,
more, the Epistle (for I let alone the Gospel) contains
neither mention nor thought of the Apocalypse, nor yet the
Apocalypse of the Epistle, whereas Paul by his Epistles
signified something even of his visions, which he did not
separately insert. Moreover, we may conjecture from the
diction the difference of the Gospel and the Epistle from
the Apocalypse. For the former are written not only
without error, as regards the rules of Greek, but very
elegantly in words, in reasonings, and in arrangement of
the explanations. We are very far from finding in them
a barbarous word or a solecism, or any vulgarism at all.
For he had, as it appears, both the one word and the other,
as the Lord had granted both to him—that of knowledge,
and that of expression. That the other saw a revelation

καὶ γνῶσιν εἰληφέναι καὶ προφητείαν, οὐκ ἀντερῶ· διάλεκτον μέντοι καὶ γλῶσσαν οὐκ ἀκριβῶς ἑλληνίζουσαν αὐτοῦ βλέπω, ἀλλ' ἰδιώμασίν τε βαρβαρικοῖς χρώμενον, καί που καὶ σολοικίζοντα. ἅπερ οὐκ ἀναγκαῖον νῦν ἐκλέγειν·
5 οὐδὲ γὰρ ἐπισκώπτων, μή τις νομίσῃ, ταῦτα εἶπον, ἀλλὰ μόνον τὴν ἀνομοιότητα διευθύνων τῶν γραφῶν.

EUSEBIUS, *Hist. Eccles.* vii. 25.

LXIV.

Αὐτοκράτωρ Καῖσαρ Πούπλιος Λικίνιος Γαλλιηνός, εὐσεβής, εὐτυχής, σεβαστός, Διονυσίῳ καὶ Πίννᾳ καὶ Δημητρίῳ, καὶ τοῖς λοιποῖς ἐπισκόποις. τὴν εὐεργεσίαν
10 τῆς ἐμῆς δωρεᾶς διὰ παντὸς τοῦ κόσμου ἐκβιβασθῆναι προσέταξα· ὅπως ἀπὸ τόπων τῶν θρησκευσίμων ἀποχωρήσωσι. καὶ διὰ τοῦτο καὶ ὑμεῖς τῆς ἀντιγραφῆς τῆς ἐμῆς τῷ τύπῳ χρῆσθαι δύνασθε, ὥστε μηδένα ὑμῖν ἐνοχλεῖν. καὶ τοῦτο ὅπερ κατὰ τὸ ἐξὸν δύναται ὑφ'
15 ὑμῖν ἀναπληροῦσθαι, ἤδη πρὸ πολλοῦ ὑπ' ἐμοῦ συγκεχώρηται. καὶ διὰ τοῦτο Αὐρήλιος Κυρήνιος, ὁ τοῦ μεγίστου πράγματος προστατεύων, τὸν τύπον τὸν ὑπ' ἐμοῦ δοθέντα διαφυλάξει.

Ibid. 13.

LXV.

Τοῦ δὴ οὖν Παύλου σὺν καὶ τῇ τῆς πίστεως ὀρθοδοξίᾳ
20 τῆς ἐπισκοπῆς ἀποπεπτωκότος, Δόμνος, ὡς εἴρηται, τὴν λειτουργίαν τῆς κατὰ Ἀντιόχειαν ἐκκλησίας διεδέξατο. ἀλλὰ γὰρ μηδαμῶς ἐκστῆναι τοῦ Παύλου τοῦ τῆς ἐκκλησίας οἴκου θέλοντος, βασιλεὺς ἐντευχθεὶς Αὐρηλιανὸς αἰσιώτατα περὶ τοῦ πρακτέου διείληφε, τούτοις νεῖμαι
25 προστάττων τὸν οἶκον, οἷς ἂν οἱ κατὰ τὴν Ἰταλίαν καὶ τὴν Ῥωμαίων πόλιν ἐπίσκοποι τοῦ δόγματος ἐπιστέλλοιεν.

Ibid 30.

and received knowledge and prophecy, I will not dispute: howbeit I see that his dialect and language are not accurately Greek, but that he used barbarous vulgarisms, and in some places downright solecisms. But these I need not now pick out; for I do not write this in mockery—let no man think it—but only to show plainly the unlikeness of the writings.

Rescript of Gallienus.

THE Emperor Caesar Publius Licinius Gallienus, Pius, Felix, Augustus, to Dionysius, Pinnas, Demetrius, and the other bishops. I have ordered the bounty of my gift to be declared through all the world, that they may depart from the places of religious worship. And for this purpose you may use this copy of my rescript, that no one may molest you. And this which you are now enabled lawfully to do, has already for a long time been conceded by me. Therefore Aurelius Cyrenius, who is the chief administrator of affairs, will keep this copy which I have given.

N. L.

Aurelian's Decision of the Bishopric of Antioch.

So then, as Paul had fallen from the bishopric as well as from the orthodox faith, Domnus as was said before succeeded him as bishop of the Church of Antioch. But as Paul entirely refused to leave the church-house, petition was made to the emperor Aurelian, and he gave a very just decision of the matter, by ordering the house to be given up to those with whom the bishops of the religion in Italy and Rome held intercourse.

LXVI.

Ἔτος τοῦτο ἦν ἐννεακαιδέκατον τῆς Διοκλητιανοῦ βασιλείας, Δύστρος μήν, λέγοιτο δ᾽ ἂν οὗτος Μάρτιος κατὰ Ῥωμαίους, ἐν ᾧ, τῆς τοῦ σωτηρίου πάθους ἑορτῆς εἰσελαυνούσης, ἥπλωτο πανταχόσε βασιλικὰ γράμματα, τὰς μὲν ἐκκλησίας εἰς ἔδαφος φέρειν, τὰς δὲ γραφὰς ἀφανεῖς πυρὶ γενέσθαι προστάττοντα, καὶ τοὺς μὲν τιμῆς ἐπειλημμένους, ἀτίμους, τοὺς δὲ ἐν οἰκετίαις, εἰ ἐπιμένοιεν τῇ τοῦ Χριστιανισμοῦ προθέσει, ἐλευθερίας στερεῖσθαι[1] προαγορεύοντα. καὶ ἡ μὲν πρώτη καθ᾽ ἡμῶν γραφὴ τοιαύτη τις ἦν· μετ᾽ οὐ πολὺ δὲ ἑτέρων ἐπιφοιτησάντων γραμμάτων, προσετάττετο τοὺς τῶν ἐκκλησιῶν προέδρους πάντας τοὺς κατὰ πάντα τόπον πρῶτα μὲν δεσμοῖς παραδίδοσθαι, εἶθ᾽ ὕστερον πάσῃ μηχανῇ θύειν ἐξαναγκάζεσθαι.

Ibid. viii. 2.

LXVII.

'MAGUS fuit, clandestinis artibus omnia illa perfecit, Aegyptiorum ex adytis angelorum potentium nomina et remotas furatus est disciplinas.' Quid dicitis, o parvuli, incomperta vobis et nescia temerariae vocis loquacitate garrientes? Ergone illa quae gesta sunt daemonum fuere praestigiae et magicarum artium ludi? Potestis aliquem nobis designare, monstrare ex omnibus illis magis, qui umquam fuere per saecula, consimile aliquid Christo millesima ex parte qui fecerit? ...

Unus fuit e nobis, qui redire in corpora iamdudum animas praecipiebat efflatas, prodire ab aggeribus conditos et post dum funeris tertium pollinctorum velaminibus expediri? Unus fuit e nobis, qui quid singuli voluerint, quid sub obscuris cogitationibus continerent tacitorum in cordibus pervidebat? ...

Nihil ut remini magicum, nihil humanum, praestigiosum

[1] Lact. *de Mort. Pers.* 13 'ut religionis illius homines carerent omni honore ac dignitate ... libertatem denique ac vocem non haberent.'

The Edicts of Diocletian.

THIS year was the nineteenth of the reign of Diocletian, the month Dystrus, which is called March by the Romans, when as the feast of the Saviour's Passion was approaching, imperial edicts were published everywhere, commanding the churches to be levelled with the ground and the Scriptures to be destroyed with fire, and ordering that those possessed of honour should lose their position, and that they of Caesar's household, if they held to their profession of Christianity, should be deprived of freedom. Such was the first edict against us; and before long by other edicts following it was ordered that all the rulers of the Churches everywhere should first be committed to bonds, and afterwards by every art be made to sacrifice.

Our Lord's Miracles.

JESUS was a Magian; He effected all these things by secret arts. From the shrines of the Egyptians he stole the names of angels of might, and the rules of a secret craft. Why, O witlings, do you speak of things which you have not examined, and which are unknown to you, prating with the garrulity of a rash tongue? Were, then, those things which were done, the freaks of demons, and the tricks of magical arts? Can you specify and point out to me any one of all those magicians who have ever existed in past ages that did anything similar in the thousandth degree to Christ?...

Was He one of us, who ordered souls once breathed forth to return to the body, persons buried to come forth from the tomb, and after three days to be loosed from the swathings of the undertaker? Was He one of us, who saw clearly in the hearts of the silent what each was pondering, what each had in his secret thoughts?...

There was nothing magical, as you suppose, nothing

aut subdolum, nihil fraudis delituit in Christo, derideatis
licet ex more atque in lasciviam dissolvamini cachinnorum.
Deus ille sublimis fuit, deus radice ab intima, deus ab
incognitis regnis et ab omnium principe deo sospitator
5 est missus.

ARNOBIUS, *Adv. Nationes*, i. 43-53.

LXVIII.

Ex iis qui mihi noti sunt Minucius Felix non ignobilis
inter causidicos loci fuit. Huius liber, cui Octavio titulus
est, declarat quam idoneus veritatis assertor esse potuisset,
si se totum ad id studium contulisset. Septimius quoque
10 Tertullianus fuit omni genere litterarum peritus, sed in
eloquendo parum facilis et mi us comptus et multum
obscurus fuit. Ergo ne hic quidem satis celebritatis
invenit. Unus igitur praecipuus et clarus exstitit Cyprianus, quoniam et magnam sibi gloriam ex artis oratoriae
15 professione quaesierat et admodum multa conscripsit in
suo genere miranda. Erat enim ingenio facili copioso
suavi et, quae sermonis maxima est virtus, aperto, ut
discernere non queas, utrumne ornatior in eloquendo an
felicior in explicando an potentior in persuadendo fuerit.
20 Hic tamen placere ultra verba sacramentum ignorantibus
non potest, quoniam mystica sunt quae locutus est et ad
id praeparata, ut a solis fidelibus audiantur: denique a
doctis huius saeculi, quibus forte scripta eius innotuerunt,
derideri solet.

LACTANTIUS, *Div. Inst.* v. 1.

LXIX.

25 DIOCLETIANUS, qui scelerum inventor et malorum machi-
nator fuit, cum disperderet omnia, ne a deo quidem

human trickery in Christ; no deceit lurked in him, although you smile in derision, as your wont is, and though you split with roars of laughter. He was God on high, God in His inmost root, God from unknown realms, sent by the ruler of all as a Saviour.

R.

Lactantius criticizing earlier Apologists.

OF those who are known to me, Minucius Felix was of no mean rank among pleaders. His book, which is entitled *Octavius*, shows how doughty a champion of the truth he could have been, if he had devoted himself entirely to that occupation. Septimius Tertullianus too was skilled in every sort of literature, but in eloquence he had little readiness, with small polish and much obscurity. So neither did he find much popularity. Cyprianus therefore was the one more than others conspicuous and eminent, for he had won to himself much glory from his profession of the art of oratory, and he has written a great number of things in their own sort worthy of admiration. For he was of a ready spirit, fluent, agreeable, and (what is a very great excellence of language) plain, so that you cannot decide whether he was more elegant in language, or happier in explanation, or stronger in persuasion. Yet even he cannot please—further than his words—those who do not know the mystery, since the words he has spoken are mystical, and shaped to the end that they may be understood of the faithful only: in short, by the learned of this world to whom his writings have by chance become known, he is commonly ridiculed.

Misgovernment of Diocletian.

WHEN Diocletian, that inventor of crimes and deviser of evils, was ruining all things, he could not refrain his

manus potuit abstinere. Hic orbem terrae simul et
avaritia et timiditate subvertit. Tres enim participes regni
sui fecit, in quatuor partes orbe diviso, et multiplicatis
exercitibus, cum singuli eorum longe maiorem numerum
5 militum habere contenderunt, quam priores principes
habuerant, cum soli rempublicam gererent. Adeo maior
esse coeperat numerus accipientium, quam dantium, ut
enormitate indictionum consumptis viribus colonorum, de-
sererentur agri et culturae verterentur in silvam. Et ut
10 omnia terrore complerentur, provinciae quoque in frusta
concisae: multi praesides et plura officia singulis regioni-
bus ac paene iam civitatibus incubare; item rationales
multi, et magistri, et vicarii praefectorum, quibus omnibus
civiles actus admodum rari, sed condemnationes tantum
15 et proscriptiones frequentes, exactiones rerum innumera-
bilium, non dicam crebrae, sed perpetuae, et in exactioni-
bus iniuriae non ferendae. Haec quoque tolerari possunt
quae ad exhibendos milites spectant. Idem insatiabili
avaritia thesauros nunquam minui volebat, sed semper
20 extraordinarias opes ac largitiones congerebat, ut ea quae
recondebat, integra atque inviolata servaret. Idem cum
variis iniquitatibus immensam faceret caritatem, legem
pretiis rerum venalium statuere conatus est. Tunc ob
exigua et vilia multus sanguis effusus, nec venale quid-
25 quam metu apparebat, et caritas multo deterius exarsit,
donec lex necessitate ipsa post multorum exitium solveretur. Huc accedebat infinita quaedam cupiditas aedi-
ficandi, non minor provinciarum exactio in exhibendis
operariis, et artificibus, et plaustris omnibusque quaecumque

hands even from God. He was the man who overturned the whole world, partly by avarice and partly by cowardice. He made three partners in his government, dividing the Empire into four parts, so that armies were multiplied, because each of the four endeavoured to have a much greater number of soldiers than former emperors had when they ruled the state alone. Thus the receivers of taxes began to be more in number than the payers, so that by reason of the consumption of husbandmen's goods by the excess of land-taxes, the farms were left waste and tilled lands turned into forest. In order too that all places might be filled with terror the provinces also were cut up into fragments, and many presidents and sundry companies of officials lay heavy on every territory, and indeed almost on every city; and there were many receivers besides and secretaries and deputies of the prefects. All these very seldom had civil cases before them, only condemnations and continual confiscations and requisitions—I will not say frequent, but unceasing—of every kind of property, and in the levying intolerable wrongs. Even these might be borne if they were intended to provide pay for the soldiers; but Diocletian in his insatiable avarice would never let his treasures be diminished, but was always heaping up extraordinary aids and benevolences, in order to keep his hoards untouched and inviolate. Again, when by various evil deeds he caused a prodigious scarcity, he essayed by law to fix the prices of goods in the market. Then much blood was shed for trifling and paltry wares, and through fear nothing appeared in the market, so that the scarcity was made much worse, till after the law had ruined multitudes it was of sheer necessity abolished. In addition to this he had an unlimited taste for building, and levied of the provincials as unlimited exactions for the wages of workmen and artificers, and the supplying of wagons and

sint fabricandis operibus necessaria. Hic basilicae, hic
circus, hic moneta, hic armorum fabrica, hic uxori domus,
hic filiae. Repente magna pars civitatis exceditur. Migra-
bant omnes cum coniugibus ac liberis, quasi urbe ab
5 hostibus capta. Et cum perfecta haec fuerant cum interitu
provinciarum, Non recte facta sunt, aiebat; alio modo
fiant. Rursus dirui ac mutari necesse erat, iterum fortasse
casura. Ita semper dementabat, Nicomediam studens
urbi Romae coaequare. Iam illud praetereo, quam multi
10 perierint possessionum, aut opum gratia. Hoc enim usi-
tatum et fere licitum consuetudine malorum. Sed in hoc
illud fuit praecipuum, quod ubicunque cultiorem agrum
viderat, aut ornatius aedificium, iam parata domino ca-
lumnia et poena capitalis, quasi non posset rapere aliena
15 sine sanguine.

ID. *De Mort. Pers.* 7.

LXX.

INTER caetera, quae pro rei publicae semper commodis
atque utilitate disponimus, nos quidem volueramus antehac,
iuxta leges veteres et publicam disciplinam Romanorum,
cuncta corrigere, atque id providere, ut etiam Christiani,
20 qui parentum suorum reliquerant sectam, ad bonas mentes
redirent: siquidem quadam ratione tanta eosdem Christianos voluntas invasisset et tanta stultitia occupasset, ut
non illa veterum instituta sequerentur, quae forsitan primum parentes eorundem constituerant; sed pro arbitrio
25 suo atque ut iisdem erat libitum, ita sibimet leges

everything else that was wanted for the works in hand. Here were public offices, there a circus, here a mint, there a factory of arms, here a palace for his wife, and there one for his daughter. On a sudden a large part of the city is turned out of doors: they all had to remove with wives and children, as if the city had been taken by enemies. And when the works had been finished at the cost of ruin to the provinces—'They are not done right,' he used to say; 'let them be done another way.' So they had to be pulled down and altered, perhaps only to be demolished again. Thus he always played the madman in his endeavour to equal Nicomedia with imperial Rome. I leave untold how many perished on account of their estates or wealth, for by the custom of evil men this was become frequent and almost lawful. Yet the worst of it was this, that wherever he saw a field more carefully tilled or a house more elegantly adorned than usual, straightway an accusation and capital sentence was prepared for the owner as though he could not spoil his neighbour's goods without shedding of blood.

The Toleration Edict of Galerius.

AMONGST our other arrangements, which we are always making for the use and profit of the commonwealth, we for our part had heretofore endeavoured to set all things right according to the ancient laws and public order of the Romans, and to compass this also that the Christians too who had left the persuasion of their own fathers should return to a better mind; seeing that through some strange reasoning such wilfulness had seized the Christians and such folly possessed them, that, instead of following those constitutions of the ancients which peradventure their own ancestors had first established, they were making themselves laws for their own observance, merely according to their own judgement and as their

facerent, quas observarent, et per diversa varios populos congregarent. Denique cum eiusmodi nostra iussio exstitisset, ut ad veterum se instituta conferrent, multi periculo subiugati, multi etiam deturbati sunt; atque cum plurimi in proposito perseverarent, ac videremus, nec diis eosdem cultum ac religionem debitam exhibere, nec Christianorum deum observare, contemplatione mitissimae nostrae clementiae intuentes et consuetudinem sempiternam, qua solemus cunctis hominibus veniam indulgere, promptissimam in his quoque indulgentiam nostram credidimus porrigendam; ut denuo sint Christiani, et conventicula sua componant, ita ut ne quid contra disciplinam agant. Per aliam autem epistolam iudicibus significaturi sumus, quid debeant observare. Unde iuxta hanc indulgentiam nostram debebunt deum suum orare pro salute nostra, et rei publicae, ac sua, ut undiqueversum res publica praestetur incolumis, et securi vivere in sedibus suis possint.

Ibid. 34.

LXXI.

Litterae Licinii.

Cum feliciter tam ego Constantinus Augustus, quam etiam ego Licinius Augustus apud Mediolanum convenissemus, atque universa, quae ad commoda et securitatem publicam pertinerent, in tractatu haberemus, haec inter caetera quae videbamus pluribus hominibus profutura, vel in primis ordinanda esse credidimus, quibus divinitatis reverentia continebatur, ut daremus et Christianis et omnibus liberam potestatem sequendi religionem, quam quisque voluisset, quo quidquid divinitatis in sede coelesti[1], nobis atque omnibus, qui sub potestate nostra sunt constituti, placatum ac propitium possit existere. Itaque hoc consilium salubri ac rectissima ratione ineundum esse

---

[1] Eus. *H. E.* x. 5 ὅ, τί ποτέ ἐστι θειότητος καὶ οὐρανίου πράγματος.

pleasure was, and in divers places were assembling sundry sorts of peoples. In short, when a command of ours had been set forth to the effect that they were to betake themselves to the institutions of the ancients, many of them were subdued by danger, many also ruined; yet when great numbers held to their determination, and we saw that they neither gave worship and due reverence to the gods, nor yet regarded the god of the Christians—we therefore in consideration of our most mild clemency, and of the unbroken custom whereby we are used to grant pardon to all men, have thought it right in this case also to offer our speediest indulgence, that Christians may exist again, and may establish their meetings, yet so that they do nothing contrary to good order. By another letter we shall signify to magistrates, how they should proceed. Wherefore, in accordance with this indulgence of ours, they will be bound to pray their god for our good estate, and that of the commonwealth, and their own, that the commonwealth may endure on every side unharmed, and they may be able to live securely in their own homes.

The 'Edict of Milan.'

WHEN we, Constantine Augustus and Licinius Augustus, had happily met together at Milan, and were holding consideration of all things which concern the advantage and security of the state, we thought that amongst other things which seemed likely to profit men generally, we ought in the very first place to set in order the conditions of the reverence paid to the Divinity, by giving to the Christians and all others full authority to follow whatever worship any man has chosen; whereby whatsoever Divinity dwells in heaven may be benevolent and propitious to us, and to all who are placed under our authority. Therefore we thought it good with sound counsel and very right

credidimus, ut nulli omnino facultatem abnegandam putaremus, qui vel observationi Christianorum, vel ei religioni mentem suam dederet, quam ipse sibi aptissimam esse sentiret; ut possit nobis summa divinitas, cuius religioni
5 liberis mentibus obsequimur, in omnibus solitum favorem suum benevolentiamque praestare. Quare scire dicationem tuam convenit, placuisse nobis, ut amotis omnibus[1] omnino conditionibus, quae prius scriptis ad officium tuum datis super Christianorum nomine videbantur, nunc libere
10 ac simpliciter unusquisque eorum, qui eandem observandae religioni Christianorum gerunt voluntatem, citra ullam inquietudinem ac molestiam sui id ipsum observare contendant. Quae sollicitudini tuae plenissime significanda esse credidimus, quo scires, nos liberam atque
15 absolutam colendae religionis suae facultatem iisdem Christianis dedisse. Quod cum iisdem a nobis indultum esse pervideas, intelligit dicatio tua, etiam aliis religionis suae vel observantiae potestatem similiter apertam et liberam pro quiete temporis nostri esse concessam,
20 ut in colendo, quod quisque delegerit, habeat liberam facultatem, quod nobis placuit, ut neque cuiquam honori, neque cuiquam religioni aliquid a nobis detractum videatur. Atque hoc insuper in persona Christianorum statuendum esse censuimus, quod si eadem loca,
25 ad quae antea convenire consuerant, de quibus etiam datis ad officium tuum litteris certa antehac forma fuerat comprehensa, priore tempore aliqui vel a fisco nostro, vel ab alio quocunque videntur esse mercati, eadem Christianis sine pecunia et sine-ulla pretii petitione, póstposita
30 omni frustratione atque ambiguitate, restituantur. Qui etiam dono fuerunt consecuti, eadem similiter iisdem Christianis quantocius reddant. Et iam vel hi qui emerunt, vel qui dono fuerunt consecuti, si petiverint de nostra

[1] Eus. *H. E.* x. 5 ἀφαιρεθεισῶν παντελῶς τῶν αἱρέσεων.

reason to lay down this law, that no man whatever should be refused any legal facility, who has given up his mind either to the observance of Christianity, or to the worship which he personally feels best suited to himself; to the end that the supreme Divinity, whose worship we freely follow, may continue in all things to grant us his wonted favour and goodwill. Wherefore your Devotion should know that it is our pleasure to abolish all conditions whatever which appeared in former charters directed to your office about the Christians, that every one of those who have a common wish to observe the Christian worship may now freely and unconditionally endeavour to observe the same without any annoyance or disquiet. These things we thought good to signify in the fullest manner to your Carefulness, that you might know that we have given freely and unreservedly to the said Christians authority to practise their worship. And when you perceive that we have made this grant to the said Christians, your Devotion understands that to others also freedom for their own worship and observance is likewise left open and freely granted, as befits the quiet of our times, that every man may have freedom in the practice of whatever worship he has chosen, for it is not our will that aught be diminished from the honour of any worship. Moreover in regard to the Christians we have thought fit to ordain this also, that if any appear to have bought, whether from our exchequer or from any others, the places at which they were used formerly to assemble, concerning which definite orders have been given before now, and that by letters issued to your office—that the same be restored to the Christians, setting aside all delay and doubtfulness, without any payment or demand of price. Those also who have obtained them by gift shall restore them in like manner without delay to the said Christians; and those moreover who have bought them, as well as those who have obtained them by gift, if they request anything of our

benevolentia aliquid, vicarium postulent, quo et ipsis per
nostram clementiam consulatur. Quae omnia corpori
Christianorum protinus per intercessionem tuam ac sine
mora tradi oportebit. Et quoniam iidem Christiani non
5 ea loca tantum, ad quae convenire consuerunt, sed alia
etiam habuisse noscuntur, ad ius corporis eorum, id est
ecclesiarum, non hominum singulorum, pertinentia; ea
omnia lege, qua superius comprehendimus; citra ullam
prorsus ambiguitatem, vel controversiam iisdem Chris-
10 tianis, id est, corpori et conventiculis eorum reddi iubebis:
supra dicta scilicet ratione servata, ut ii, qui eadem sine
pretio, sicut diximus, restituant, indemnitatem de nostra
benevolentia sperent. In quibus omnibus supra dicto corpori Christianorum intercessionem tuam efficacissimam
15 exhibere debebis, ut praeceptum nostrum quantocius
compleatur; quo etiam in hoc per clementiam nostram
quieti publicae consulatur. Hactenus fiet, ut sicut superius comprehensum est, divinus iuxta nos favor, quem
in tantis sumus rebus experti, per omne tempus prospere
20 successibus nostris cum beatitudine publica perseveret.
Ut autem huius sanctionis et benevolentiae nostrae
forma ad omnium possit pervenire notitiam, prolata pro-
grammate tuo haec scripta et ubique proponere, et ad
omnium scientiam te perferre conveniet, ut huius bene-
25 volentiae nostrae sanctio latere non possit.

Ibid. 48.

LXXII.

*Εὐχομένῳ δὲ ταῦτα καὶ λιπαρῶς ἱκετεύοντι τῷ βασιλεῖ,
θεοσημία τις ἐπιφαίνεται παραδοξοτάτη· ἣν τάχα μὲν*

benevolence, they shall apply to the Vicarius, that order
may be taken for them too by our Clemency. All these
things must be delivered over at once and without delay
by your intervention to the corporation of the Christians.
And since the said Christians are known to have possessed, not those places only whereto they were used to
assemble, but others also belonging to their corporation,
namely the churches, and not to individuals, we comprise
them all under the above law, so that you will order them
to be restored without any doubtfulness or dispute to
the said Christians, that is to their corporation and
assemblies; provided always as aforesaid, that those
who restore them without price, as we said, shall expect
a compensation from our benevolence. In all these things
you must give the aforesaid Christians your most effective
intervention, that our command may be fulfilled as soon
as may be, and that in this matter, as well as others, order
may be taken by our Clemency for the public quiet. So
far we will ensure that, as is already said, the Divine
favour which we have already experienced in so many
affairs shall continue for all time to give us prosperity
and successes, together with happiness for the State.
But that it may be possible for this command of our
benevolence to come to the knowledge of all men, it will
be your duty by a proclamation of your own to publish
everywhere and bring to the notice of all men this present
document when it reaches you, that the command of this
our benevolence may not be hidden.

Constantine's Cross.

[ACCORDINGLY he called on him with earnest prayer and
supplications that he would reveal to him who he was,
and stretch forth his right hand to help him in his present
difficulties.] And while he was thus praying with fervent
entreaty, a most marvellous sign appeared to him from

ἄλλου λέγοντος, οὐ ῥᾴδιον ἦν ἀποδέξασθαι, αὐτοῦ δὲ τοῦ νικητοῦ βασιλέως, τοῖς τὴν γραφὴν διηγουμένοις ἡμῖν μακροῖς ὕστερον χρόνοις, ὅτε ἠξιώθημεν τῆς αὐτοῦ γνώσεώς τε καὶ ὁμιλίας, ἐξαγγείλαντος, ὅρκοις τε πιστω-
5 σαμένου τὸν λόγον, τίς ἂν ἀμφιβάλοι μὴ οὐχὶ πιστεῦσαι τῷ διηγήματι; μάλισθ᾽ ὅτε καὶ ὁ μετὰ ταῦτα χρόνος ἀληθῆ τῷ λόγῳ παρέσχε τὴν μαρτυρίαν. ἀμφὶ μεσημβρινὰς ἡλίου ὥρας, ἤδη τῆς ἡμέρας ἀποκλινούσης, αὐτοῖς ὀφθαλμοῖς ἰδεῖν ἔφη ἐν αὐτῷ οὐρανῷ ὑπερκείμενον τοῦ
10 ἡλίου σταυροῦ τρόπαιον, ἐκ φωτὸς συνιστάμενον, γραφήν τε αὐτῷ συνῆφθαι, λέγουσαν· Τούτῳ νίκα. θάμβος δ᾽ ἐπὶ τῷ θεάματι κρατῆσαι αὐτόν τε καὶ τὸ στρατιωτικὸν ἅπαν, ὃ δὴ στελλομένῳ ποι πορείαν συνείπετό τε καὶ θεωρὸν ἐγίνετο θαύματος.
15 Καὶ δὴ διαπορεῖν πρὸς ἑαυτὸν ἔλεγε, τί ποτε εἴη τὸ φάσμα. ἐνθυμουμένῳ δ᾽ αὐτῷ καὶ ἐπὶ πολὺ λογιζομένῳ νὺξ ἐπῄει καταλαβοῦσα· ἐνταῦθα δὴ ὑπνοῦντι αὐτῷ, τὸν Χριστὸν τοῦ Θεοῦ σὺν τῷ φανέντι κατ᾽ οὐρανὸν σημείῳ ὀφθῆναί τε καὶ παρακελεύσασθαι, μίμημα ποιησά-
20 μενον τοῦ καθ᾽ οὐρανὸν ὀφθέντος σημείου, τούτῳ πρὸς τὰς τῶν πολεμίων συμβολὰς ἀλεξήματι χρῆσθαι.

EUSEBIUS, *Vita Const.* i. 28, 29.

LXXIII.

Τὰ περὶ τῆς ἐκκλησιαστικῆς πίστεως πραγματευθέντα κατὰ τὴν μεγάλην σύνοδον τὴν ἐν Νικαίᾳ συγκροτηθεῖσαν εἰκὸς μὲν ὑμᾶς καὶ ἄλλοθεν μεμαθηκέναι, τῆς φήμης
25 προτρέχειν εἰωθυίας τὸν περὶ τῶν πεπραγμένων ἀκριβῆ λόγον. Ἀλλ᾽ ἵνα μὴ ἐκ τοιαύτης ἀκοῆς τὰ τῆς ἀληθείας ἑτέρως ὑμῖν ἀπαγγέλληται, ἀναγκαίως διεπεμψάμεθα ὑμῖν πρῶτον μὲν τὴν ὑφ᾽ ἡμῶν προτεθεῖσαν περὶ τῆς

heaven, the account of which it might have been hard to believe had it been related by any other person. But since the victorious emperor himself long afterwards declared it to the writer of this history, when he was honoured with his acquaintance and society, and confirmed his statement by an oath, who could hesitate to accredit the relation, especially since the testimony of after-time has established its truth? He said that about noon, when the day was already beginning to decline, he saw with his own eyes the trophy of a cross of light in the heavens, above the sun, and bearing the inscription, CONQUER BY THIS. At this sight he himself was struck with amazement, and his whole army also, which followed him on this expedition, and witnessed the miracle.

He said, moreover, that he doubted within himself what the import of this apparition could be. And while he continued to ponder and reason on its meaning, night came on; then in his sleep the Christ of God appeared to him with the same sign which he had seen in the heavens, and commanded him to make a likeness of that sign which he had seen in the heavens, and to use it as a safeguard in all engagements with his enemies.

N. L.

The Letter of Eusebius.

'You will have probably learnt from other sources what was decided respecting the faith of the Church at the General Council of Nicaea, for the fame of great transactions generally outruns the accurate account of them: but lest rumours not in strict accordance with the truth should reach you, we think it necessary to send to you, first, the formulary of faith originally proposed by us, and next, the

πίστεως γραφήν, ἔπειτα τὴν δευτέραν, ἣν ταῖς ἡμετέραις
φωναῖς προσθήκας ἐπιβαλόντες ἐκδεδώκασι. Τὸ μὲν οὖν
παρ' ἡμῶν γράμμα ἐπὶ παρουσίᾳ τοῦ θεοφιλεστάτου
βασιλέως ἡμῶν ἀναγνωσθέν, εὖ τε ἔχειν καὶ δοκίμως
5 ἀποφανθέν, τοῦτον ἔχει τὸν τρόπον.

Ἡ ὑφ' ἡμῶν ἐκτεθεῖσα πίστις. Καθὼς παρελάβομεν
παρὰ τῶν πρὸ ἡμῶν ἐπισκόπων, καὶ ἐν τῇ πρώτῃ κατη-
χήσει, καὶ ὅτε τὸ λουτρὸν ἐλαμβάνομεν, καθὼς ἀπὸ τῶν
θείων γραφῶν μεμαθήκαμεν, καὶ ὡς ἐν αὐτῷ τῷ πρεσ-
10 βυτερίῳ καὶ ἐν αὐτῇ τῇ ἐπισκοπῇ ἐπιστεύομέν τε καὶ
ἐδιδάσκομεν, οὕτω καὶ νῦν πιστεύοντες τὴν ἡμετέραν
πίστιν προσαναφέρομεν. Ἔστι δὲ αὕτη. Πιστεύω εἰς
ἕνα Θεόν, Πατέρα παντοκράτορα, τὸν τῶν ἁπάντων
ὁρατῶν τε καὶ ἀοράτων ποιητήν, καὶ εἰς ἕνα Κύριον
15 Ἰησοῦν Χριστόν, τὸν τοῦ Θεοῦ Λόγον, Θεὸν ἐκ Θεοῦ,
φῶς ἐκ φωτός, ζωὴν ἐκ ζωῆς, Υἱὸν μονογενῆ, πρωτότοκον
πάσης τῆς κτίσεως, πρὸ πάντων τῶν αἰώνων ἐκ τοῦ
Πατρὸς γεγεννημένον· δι' οὗ καὶ ἐγένετο πάντα· τὸν διὰ
τὴν ἡμετέραν σωτηρίαν σαρκωθέντα καὶ ἐν ἀνθρώποις
20 πολιτευσάμενον, καὶ παθόντα, καὶ ἀναστάντα τῇ τρίτῃ
ἡμέρᾳ, καὶ ἀνελθόντα πρὸς τὸν Πατέρα, καὶ ἥξοντα
πάλιν ἐν δόξῃ κρῖναι ζῶντας καὶ νεκρούς. Πιστεύομεν
καὶ εἰς ἓν Πνεῦμα ἅγιον.

Τούτων ἕκαστον εἶναι καὶ ὑπάρχειν πιστεύοντες,
25 Πατέρα, ἀληθινῶς Πατέρα· καὶ Υἱόν, ἀληθινῶς Υἱόν·
Πνεῦμά τε ἅγιον, ἀληθινῶς Πνεῦμα ἅγιον, καθὰ καὶ ὁ
Κύριος ἡμῶν ἀποστέλλων εἰς τὸ κήρυγμα τοὺς ἑαυτοῦ
μαθητὰς εἶπε. Πορευθέντες μαθητεύσατε πάντα τὰ ἔθνη,
βαπτίζοντες αὐτοὺς εἰς τὸ ὄνομα τοῦ Πατρός, καὶ τοῦ
30 Υἱοῦ, καὶ τοῦ ἁγίου Πνεύματος· περὶ ὧν καὶ διαβεβαιού-
μεθα οὕτως ἔχειν, καὶ οὕτως φρονεῖν, καὶ πάλαι οὕτως
ἐσχηκέναι, καὶ μέχρι θανάτου ὑπὲρ ταύτης συνίστασθαι
τῆς πίστεως, ἀναθεματίζοντες πᾶσαν ἄθεον αἵρεσιν.

second, published with additions made to our terms. The following is our formulary, which was read in the presence of our most pious emperor, and declared to be couched in right and proper language.

The Faith put forth by us.

'"As in our first catechetical instruction, and at the time of our baptism, we received from the bishops who were before us and as we have learnt from the Holy Scriptures, and, alike as presbyters, and as bishops, were wont to believe and teach; so we now believe and thus declare our faith. It is as follows:—

' "I believe in one God, Father Almighty, the Maker of all things, visible and invisible; and in one Lord Jesus Christ, the Word of God, God of God, Light of Light, Life of Life, Only-begotten Son, First-born of every creature, begotten of the Father before all worlds; by Whom all things were made; Who for our salvation was incarnate, and lived among men. He suffered and rose again the third day, and ascended to the Father; and He will come again in glory to judge the quick and the dead. We also believe in one Holy Ghost.

' "I believe in the being and continual existence of each of these; that the Father is in truth the Father; the Son in truth the Son; the Holy Ghost in truth the Holy Ghost; as our Lord, when sending out His disciples to preach the Gospel, said, *Go forth and teach all nations, baptizing them into the name of the Father, and of the Son, and of the Holy Ghost.* We positively affirm that we hold this faith, that we have always held it, and that we adhere to it even unto death, condemning all ungodly heresy. We testify, as before God, the Almighty and our Lord Jesus Christ, that we have thought thus from the heart, and from the soul, ever since we can remember: and we

Ταῦτα ἀπὸ καρδίας καὶ ψυχῆς πεφρονηκέναι, ἐξ οὗπερ ἴσμεν ἑαυτούς, καὶ νῦν φρονεῖν τε καὶ λέγειν ἐξ ἀληθείας, ἐπὶ τοῦ Θεοῦ τοῦ παντοκράτορος καὶ τοῦ Κυρίου ἡμῶν Ἰησοῦ Χριστοῦ μαρτυρόμεθα· δεικνύναι ἔχοντες καὶ δι'
5 ἀποδείξεως καὶ πείθειν ὑμᾶς ὅτι καὶ τοὺς παρεληλυθότας χρόνους οὕτως ἐπιστεύομέν τε καὶ ἐκηρύσσομεν.

Ταύτης ὑφ' ἡμῶν ἐκτεθείσης τῆς πίστεως, οὐδεὶς παρῆν ἀντιλογίας τόπος. Ἀλλ' αὐτός τε πρῶτος ὁ θεοφιλέστατος ἡμῶν βασιλεὺς ὀρθότατα περιέχειν αὐτὴν ἐμαρτύ-
10 ρησεν· οὕτω τε καὶ ἑαυτὸν φρονεῖν συνωμολόγησε, καὶ ταύτῃ τοὺς πάντας συγκατατίθεσθαι ὑπογράφειν τε τοῖς δόγμασι καὶ συμφρονεῖν τούτοις αὐτοῖς παρεκελεύετο ἑνὸς μόνου προσεγγραφέντος ῥήματος τοῦ ὁμοουσίου, ὃ καὶ αὐτὸ ἡρμήνευσε λέγων ὅτι μὴ κατὰ σωμάτων πάθη λέγοιτο
15 ὁμοούσιος, οὔτε κατὰ διαίρεσιν, οὔτε κατά τινα ἀποτομὴν ἐκ Πατρὸς ὑποστῆναι. Μηδὲ γὰρ δύνασθαι τὴν ἄϋλον καὶ νοερὰν καὶ ἀσώματον φύσιν σωματικόν τι πάθος ὑφίστασθαι· θείοις δὲ καὶ ἀπορρήτοις λόγοις προσήκει τὰ τοιαῦτα νοεῖν. Καὶ ὁ μὲν σοφώτατος ἡμῶν καὶ εὐσε-
20 βέστατος βασιλεὺς τὰ τοιαῦτα διεφιλοσόφει· οἱ δὲ προφάσει τῆς τοῦ ὁμοουσίου προσθήκης τήνδε τὴν γραφὴν πεποιήκασιν.

Ἡ ἐν τῇ συνόδῳ ὑπαγορευθεῖσα πίστις.

Πιστεύομεν εἰς ἕνα Θεὸν Πατέρα παντοκράτορα, πάν-
25 των ὁρατῶν τε καὶ ἀοράτων ποιητήν· καὶ εἰς ἕνα Κύριον Ἰησοῦν Χριστὸν τὸν Υἱὸν τοῦ Θεοῦ, γεννηθέντα ἐκ τοῦ Πατρὸς μονογενῆ, τουτέστιν ἐκ τῆς οὐσίας τοῦ Πατρός, Θεὸν ἐκ Θεοῦ, καὶ φῶς ἐκ φωτός, Θεὸν ἀληθινὸν ἐκ Θεοῦ ἀληθινοῦ, γεννηθέντα οὐ ποιηθέντα, ὁμοούσιον τῷ Πατρί·
30 δι' οὗ τὰ πάντα ἐγένετο, τά τε ἐν τῷ οὐρανῷ καὶ τὰ ἐν τῇ γῇ· τὸν δι' ἡμᾶς τοὺς ἀνθρώπους καὶ διὰ τὴν ἡμετέραν σωτηρίαν κατελθόντα, καὶ σαρκωθέντα, ἐνανθρωπήσαντα· παθόντα καὶ ἀναστάντα τῇ τρίτῃ ἡμέρᾳ· ἀνελθόντα εἰς

have the means of showing, and, indeed, of convincing you, that we have always during the past thus believed and preached."

'When this formulary had been set forth by us, there was no room to gainsay it; but our beloved emperor himself was the first to testify that it was most orthodox, and that he coincided in opinion with it; and he exhorted the others to sign it, and to receive all the doctrine it contained, with the single addition of one word—"consubstantial." He explained that this term implied no bodily condition or change, for that the Son did not derive His existence from the Father either by means of division or of abscission, since an immaterial, intellectual, and incorporeal nature could not be subject to any bodily condition or change. These things must be understood as bearing a divine and mysterious signification. Thus reasoned our wisest and most religious emperor. The addition of the word *consubstantial* has given occasion for the composition of the following formulary :—

The Creed published by the Council.

'"We believe in one God, Father Almighty, Maker of all things visible and invisible. And in one Lord Jesus Christ, the Son of God, begotten of the Father; only-begotten, that is, of the substance of the Father, God of God, Light of Light, Very God of Very God, begotten not made, being of one substance with the Father: by Whom all things were made both in heaven and on earth: Who for us men, and for our salvation, came down, and was incarnate, and was made man; He suffered, and rose again the third day; He ascended into heaven, and is coming to judge both quick and dead. And (we believe) in the Holy Ghost. The Holy Catholic

τοὺς οὐρανούς, ἐρχόμενον κρῖναι ζῶντας καὶ νεκρούς. Καὶ εἰς τὸ ἅγιον Πνεῦμα. Τοὺς δὲ λέγοντας ὅτι ἦν ποτὲ ὅτε οὐκ ἦν, καὶ πρὶν γεννηθῆναι οὐκ ἦν, καὶ ὅτι ἐξ οὐκ ὄντων ἐγένετο, ἢ ἐξ ἑτέρας ὑποστάσεως ἢ οὐσίας φάσκοντας
5 εἶναι, τρεπτὸν ἢ ἀλλοιωτὸν τὸν Υἱὸν τοῦ Θεοῦ, ἀναθεματίζει ἡ ἁγία καθολικὴ καὶ ἀποστολικὴ ἐκκλησία.

Καὶ δὴ ταύτης τῆς γραφῆς ὑπ᾽ αὐτῶν ὑπαγορευθείσης, ὅπως εἴρηται αὐτοῖς τὸ ἐκ τῆς οὐσίας τοῦ Πατρὸς καὶ τὸ τῷ Πατρὶ ὁμοούσιον, οὐκ ἀνεξέταστον αὐτοῖς καταλιμ-
10 πάνομεν. Ἐρωτήσεις τοιγαροῦν καὶ ἀποκρίσεις ἐντεῦθεν ἀνεκινοῦντο· ἐβασανίζετο ὁ λόγος τῆς διανοίας τῶν εἰρημένων. Καὶ δὴ τὸ ἐκ τῆς οὐσίας ὡμολόγητο πρὸς αὐτῶν δηλωτικὸν εἶναι τοῦ ἐκ μὲν τοῦ Πατρὸς εἶναι, οὐ μὴν ὡς μέρος ὑπάρχειν τοῦ Πατρός. Ταύτῃ καὶ ἡμῖν ἐδόκει
15 καλῶς ἔχειν συγκατατίθεσθαι τῇ διανοίᾳ, τῆς εὐσεβοῦς διδασκαλίας ὑπαγορευούσης ἐκ τοῦ Πατρὸς εἶναι τὸν Υἱόν, οὐ μὴν μέρος τῆς οὐσίας αὐτοῦ τυγχάνειν. Διόπερ ταύτῃ τῇ διανοίᾳ καὶ αὐτοὶ συνετιθέμεθα, οὐδὲ τὴν φωνὴν παραιτούμενοι, τοῦ τῆς εἰρήνης σκοποῦ πρὸ ὀφθαλμῶν
20 ἡμῶν κειμένου, καὶ τοῦ μὴ τῆς ὀρθῆς ἐκπεσεῖν διανοίας. Κατὰ ταυτὰ δὲ καὶ τὸ γεννηθέντα οὐ ποιηθέντα κατεδεξάμεθα· ἐπειδὴ τὸ ποιηθέντα κοινὸν ἔφασκον εἶναι πρόσρημα τῶν λοιπῶν κτισμάτων τῶν διὰ τοῦ Υἱοῦ γενομένων, ὧν οὐδὲν ὅμοιον ἔχειν τὸν Υἱόν. Δι᾽ ὃ δὴ μὴ εἶναι αὐτὸν
25 ποίημα τοῖς δι᾽ αὐτοῦ γενομένοις ἐμφερές, κρείττονος δὲ ἢ κατὰ πᾶν ποίημα τυγχάνειν οὐσίας, ἣν ἐκ τοῦ Πατρὸς γεγεννῆσθαι διδάσκει τὰ θεῖα λόγια, τοῦ τρόπου τῆς γεννήσεως καὶ ἀνεκφράστου καὶ ἀνεπιλογίστου πάσῃ γεννητῇ φύσει τυγχάνοντος. Οὕτω δὲ καὶ τό, ὁμοούσιον
30 εἶναι τοῦ Πατρὸς τὸν Υἱόν, ἐξεταζόμενος ὁ λόγος συνίστη, οὐ κατὰ τὸν τῶν σωμάτων τρόπον, οὐδὲ τοῖς θνητοῖς ζώοις παραπλησίως. Οὔτε γὰρ κατὰ διαίρεσιν τῆς οὐσίας, οὔτε κατὰ ἀποτομήν, ἀλλ᾽ οὐδὲ κατά τι πάθος ἢ τροπὴν

and Apostolic Church anathematizes all who say there was a time when the Son of God was not; that before He was begotten He was not; that He was made out of the non-existent; or that He is of a different essence and of a different substance from the Father; and is susceptible of variation or change.'

'When they had set forth this formulary, we did not leave without examination that passage in which it is said that the Son is of the substance of the Father and consubstantial with the Father. Questions and arguments thence arose, and the meaning of the terms was exactly tested. Accordingly they were led to confess that the word consubstantial signifies that the Son is of the Father, but not as being a part of the Father. We deemed it right to receive this opinion: for that is sound doctrine which teaches that the Son is of the Father, but not part of His substance. From the love of peace, and lest we should fall from the true belief, we also accept this view, neither do we reject the term "consubstantial." For the same reason we admitted the expression, "begotten, but not made"; for they alleged that the word "made" applies generally to all things which were created by the Son, to which the Son is in no respect similar; and that consequently He is not a created thing, like the things made by Him, but is of a substance superior to all created objects, which the Holy Scriptures teach to be begotten of the Father, by a mode of generation which is incomprehensible and inexplicable to all created beings. So also the term "of one substance with the Father," when investigated, was accepted not in accordance with bodily relations or similarity to mortal beings. For it was also shown that it does not either imply division of substance, nor abscission, nor any modification or change or alteration in the power of the Father, all of which are alien from the nature of the

ἢ ἀλλοίωσιν τῆς τοῦ Πατρὸς δυνάμεως· τούτων γὰρ ἁπάντων ἀλλότριον εἶναι τὴν τοῦ ἀγεννήτου Πατρὸς φύσιν. Παραστατικὸν δ' εἶναι τὸ ὁμοούσιον τῷ Πατρὶ τοῦ μηδεμίαν ἐμφέρειαν πρὸς τὰ γενητὰ κτίσματα τὸν Υἱὸν τοῦ
5 Θεοῦ φέρειν, μόνον δὲ τῷ Πατρὶ τῷ γεγεννηκότι κατὰ πάντα τρόπον ὅμοιον· καὶ μὴ εἶναι ἐξ ἑτέρας τινὸς ὑποστάσεώς τε καὶ οὐσίας ἀλλ' ἐκ τῆς τοῦ Πατρός. ⁷Ωι καὶ αὐτῷ τοῦτον ἑρμηνευθέντι τὸν τρόπον καλῶς ἔχειν ἐφάνη συγκατατίθεσθαι· ἐπεὶ καὶ τῶν παλαιῶν λογίους τινὰς
10 καὶ ἐπιφανεῖς ἐπισκόπους καὶ συγγραφέας ἔγνωμεν ἐπὶ τῆς τοῦ Πατρὸς καὶ Υἱοῦ θεολογίας τῷ τοῦ ὁμοουσίου συγχρησαμένους ὀνόματι.

Ταῦτα μὲν περὶ τῆς ἐκτεθείσης εἰρήσθω πίστεως·· ᾗ συνεφωνήσαμεν οἱ πάντες, οὐκ ἀνεξετάστως, ἀλλὰ κατὰ
15 τὰς ἀποδοθείσας διανοίας ἐπ' αὐτοῦ τοῦ θεοφιλεστάτου βασιλέως ἐξετασθείσας, καὶ τοῖς εἰρημένοις λογισμοῖς συνομολογηθείσας. Καὶ τὸν ἀναθεματισμὸν δὲ τὸν μετὰ τὴν πίστιν πρὸς αὐτῶν τιθέντα δεκτὸν εἶναι ἡγησάμεθα, διὰ τὸ ἀπείργειν ἀγράφοις χρῆσθαι φωναῖς, δι' ἃς σχεδὸν
20 ἡ πᾶσα ἐγεγόνει σύγχυσις καὶ ἀκαταστασία τῆς ἐκκλησίας. Μηδεμιᾶς γοῦν θεοπνεύστου γραφῆς τῷ ἐξ οὐκ ὄντων, καὶ τῷ, ἦν ποτὲ ὅτε οὐκ ἦν, καὶ τοῖς ἑξῆς ἐπιλεγομένοις κεχρημένης, οὐκ εὔλογον ἐφάνη ταῦτα λέγειν καὶ διδάσκειν. ⁷Ωι καὶ αὐτῷ καλῶς δόξαντι συνεθέμεθα,
25 ἐπεὶ μηδὲ ἐν τῷ πρὸ τούτου χρόνῳ τούτοις εἰώθειμεν συγχρῆσθαι τοῖς ῥήμασιν. [῎Ετι μὴν τὸ ἀναθεματίζεσθαι τὸ πρὸ τοῦ γεννηθῆναι οὐκ ἦν οὐκ ἄτοπον ἐνομίσθη, τῷ παρὰ πᾶσι μὲν ὁμολογεῖσθαι εἶναι αὐτὸν Υἱὸν τοῦ Θεοῦ καὶ πρὸ τῆς κατὰ σάρκα γεννήσεως. ῎Ηδη δὲ ὁ θεοφιλέ-
30 στατος ἡμῶν βασιλεὺς τῷ λόγῳ κατεσκεύαζε καὶ κατὰ τὴν ἔνθεον αὐτοῦ γέννησιν τὸ πρὸ πάντων αἰώνων εἶναι αὐτόν· ἐπεὶ καὶ πρὶν ἐνεργείᾳ γεννηθῆναι, δυνάμει ἦν ἐν τῷ Πατρὶ ἀγεννήτως, ὄντος τοῦ Πατρὸς ἀεὶ Πατρός, ὡς καὶ

unbegotten Father. It was concluded that the expression *being of one substance with the Father*, implies that the Son of God does not resemble, in any one respect, the creatures which He has made; but that to the Father alone, who begat Him, He is in all points perfectly like: for He is of the essence and of the substance of none save of the Father. This interpretation having been given of the doctrine, it appeared right to us to assent to it, especially as we were aware that of the ancients some learned and celebrated bishops and writers have used the term "consubstantial" with respect to the divinity of the Father and of the Son.

'These are the circumstances which I had to communicate respecting the published formulary of the faith. To it we all agreed, not without investigation, but, in the above sense, after having subjected it to thorough examination in the presence of our most beloved emperor, and agreed to it in accordance with the above reasons. We also allowed that the anathema appended by them to their formulary of faith should be accepted, because it prohibits the use of words which are not scriptural; through which almost all the disorder and troubles of the Church have arisen. And since no passage of the inspired Scripture uses the terms "out of the non-existent," or that "there was a time when He was not," nor indeed any of the other phrases of the same class, it did not appear reasonable to assert or to teach such things. In this opinion, therefore, we judged it right to agree; since, indeed, we had never, at any former period, been accustomed to use such terms. [Moreover, the condemnation of the assertion that before He was begotten He was not, did not appear to involve any incongruity, because all assent to the fact that He was the Son of God before He was begotten according to the flesh. And here our emperor, most beloved by God,

βασιλέως ἀεὶ καὶ σωτῆρος καὶ δυνάμει πάντα ὄντος, ἀεί τε καὶ κατὰ τὰ αὐτὰ καὶ ὡσαύτως ἔχοντος.] Ταῦτα ὑμῖν ἀναγκαίως διεπεμψάμεθα, ἀγαπητοί, τὰ κεκριμένα τῆς ἡμετέρας ἐξετάσεώς τε καὶ συγκαταθέσεως φανερὰ καθ-
5 ιστῶντες· ὡς εὐλόγως τότε μὲν καὶ μέχρις ὑστάτης ὥρας ἱστάμεθα, ὅθ' ἡμῖν τὰ ἑτεροίως γραφέντα προσέκοπτε, τότε δὲ ἀφιλονείκως τὰ μὴ λυποῦντα κατεδεξάμεθα, ὅθ' ἡμῖν εὐγνωμόνως τῶν λόγων ἐξετάζουσι τὴν διάνοιαν ἐμφανῆ σύμπραξιν ἔχειν ἔδοξε τοῖς ὑφ' ἡμῶν αὐτῶν ἐν τῇ
10 προεκτεθείσῃ πίστει ὡμολογημένοις.

THEODORET, *Hist. Eccl.* i. 12.

LXXIV.

Can. 26. *Ut omni sabbato ieiunetur*. Errorem placuit corrigi, ut omni sabbati die superpositiones celebremus.

Can. 33. *De episcopis et ministris ut ab uxoribus abstineant*. Placuit in totum prohibere episcopis, pres-
15 byteris et diaconibus vel omnibus clericis positis in ministerio abstinere se a coniugibus suis et non generare filios: quicunque vero fecerit, ab honore clericatus exterminetur.

Can. 36. *Ne picturae in ecclesia fiant*. Placuit picturas
20 in ecclesia non esse debere, ne quod colitur et adoratur in parietibus depingatur.

Can. 49. *De frugibus fidelium ne a Iudaeis benedicantur*. Admoneri placuit possessores, ut non patiantur fructus suos ... a Iudaeis benedici, ne nostram irritam
25 et infirmam faciant benedictionem.

began to reason concerning His divine origin, and His existence before all ages. He was virtually in the Father without generation, even before He was actually begotten, the Father having always been the Father, just as He has always been a King and a Saviour, and, virtually, all things, and has never known any change of being or action.]

'We have thought it requisite, beloved brethren, to transmit you an account of these circumstances, in order to show you what examination and investigation we bestowed on all the questions which we had to decide; and also to prove how at one time we reasonably resisted, even to the last hour, when doctrines improperly expressed offended us, and, at another time, we, without contention, accepted the articles which contained nothing objectionable, when after a thorough and candid investigation of their signification, they appeared perfectly conformable with what had been confessed by us in the formulary of faith which we had published.'

N. L.

Select Canons of Councils.

ELVIRA.

Can. 26. It has seemed good that we correct an error, that we fast strictly every sabbath day.

Can. 33. It has seemed good entirely to interdict bishops, presbyters, and deacons and all clerics engaged in sacred offices from intercourse with their wives and procreation of children. Whoso disobeys is to be degraded from the clerical office.

Can. 36. It has seemed good that there be no pictures in the church, lest what is worshipped and adored be painted on the walls.

Can. 49. It has seemed good that landowners be warned that they suffer not their crops to be blessed by Jews, lest they make our blessing invalid or weak.

Can. 60. *De his qui destruentes idola occiduntur.* Si quis idola fregerit et ibidem fuerit occisus, quatenus in Evangelio scriptum non est neque invenietur sub apostolis unquam factum, placuit in numero eum non recipi martyrum.

Can. 3. Ἀπηγόρευσεν καθόλου ἡ μεγάλη σύνοδος μήτε ἐπισκόπῳ μήτε πρεσβυτέρῳ μήτε διακόνῳ μήτε ὅλως τινὶ τῶν ἐν τῷ κλήρῳ ἐξεῖναι συνείσακτον ἔχειν, πλὴν εἰ μὴ ἄρα μητέρα ἢ ἀδελφὴν ἢ θείαν, ἢ ἃ μόνα πρόσωπα πᾶσαν ὑποψίαν διαπέφευγε.

Can. 6. Ecclesia Romana semper habuit primatum. τὰ ἀρχαῖα ἔθη κρατείτω τὰ ἐν Αἰγύπτῳ καὶ Λιβύῃ καὶ Πενταπόλει, ὥστε τὸν Ἀλεξανδρείας ἐπίσκοπον πάντων τούτων ἔχειν τὴν ἐξουσίαν, ἐπειδὴ καὶ τῷ ἐν τῇ Ῥώμῃ ἐπισκόπῳ τοῦτο σύνηθές ἐστιν· ὁμοίως δὲ καὶ κατὰ τὴν Ἀντιόχειαν καὶ ἐν ταῖς ἄλλαις ἐπαρχίαις τὰ πρεσβεῖα σώζεσθαι ταῖς ἐκκλησίαις . . .

Can. 17. Ἐπειδὴ πολλοὶ ἐν τῷ κανόνι ἐξεταζόμενοι τὴν πλεονεξίαν καὶ τὴν αἰσχροκέρδειαν διώκοντες ἐπελάθοντο τοῦ θείου γράμματος λέγοντος· Τὸ ἀργύριον αὐτοῦ οὐκ ἔδωκεν ἐπὶ τόκῳ· . . . ἐδικαίωσεν ἡ ἁγία καὶ μεγάλη σύνοδος ὡς εἴ τις εὑρεθείη μετὰ τὸν ὅρον τοῦτον τόκους λαμβάνων . . . καθαιρεθήσεται τοῦ κλήρου καὶ ἀλλότριος τοῦ κανόνος ἔσται.

Can. 19. Περὶ τῶν Παυλιανισάντων, εἶτα προσφυγόντων τῇ καθολικῇ ἐκκλησίᾳ, ὅρος ἐκτεθεῖται, ἀναβαπτίζεσθαι αὐτοὺς ἐξάπαντος . . .

Can. 20. ἐπειδή τινές εἰσιν ἐν τῇ κυριακῇ γόνυ κλίνοντες καὶ ἐν ταῖς τῆς πεντηκοστῆς ἡμέραις· ὑπὲρ τοῦ πάντα ἐν πάσῃ παροικίᾳ φυλάττεσθαι, ἑστῶτας ἔδοξε τῇ ἁγίᾳ συνόδῳ τὰς εὐχὰς ἀποδιδόναι τῷ Θεῷ.

Can. 60. If anyone shall have destroyed idols and been slain on the spot, it has seemed good that he be not included among the martyrs, seeing that it is not so commanded in the Gospel, and will not be found ever to have been done in the Apostles' time.

NICAEA.

Can. 3. The great council entirely forbids it to be lawful for either bishop or elder or deacon or any at all of the clergy to have [in his house] a spiritual sister; only a mother or sister or aunt, or such persons only as are past all suspicion.

Can. 6. Let the old customs prevail—those current in Egypt and Libya and Pentapolis, that the bishop of Alexandria have power over all these, for this is the practice with the Roman bishop also. Likewise in the case of Antioch and the other provinces let their prerogatives be preserved to the churches. . . .

Can. 17. Seeing that many on the roll of the Church in following after covetousness and filthy lucre have forgotten the divine scripture (Ps. xv. 5) which says, He hath not given his money upon usury . . . the great and holy synod determines that if any be found after this decision taking usury, . . . he shall be deposed from the clergy and struck off the roll.

Can. 19. Concerning former Paulianists who have betaken themselves to the Catholic Church, a rule has been put forth [by the Council itself], that they are without exception to be rebaptized . . .

Can. 20. Seeing that there are some who kneel on Sunday and in the days of Pentecost, it has seemed good to the holy council (that all things may be observed in every diocese) that men should offer their prayers to God standing.

Can. 11. Περὶ τοῦ μὴ δεῖν τὰς λεγομένας πρεσβύτιδας ἤτοι προκαθημένας ἐν ἐκκλησίᾳ καθίστασθαι.

Can. 13. Περὶ τοῦ μὴ τοῖς ὄχλοις ἐπιτρέπειν τὰς ἐκλογὰς ποιεῖσθαι τῶν μελλόντων καθίστασθαι εἰς ἱερατεῖον.

Can. 28. Ὅτι οὐ δεῖ ἐν τοῖς κυριακοῖς ἢ ἐν ταῖς ἐκκλησίαις ἀγάπας ποιεῖν καὶ ἐν τῷ οἴκῳ τοῦ θεοῦ ἐσθίειν καὶ ἀκούβιτα στρωννύειν.

Can. 29. Ὅτι οὐ δεῖ Χριστιανοὺς ἰουδαΐζειν καὶ ἐν τῷ σαββάτῳ σχολάζειν, ἀλλὰ ἐργάζεσθαι αὐτοὺς ἐν τῇ αὐτῇ ἡμέρᾳ, τὴν δὲ κυριακὴν προτιμῶντας εἴγε δύναιντο σχολάζειν ὡς Χριστιανοί.

Can. 3. Τὸν μέντοι Κωνσταντινουπόλεως ἐπίσκοπον ἔχειν τὰ πρεσβεῖα τῆς τιμῆς μετὰ τὸν τῆς Ῥώμης ἐπίσκοπον, διὰ τὸ εἶναι αὐτὴν νέαν Ῥώμην.

LXXV.
Roman Religion.

1. Separatim nemo habessit deos, neve novos sive advenas nisi publice adscitos privatim colunto. *XII Tabb.*

2. Est enim pietas iustitia adversus deos, . . . sanctitas autem scientia colendorum sacrorum. Cic. *De Nat. Deor.* i. 41.

3. τὸ μὲν θεῖον πάντῃ πάντως αὐτός τε σέβου κατὰ τὰ πάτρια καὶ τοὺς ἄλλους τιμᾶν ἀνάγκαζε, τοὺς δὲ δὴ ξενίζοντάς τι περὶ αὐτὸ καὶ μίσει καὶ κόλαζε, μὴ μόνον τῶν θεῶν ἕνεκα, ὧν ὁ καταφρονήσας οὐδ' ἄλλου ἄν τινος προτιμήσειεν, ἀλλ' ὅτι καὶ καινά τινα δαιμόνια οἱ τοιοῦτοι ἀντεσφέροντες πολλοὺς ἀναπείθουσιν ἀλλοτριονομεῖν, κἀκ τούτου

LAODICEA.

Can. 11. That there be no ordination of the so-called female elders or presidents in the church.

Can. 13. That the multitude be not allowed to make the choice of those to be appointed to priestly office.

Can. 28. That it be not lawful to hold *agapae* in the Lord's houses or the churches, or to eat in the house of God or lay couches.

Can. 29. That Christians must not play Jews by ceasing work on the Sabbath, but that they work on that day and prefer the Lord's day by ceasing work as Christians if they can.

CONSTANTINOPLE (381).

Can. 3. The bishop however of Constantinople to have precedence of honour after the bishop of Rome, because Constantinople is New Rome.

καὶ συνωμοσίαι καὶ συστάσεις ἑταιρεῖαί τε γίγνονται, ἅπερ ἥκιστα μοναρχίᾳ συμφέρει. (MAECENAS) DIO CASS. *Hist.* lii. 36.

4. Iudaeos fieri sub gravi poena vetuit. Idem etiam de Christianis sanxit. *Vita Severi*, 17.

5. Cum Christiani quendam locum, qui publicus fuerat, occupassent, contra popinarii dicerent, sibi eum deberi, rescripsit, melius esse, ut quemadmodumcunque illic deus colatur, quam propinariis dedatur. *Vita Alexandri Severi*, 49.

6. †Impp. Maximianus, Diocletianus et Maximinus nobilissimi A. A. A. Iuliano proconsuli Africae † . . . neque reprehendi a nova vetus religio debet. Maximi enim criminis est, retractare, quae semel ab antiquitate statuta et definita, suum cursum tenent ac possident . . . Iubemus namque, auctores quidem et principes una cum abominandis scripturis eorum severiori poenae subici, ita ut flammeis ignibus exurantur : consectaneos vero . . . capita puniri praecipimus . . . si qui sane etiam honorati . . . ad hanc . . . doctrinam Persarum se transtulerint, eorum patrimonia fisco nostro adsociari facies, ipsosque . . . metallis dari. Dat. pridie Kal. Aprilis, Alexandriae.

Mos. et Rom. Legum Collatio, xv. 3.

7. . . . AEDuo SUMMIS honoribus APUD SUOS FUNCTO SACERDOTI AD TEMPL ROM ET AUG AD CONFLUENT ARARIS ET RHODANI. (WILMANNS, *Inscr.* 2220.)

8. DIS MAGNIS ULPIUS EGNATIUS FAVENTINUS V C AUGUR PUB P R Q PATER ET HIEROCERYX D S I M ARCHIBUCOLUS DEI LIBERI HIEROFANTA HECATAE SACERDOS ISIDIS PERCEPTO TAUROBOLIO CRIOBOLIOQ IDIBUS AUGUSTIS D D N N VALENTE AUG V ET VALENTINIANO CONSS FELICITER. (WILMANNS, *Inscr.* 111.)

INDEX

Acts, of Peter, 32.
— of Paul, 34, 36.
— of Apostles (Eus.), 36; (*Mur.*), 84.
Agapé, described, 20; forbidden in churches, 190.
Alburnus, an unknown god, 110.
Alexandria, Nicene Canon on, 188.
Allegorical interpretation, samples from Justin, 56 sq.; Origen on, 132; Porphyry on, 142, 164.
Ambrosius, 130.
Anicetus, bishop of Rome, 60, 102 *bis*.
Antichrist, 88, 114 (?).
Antioch, Aurelian's decision, 160.
Apocalypse: of John (*Eus.*), 36, 40; (*Mur.*), 86; (Irenaeus), 88; (Dion. Al.), 156.
— of Peter, 36; (*Mur.*), 86.
Apocryphal books: (Eus.), 36, 60, 64; (*Mur.*), 86 sq.
Apostles: in *Teaching*, 22.
Aristides, 44.
Aristion, 40.
Arnobius, on our Lord's miracles, 162.
Attalus, martyr, 70, 72.
Aurelian, decision about Antioch, 160.
Aurelius, illiterate confessor, 148.
ἀπομνημονεύματα τῶν ἀπ., 52.

Baptism, the *Teaching*, 18; Justin, 50; Tert., 118; of infants, 128; repeated, 130; schismatic, worthless, 152; heretical, 142 sq., 189.
Basilides, 88.
Bishops in Clement, 8 sq.; in *Teaching*, 26; sinful, to be retained (Callistus), 130, to be deposed (Cyprian), 150; Cyprian's theory of, 146 sq.; appointment, 26, 150, 190.
Blandina, martyr, 70 sq.

Caesarea, Creed of, 178.
Caesariani, 154, 162 (?).
Callistus, bp. of Rome; misdeeds of, 128.
Celsus, 132 sq.
Cerdon, 96.
Cerinthus and St. John, 104.
Chiliasm, 40.
Christian life, accounts of (*ad Diogn.*), 12 sq.; (Aristides), 46; (Tertullian), 116.
Christian worship: (Justin), 50; (Tert.), 116.
Christians, in the world, 12, 46; before Christ, 48, 50; not disloyal, 114; numbers of, 114; do not specially address fools, 134.
Church discipline, 116; confounded by heretics, 122; Roman bp.'s edict, 124; relaxed by Callistus, 128; Novatian, 146; and the Confessors, 148 sq.; of sinful bps., 130, 150; Canons of Councils, 186 sq.
— government, 6 sq., 12, 26; Cyprian's theory, 146, 150.
— no forgiveness outside, 146, 152.
Clement of Rome; Letter to Corinthians, 2 sq., 60, 64, 100; wrote Ep. Hebr., 142.
Constantine, Edict of Milan, 170; vision of Cross, 174; at Nicaea, 180.
Corinth, church of: Clement's letter to, 2 sq.

o

Index.

Corpus (*Christianorum*), 116, 174.
Creed, traces of, 152; of Caesarea, 178; of Nicaea, 180.
Cross, sign of, 118; vision of, 174.
Cyprian, on Church unity, 146 sq.; Lactantius on, 164.

Deaconesses, 28.
Deacons, in *Teaching*, 26.
Demons, authors of heathenism, 46; imitated Eucharist, 52.
Diatessaron of Tatian, 62.
Diocletian: edicts, 160; misgovernment, 164.
Dionysius of Alexandria, on Novatian, 146; on Apocalypse, 156, 160.
— of Corinth, 32, 58, 62.
Docetism, Ignatius on, 12.
Domnus, bp. of Antioch, 160.
Δαναΐδες καὶ Δίρκαι, 6.

Easter Question: Polycrates, 94; Polycarp, 102; Firmilian, 154.
Egregii viri, 156.
Elders, 10, 12; (female), 190.
Eleutherus, bp. of Rome, 60, 102.
Elvira, Council of, 186.
Encratites, 62.
Epistles: of St. Paul, fourteen (Eus.), 34, 36; (*Mur.*), 84; mutilated by Marcion, 98.
— to Hebrews (Eus.), 34; (Origen), 142.
— to Laodicenes (*Mur.*), 86.
— of Clement, 2 sq., 60, 64, 100.
— of Polycarp, 104.
— James (Eus.), 36.
— 1 Peter (Eus.), 32, 46; (Papias), 44; (*Mur.?*), 86; (Iren.), 90.
— 2 Peter (Eus.), 32, 36; (*Mur.?*), 86; (Firmilian?), 154.
— 1 John (Eus.), 36; (Papias), 44; (*Mur.*), 84; (Iren.), 90.
— 2 & 3 John (Eus.), 36; (*Mur.*), 86.
— Jude (Eus.), 36; (*Mur.*), 86.
— Barnabas (Eus.), 36.
Eucharist, in *Teaching*, 20; Justin, 52 sq.; Tert., 118, 126.
— unbaptized excluded from, 20, 52.
— reserved, 54.

Eusebius: on Epistles, 34; on the Canon, 36; on Papias, 38 sq.; intercourse with Constantine, 176; Letter of, 176 sq.
ἐπιμονήν, 10.

Faith and knowledge, 108.
Fasts: the *Teaching*, 18; Montanists, 92.
Firmilian, letter of, 154.
Flavia Domitilla, 10.
Flavius Clemens, 10.
Florinus, 92.

Gaius of Rome, 32.
Galerius, edict of, 168.
Gallienus, Rescript of, 160.
Glabrio, 10.
Gospels: Canonical, Eus., 36; Irenaeus, 88.
— spurious, 36.
— of Matthew (Papias), 44; (Ir.), 88.
— of Mark (Papias), 42; (*Mur.*), 82; (Ir.), 88.
— of Luke (*Mur.*), 82; (Ir.), 88; (Marcion), 98.
— of John (*Mur.*), 84; (Ir.), 88.

Heathenism, work of demons, 46.
Hebrews, Gospel acc. to, 36, 44.
Hegesippus, 58 sq.
Heretics, misuse of Scripture, 108; not to be argued with, 120; disorderly worship, 122.
Hermas, *Shepherd* of, 34, 86, 90.
Hyginus, bp. of Rome, 96, 102 sq.

Idols, destroyers of, 188.
Ignatius: on episcopacy, 12; on Docetism, 12; ref. by Irenaeus, 90.
Inspiration: of O.T., 136; of N.T., 136.
Irenaeus, on Papias, 38; chiliastic, 48; on Tatian, 62; on Gospels and Apoc., &c., 88; to Florinus, 92; on Marcion, 96; on tradition, 98; on Polycarp, 102.

Index

Jesus Christ, put to death, 2; Incarnation real, 12; Reason incarnate, 48 sq.; date of, 48; instituted Eucharist, 52; rose again on Sunday, 56; Temptation parabolical, 138; miracles, 162.
Jews, not to bless crops, 186.
Jewish interpretations, 56.
John, the apostle: see *Gospels, Epistles, Apocalypse,* Papias, Polycrates, Cerinthus.
— the Elder, 40.
Jugglers, the works of, 134.
Justin Martyr, on heathenism, 46 sq., on Christian worship, 50; Tatian his disciple, 62; ref. by Ir., 90.
Justus (Barsabas), 40.

κυριακός, 26, 38, 44.

Lactantius on earlier Apologists, 164.
Laodicea, Council of, 190.
Lapsi (Pliny), 28; (Decian), 144, 148.
Libelli, 144, 148.
Licinius, Emperor, 170.
Linus, bp. of Rome, 100.
Lord's Prayer in *Teaching,* 20.
Lucian, confessor: recklessness of, 148 sq.
Lyons and Vienne: persecution, 66 sq.

Mappalicus, martyr, 148.
Marcion, 62, 88 (?), 96 sq., 102; and Polycarp, 104, 118.
Marriages, mixed, 124; of clergy, 130, 186; unequal, 130.
Matthias, 40.
Maturus, martyr, 70, 72.
Melito, 58, 96.
Memoirs of Apostles, 52, 54.
Messianic Prophecies, 56 sq.
Milan, Edict of, 170.
Minucius Felix, 164.
Miracles, argument from: (Quadratus), 44; (Origen), 132; (Arnobius), 162.
Mithras, 52.
Montanus, 90, 128.
μαρὰν ἀθά, 22.
μυστήριον κοσμικόν, 24.

Nicaea, Council of, 176–186, 188.
Noetians, 92.
Novatian: Dion. Al. on, 146; his baptism worthless, 152.

Origen, 130 sq.
ὁμοούσιον, 180 sq.

Papias, 38 sq.
Papirius, 96.
Paul, apostle: at Rome (Clement), 4; (Eus.), 30; (*Mur.*), 84; (Ir.), 100.
— confessor, 148.
— of Samosata, 160; followers of, 188.
Pericope adulterae (?) in Papias, 44.
Persecution, futility of, 16, 18, 114.
Persecutions: Nero, 2, 4, 30, 110.
— Domitian, 2, 10, 110.
— Trajan, 26, 112.
— Marcus Aurelius, 110.
— Decius: *libellus* of, 144; *lapsi,* 148.
— Valerian, 154, 160.
— Diocletian, 162, 168, 170.
Peter, apostle: put to death, 4 (Clement), 30 (Eusebius), at Rome, 32; *Preaching* of, 32; mention by Papias, 38; Gospel of, 32; *Apocalypse* of, 32.
Philip at Hierapolis, 40, 94.
Philosophy: preparation for the Gospel, 106; mother of heresy, 118.
Pictures, not in church, 186.
Pinytus, bp., 58.
Pius, bp. of Rome, 86, 102.
Pliny, 26 sq.
Polycarp, martyr, 96; Irenaeus on, 102; and Marcion, 104.
Polycrates, bp. of Ephesus, 94.
Ponticus, martyr, 74.
Pontifex maximus, 124.
Porphyry, on allegorical interpretations, 142.
Potentiorem principalitatem, 100
Praescriptio, 122.
Praxeas, misdeeds of, 126.
Preaching of Peter, 32.

Priscilla and Maximilla, 90, 128.
Proclus, Montanist, 32.
Prophets, in *Teaching*, 22, 24, 26; Montanist, 90.

Quadratus, 44.

Rebaptism, 152, 188.
Rome, Church of: to Corinthians, 2 sq.; apostles at, 32, 100; charity of, 62; Firmilian on, 154; Nicene Canon on, 188; Ir.'s list of bishops, 98.

Sabbath (Elv.), 186, (Laod.), 190.
Sagaris, bishop and martyr, 96.
Sanctus, martyr, 70, 72.
Saturninus (1), 62; (2), proconsul, 78; (3), 148.
Scillitan Martyrs, Acts of the, 78-82.
Scripture; misused by heretics, 108.
Shepherd of Hermas (Eus.), 34, 36; (*Mur.*), 86; (Iren.), 90.
Sinners, God's dealing with, 140.
Socrates the philosopher, condemned heathenism, 48, 50.
Soter, bp. of Rome, 60, 62 sq., 102.
Soul, Testimony of, 112.
Speratus, martyr, 78 sq.
Stephen, bp. of Rome, 154.
Subintroductae forbidden, 188.

Successus, bp., 154.
Sunday in *Teaching*, 26; Justin, 54 sq.; at Corinth, 64; no kneeling on, 118, 188; no work on, 190.

Tatian, 62; his conversion, 64.
Teaching of the Apostles, 18 sq. (Eus.), 36.
Telesphorus, bp. of Rome, martyr, 102.
Tertullian: 110-128; Lactantius on, 164.
Testimonium animae, 112.
Thraseas, bp. and martyr, 96.
Tiberius, emperor, 110.
Tradition: Irenaeus, 98; Tert., 118, 120; variety of, 154.
Travellers, reception of, 24.

Usury forbidden to clergy, 188.

Valentinus, 62, 102, 118, 120.
Victor, bp. of Rome, 94.

Wisdom, 60, 86; 90.
Women: Montanist prophetesses, 90; heretic, 122.

Zephyrinus, bp. of Rome, 32.

φωτισμός, 50.

THE END.

www.ingramcontent.com/pod-product-compliance
Lightning Source LLC
Chambersburg PA
CBHW060605230426
43670CB00011B/1983